SEE NAPLES AND DIE

The Camorra and Organised Crime

Tom Behan

TPP

TAURIS PARKE
PAPERBACKS

Published in 2009 by Tauris Parke Paperbacks
an imprint of I.B.Tauris & Co Ltd
6 Salem Road, London W2 4BU
175 Fifth Avenue, New York NY 10010
www.ibtauris.com

Distributed in the United States and Canada Exclusively by
Palgrave Macmillan
175 Fifth Avenue, New York NY 10010

First published by I.B.Tauris & Co Ltd in 2002

ISBN: 978 1 84885 018 7

A full CIP record for this book is available from the British Library
A full CIP record is available from the Library of Congress

Library of Congress Catalog Card Number: available

Printed and bound in Great Britain by CPI Group (UK) Ltd, Croydon, CR0 4YY

Tauris Parke Paperbacks is an imprint of I.B.Tauris. It is dedicated to publishing
books in accessible paperback editions for the serious general reader within
a wide range of categories, including biography, history, travel and the
ancient world. The list includes select, critically acclaimed works of top
quality writing by distinguished authors that continue to challenge, to inform
and to inspire. These are books that possess those subtle but intrinsic
elements that mark them out as something exceptional.

The Colophon of Tauris Parke Paperbacks is a representation of the ancient
Egyptian ibis, sacred to the god Thoth, who was himself often depicted in
the form of this most elegant of birds. Thoth was credited in antiquity as
the scribe of the ancient Egyptian gods and as the inventor of writing and
was associated with many aspects of wisdom and learning.

Contents

Preface to the New Edition

For decades the Neapolitan Camorra has been killing dozens if not hundreds of people every year. It is probably the biggest employer in the Naples area, and at election time can often make the difference between who wins and who loses.

One word more than any other explains why it has not been well known outside of Italy – 'Mafia' – the most powerful criminal organisation in the country during the last century. But entertainment such as *The Godfather* and *The Sopranos* have also played their part. The success of Mafia-related films and TV series often meant that around the world people thought organised crime was about the lives, loves and insecurities of glamorous, roguish but flawed gang leaders.

But there is nothing glamorous about five *Camorristi* dressing up as policemen one night in September 2008, firing 130 bullets, and killing six African migrants.

It isn't roguish to drive down main streets at night shooting up shop fronts to make sure the owners pay protection money.

People such as 'truck tyre' Vincenzo Schiavone – named because he used to kill his victims by tying them to tyres which he then set alight – are not flawed heroes but callous murderers.

In the 1990s reality started to creep in and replace
the image. Statistics from the Italian equivalent of the
FBI show how the Camorra has overtaken the Mafia. In
the period 1992–2007 police issued 1,725 arrest
warrants for Mafia membership, but 2,368 for the
Camorra. Over the same time scale police confiscated
assets worth €204 million from the Mafia, and €498
million from the Camorra.[1]

Over the last two years this hidden world has
definitively come out into the light. Surprisingly, this
occurred primarily thanks to the first book written by
a 27-year-old author, Roberto Saviano's *Gomorra*.
Initially the book's popularity spread through word
of mouth, and it quickly grew into a best seller in Italy
and then around the world. What increased its
notoriety was the author's reaction to the first threats
from the local gang – in a celebrated local meeting he
told people to rise up and drive the gangsters out of
town.

To understand why it took a young writer's first
book to blow the lid we need to look at politics. The
centre-left parties that run Naples and the surrounding area have an advantage in that they have been less
compromised with the Camorra than centre-right
ones. But destroying the Camorra's hold means
radically altering economic power – basically taking
from the rich and giving to the poor – and centre-left
governments around the world are not prepared to do
that. Recent statistics show that since the mid-1980s
incomes from work, capital and savings have become
33 per cent more unequal in Italy – the highest
increase across the thirty OECD countries.[2]

So the tendency of the centre-left has been to
condemn organised crime but do little about the
desperation that leads young people to get involved

with gangs. And many of the gang leaders have realised that if they keep a low profile, basically they can get on with business.

The attitude to legality represented by Silvio Berlusconi and other centre-right parties in parliament is qualitatively different. When Berlusconi was elected Prime Minister in 2001 he was a defendant in 17 different trials, whereas when he won the election in April 2008 he was 'only' facing five trials – and one of his first moves was to pass a law which means that as long as he is prime minister or head of state any charges against him cannot be brought to court.

This may appear shocking, but it is the history of some parliamentarians which provides the context. The most famous elder statesman of Italian politics is life senator Giulio Andreotti, who was prime minister for the Christian Democrats on seven separate occasions. Despite the fact that in 2003 the Palermo Court of Appeal found him guilty of 'cultivating personal and friendly relations with Cosa Nostra leaders' and of having a 'generic proximity to the Cosa Nostra', he never went to jail – and never for a moment thought of resigning. Because he was found guilty of this collusion only up to 1980 the 'statute of limit- ations' kicked in. This law, passed by politicians, means that you can only be punished for a crime within a certain time limit; in the case of Giulio Andreotti this period had been exceeded and so he escaped imprisonment.[3]

Another reason why the Camorra has recently started to enter the public domain outside of Italy has been the perennial crisis of rubbish collection in the Naples area – a primary source of profit for Camorra gangs. One businessman, Michele Orsi, grew tired of paying his local gang €125,000 a year in protection money to run his waste disposal business, and in late 2007 decided to talk. Authorities quickly closed down his local council – nothing unusual here because 71 councils in the Naples region have been disbanded due to Camorra infiltration since 1991 (as opposed to 48 in Sicily).[4] Investigating magistrates also placed a local MP, Mario Landolfi, under investigation for suspected links in various rubbish scams.

Two days before he was due to testify Orsi was shot three times as he was drinking a coffee in the bar next to his house. In the meantime, Landolfi had never dreamed of resigning. Furthermore, his party was now in government and he was president of the state TV control commission – in the UK the rough equivalent would be chair of the BBC board of governors. In other words, Landolfi has ultimate control over state news coverage, while Berlusconi owns the private channels.

What is even more chilling is that these linkages hardly provoke any comment; they are so common they have become relatively uncontroversial. The fact that five different Camorra supergrasses, on five different occasions, have all said that Nicola Cosentino, *Forza Italia* leader for the Naples area and under-secretary for the Economy, was helped in his election campaigns by the Camorra hardly provoked a response from his party.[5] The fact that he is also under investigation by Anti-Mafia magistrates raises just a blip on the political radar screen.

One question inevitably arises – why do people vote for these politicians? Part of the answer lies in the economic power of Camorra gangs. These organis-ations are often the biggest employers in the areas they control – which are all scarred by high unemployment and a welfare system that provides virtually no unemployment benefit. In other words, poverty and powerful criminality generally go together. For example, the Neapolitan suburb of Secondigliano/Scampia is widely recognised as being Europe's largest drugs supermarket, yet it also has the highest unemployment rate in the region (61.7 per cent).[6]

The essence of the deal these gangs make with certain parties is to offer the most precious resource imaginable for corrupt politicians – votes. Come election time, gang leaders put the word out that if people want to keep their jobs then they have to vote for 'X'. In return, corrupt politicians will offer them public sector contracts and a degree of protection from investigations and convictions.

As the world enters an economic downturn, unemployment and poverty are destined to rise, and with it the risk of increasing domination of working-class areas by powerful criminal gangs. The strength of the Camorra in the Naples region carries a warning for us all.

Notes

1. www.interno.it/dip_ps/dia/pagine/rilevazioni_stat.htm.
2. www.oecd.org/dataoecd; statistics taken from *Growing Unequal?* (OECD, 2008).
3. See T. Behan, *Defiance*, pp187–9. (I.B.Tauris, London, 2008).
4. *La Voce*, August 2007.
5. *L'Espresso*, 17 October 2008.
6. *La Repubblica*, 31 January 2005.

Acknowledgements

As the Italians say, this book *parte da lontano* – it comes from a long way back. In many ways it is the result of visiting and often living in Naples over a twenty year period, and to thank all the people who have helped me to understand a city characterised by such an uneven and combined development would simply be impossible.

However it is far easier to thank those people who have helped me to find material and who have commented on the work in draft. Apart from the individuals who agreed to be interviewed, specific thanks should go to the following: Percy Allum for guidance over the years, Max Behan, Andrea Cinquegrani and Rita Pennarola at *La Voce della Campania*, Anna Rosa Gualtieri, Tess Lee Ack for work on an earlier version, Giuliano Pennacchio for friendship and help over many years, Barbara Rampoldi for telling me I wrote too much like a Neapolitan and finally to Emma Sinclair Webb.

Introduction

*No, it was not a paradise on Earth because there were
always slum dwellers and poverty.*

Raffaele La Capria

'Politics' and 'democracy' have almost become dirty
words. Around the world, growing numbers of people
have started to switch off from conventional institutional politics.

In the 2000 US presidential elections more than 90
million Americans did not bother to vote – and the
candidate with fewer votes than his rival became
President. Out of a total of 469 seats in Congress, 440
were won by candidates who managed to raise more
money than their rivals.

Britain's general election in 2001 was an equally
spectacular example of electoral apathy. Just 59% of
the electorate bothered to vote, down from 71% in
1997 – the lowest percentage since 1918. Only one
voter in four actually voted for the party which took
power with a huge parliamentary majority – despite
the fact it had so little support in the country. Non-
voting was strongest among young people: 40% of
people aged 18–24 did not use their vote, and

membership of the Labour Party declined from 400,000 in 1997 to 280,000 in 2001.

In the 1997 EU elections, across the whole continent less than half the electorate voted – and under a quarter in the UK.

This recent increase in abstentionism probably has a lot to do with the feeling that all major parties offer very similar policies, and are in essence representatives of big business. And there can be no better example of this than the Enron Corporation, the seventh biggest company in the world until its bankruptcy in December 2001.

During his campaigns to become Governor of Texas, George W. Bush frequently flew on Enron corporate jets, as well as receiving $774,100 from the state's most powerful energy corporation. One could therefore wonder whether such generosity had any influence over the governor's deregulation of the Texas electricity market in 1999? And some people could perceive that the $1.8 million given to the Republican Party's 2000 election campaign, and the $300,000 sponsorship of Bush's inauguration party were donated in order to gain a hearing within government. Similarly, was it pure chance that Enron executives such as Larry Lindsay was appointed as one of George Bush's chief economic advisers or that Thomas White was appointed army secretary and Spencer Abraham energy secretary, both of whom had been on the Enron payroll?

The same trend has surfaced in Britain. Presumably, Enron paid £15,000 to sponsor a drinks reception and gala dinner at the Labour government's 1998 conference simply because they wanted delegates to enjoy themselves. This generosity naturally had no influence over minister Peter

Mandelson's decision, taken three weeks later, to allow Enron to buy a water company without referring the deal to the Monopolies Commission. And the frequent meetings between Enron executives and government ministers in 1998 were presumably just chats between drinking partners, and totally unconnected to Labour dropping its ban on gas-fired power stations.[1] The £36,000 of donations by Enron Europe to the first Blair government could have never had any connection with Ralph Hodge, chairman of the company, being awarded a CBE in 2001.

Just as Enron has systematically contributed to the Democrats and Republicans in the US, it has also had a close relationship with the Conservative Party. John Wakeham was Energy Secretary under Margaret Thatcher in the 1980s, and was responsible for widespread privatisation of the industry – only a few paranoid cynics could possibly see any connection between his role as a minister and his becoming an Enron director in 1994. One of the facts which emerged during Enron's collapse was that Wakeham, as chairman of the 'independent' Press Complaints Commission, had advised the company of which he was also a director, on how to gain favourable press coverage. Lord Wakeham then agreed to step down from the PCC for 'honourable' reasons, but made sure he continued to draw his £156,000 salary; presumably his £80,000 salary from Enron was not enough for the honourable aristocrat to live on.

Details such as these illustrate why it should come as no surprise that in an NOP opinion poll commissioned by Channel Four on the eve of the London Mayday demonstrations in 2001, 76% of people agreed with the statement: 'Big international companies usually care only about profits, and not the interests of the people in the countries where they operate.' Even more interesting was the fact that 67% agreed that big international companies have more influence on daily life in Britain than our own government.[2]

In Germany – a country normally associated with 'clean' politics – there has also been widespread disquiet over the investigations surrounding Helmut Kohl. who had been chancellor for 16 years during the 1980s and 1990s. He has already admitted to taking millions in secret donations to his Christian Democrat party, so much so that some of the German press has nicknamed him Don Kohleone.

In a nutshell, much of the electorate now feels disenfranchised, and is refusing to vote for the major political parties.

Italy is of course no exception to this trend. Never perhaps has the reality of modern parliamentary democracy been so accurately exposed as in Italy during the early 1990s: a reality of wall-to-wall corruption.

In less than two years, five ministers and four party leaders were forced to resign due to their alleged illegal activities, and the level of public anger and dissatisfaction was such that all political parties, including some with over a hundred years' history, either split or changed their name and policies. But even that was not enough to placate public anger; in the March 1994 elections the centre parties which had ruled Italy for nearly fifty years all but disappeared.

Even respected commentators, such as one of Italy's premier academics Ernesto Galli della Loggia, writing in the Italian equivalent of *The Times*, the *Corriere della Sera*, reflected:

> One case of corruption is one case of corruption, ten cases of corruption are ten cases of corruption, but a hundred cases of corruption is a system of corruption.
>
> *Tangentopoli* ['bribe city', the name given to the series of scandals which first emerged in Milan in 1992] has revealed this system, which in turn is divided up into a multiplicity of subsystems. The system of written laws had been replaced by a system of implicit regulations, which were nearly always in contrast with the law of the land.
>
> Italian capitalism was and is part of that system. The stubborn denial of this, the idea that only single capitalists were involved and not capitalism, is to deny that there was a system, and at this point, almost deny the light of day ...
>
> Yet the responsibility for a system cannot be individual, it must be collective.[3]

The extent of illegality was simply bewildering, and the public's anger and indignation were equally deep-seated. There can be no other country in the world where one of the most popular television programmes of 1993 was a two-hour transmission showing edited highlights of politicians squirming and wriggling their way around a prosecuting magistrate's questions. Such was the show's popularity that at one point two of the state television channels were arguing over which one had the right to broadcast the hearings.

Although most ordinary Italians had been aware that corruption was widespread, nobody imagined it was so huge and all-encompassing. Yet there was one section of the population which had always been acutely and accurately aware of the situation: the business community. In a survey among 800 members of the Confindustria, Italy's major employers' association, 85% of the respondents admitted that bribes were paid to get public sector contracts before the bubble burst in 1992.[4] In other words, those who preached the values of a 'free market' were doing anything but practising it, given that bribes were often paid to shut out a competing firm.

What clearly emerged from the *Tangentopoli* scandal was that the most powerful criminal organisation in the country was Parliament: at one point over 30% of MPs in the 1992–94 Parliament were either facing trial or under investigation. If 30% of workers in a factory were all facing similar charges, or alternatively 30% of workers in a social security office, most people would draw the inevitable conclusion that there had been an organised conspiracy. People would start to wonder, 'Surely it is impossible that only those who have been caught knew about it?' And if the accusations facing the MPs of the five parties of Italy's ruling government coalition were collated, three out of four MPs were facing serious charges. The whole institution had become nothing but a criminal conspiracy, indeed one survey revealed a real crime wave amongst the MPs of recent Parliaments, with crime levels estimated at twenty times higher than the national average.[5]

In electoral terms Italians collectively punished the parties which had managed this system. Initially this led to the growth of parties such as the racist Northern League which, from non-existence ten years previously, became the largest party in the North of the country.

But the real winner in the March 1994 elections was media magnate Silvio Berlusconi and his Forza Italia organisation, only formed at the start of that year. Despite appearances, Berlusconi was very much a man of the old guard: he had been a member of the powerful but secret P2 Freemason lodge in the early 1980s, and throughout that decade expanded his media empire thanks to his close relationship with Socialist Party leader Bettino Craxi, one of the key players in the *Tangentopoli* scandals. Berlusconi's loyalty to old friends surfaced in July 1994, when his government passed a decree law which imposed the release from custody of most of the major politicians facing trial. However the government had to rapidly withdraw the decree due to widespread protests.

In the same period his brother Paolo was arrested for corruption, while the Prime Minister himself suffered the ultimate humiliation in November. During his opening speech to a United Nations conference on organised crime, the news emerged that Berlusconi was under criminal investigation for corruption. His three-party alliance in tatters, he resigned soon after.

Writing just before Berlusconi's return to power in 2001, one academic looked back at 1994 and commented: 'He was on the ropes and instead of putting him away the Left rehabilitated him. They wanted his help for constitutional reform which came to nothing.'[6] Technically, however, there was reform. In the early 1990s millions of Italians did turn out to vote in support of electoral reform which was subsequently implemented – but by spring 2000 just 30% of the electorate bothered to vote in another referendum on electoral reform. Italians had understood that it wasn't the voting system which needed changing, but the system itself.

The victory of the centre-left coalition in the 1996 election raised enormous expectations. The largest party in the new coalition was the DS, the ex-communists: the left was finally back in power after fifty long years in opposition. Indeed ex-communist Massimo D'Alema succeeded Romano Prodi as Prime Minister in October 1998.

After the long decades of corruption and sleaze, these two governments had a huge moral mandate to clean things up, starting with establishing once and for all a clear incompatibility between Berlusconi's private ownership of a media empire, and his stated intention as future Prime Minister to radically change all aspects of state media outlets. These centre-left governments had five years to agree on, for example, the creation of blind trusts, but most of their energy was wasted in squabbles. At times the ruling government coalition consisted of up to eight different parties, all highly demanding and argumentative.

But perhaps the major reason behind the left's collapse in May 2001 was its social, foreign and economic policies. Following a path already taken by Tony Blair in Britain, Massimo D'Alema praised the market, privatising public services and decreasing employers' social security contributions. Financing for private schools was massively increased, and catholic schools gained far more official recognition. At work, changes in the law made it easier to sack people, and in foreign policy D'Alema, an ex-communist, took the unusual step of supporting NATO's bombing of Kosovo in 1999.[7]

These are just some of the reasons behind the left's electoral defeat; quite simply its traditional electorate voted for it in far lower numbers. When he became Italian Prime Minister for the second time, according to *Forbes* magazine Silvio Berlusconi was the fourteenth richest man in the world, estimated to have a personal fortune of $18.5 billion. He controls Italy's three largest private television channels, the biggest publishing company, and AC Milan, the country's most successful football team. During the election campaign he used his television companies to openly bombard the public with publicity and 'news' which was clearly biased in his support. Furthermore, 20 million copies of a Berlusconi hagiography, *An Italian Story*, were distributed to every household during the campaign. The book contained a total of 250 photographs of Berlusconi, often in soft focus: feeding one of his daughters, jogging with his son (although his mother, now divorced from Berlusconi, never appears), working out in the gym with Sylvester Stallone, picking flowers, and so on.[8]

Despite his wealth and political history, he was elected Prime Minister of the world's fifth largest economy – in coalition with two other highly dubious parties: the Northern League and the 'post-fascist' National Alliance. As in 1994, Berlusconi quickly showed his unwillingness to separate the activities of his business empire from his duties as a politician. One of the first bills announced by the government, and then passed, involved ending the crime of 'false accounting'. Before this change in the law was made Berlusconi was facing three trials as a businessman – all for false accounting. He has also called for an official parliamentary commission of inquiry into *Tangentopoli*, but not against the corrupt politicians – investigating magistrates will be scrutinised instead, to see whether they ever showed signs of 'political bias'.

Even though he is Italy's most successful 'self-made man', the international weekly of big business, *The Economist*, concluded in an editorial just before his election: 'The election of Mr Berlusconi as Prime Minister would mark a dark day for Italian democracy and the rule of law.'[9] These reservations were not just due to the nature of his business dealings, as the same editorial noted in its opening sentence; Berlusconi had also been investigated recently for 'complicity in murder, connections with the Mafia' and many other offences.

Indeed allegations of links between Forza Italia and the Mafia emerged soon after the March 1994 election; what seems clear is that Mafia bosses passed the word around that people should vote for Berlusconi's party. Among those campaigning was Pino Mandalari, who had also been the accountant of Totò Riina, the head of the Mafia at that time. One Forza Italia politician elected, Marcello Dell'Utri, had also been manager of Berlusconi's media holding company in Sicily, however he was committed for trial in October 1996 for money laundering and collusion with the Mafia. Although denying Mafia membership, he quickly admitted to attending a wedding held in London in 1980 of a presumed drug trafficker, together with three other prominent *mafiosi*. Magistrates later tried to bring further charges, but MPs refused to lift his parliamentary immunity. Despite all this, in the June 1999 EU elections Dell'Utri received a massive personal vote in Sicily.[10] He was elected as a national MP again in May 2001; indeed Forza Italia wiped the board in Sicily, winning all sixty one seats.

This is the background to a scandalous statement made soon after his election by Forza Italia Minister for Infrastructures, Pietro Lunardi, the man responsible for regulating public sector contracts, probably the economic sector from which the Mafia and the Camorra make more money than anywhere else. Who knows what kind of message he was trying to send when he said: 'The Mafia and the Camorra have always been around and will continue to be around; unfortunately they do exist. We will have to live with this reality.'[11]

This account of recent Italian politics is important because it shows that it is from this political, financial and bureaucratic cesspool that organised crime manages to find protection and to make deals.

Although the extreme economic and social problems in the South of Italy are the immediate causes of organised crime, before these can be eradicated the elected politicians and unelected big businessmen and bureaucrats have to be taken on as the first stage in the fight against organised crime. The solution to organised crime in the South cannot come from these institutions; it has to come from those ordinary people who suffer the consequences of organised crime.

Indeed, the existence of large criminal organisations in the South has historically been looked upon favourably by major southern politicians. In the postwar period a backward-looking ruling class, raised on traditions of nepotism and string-pulling, has transformed southern political life into a bureaucratic nightmare in which any public service or project is viewed as a favour, not an automatic right, and even then the service or project in question is normally only provided if there is some kind of bribe or trade-off.

The trade-off between politicians and professional criminals is quite simple: the criminals mobilise their considerable electorate around specific candidates, invest large parts of their illegal profits in legal activities which generate desperately needed jobs, and create a climate of fear and intimidation, keeping the lid on a society that often resembles a pressure cooker. The politician repays the favour in three ways: by awarding public sector contracts to companies controlled by professional criminals; guaranteeing a considerable amount of legal protection through applying specific pressure within the judiciary and the police force; and often allowing gang leaders to control the allocation of resources and personal favours to ordinary people.

The strength of the Camorra

The Camorra predates the Mafia by several decades. But its history has been less linear than its Sicilian counterpart, as at various points in its history it has been defined as being completely extinct or close to extinction: the first pronouncement of the Camorra's death occurred following a major trial in 1912; then during the interwar period the fascists claimed to have eradicated it through widespread repression, while the historian Eric Hobsbawm declared that it was approaching extinction in his 1959 book *Primitive Rebels*.

The reality, though, is that like the Mafia, the Camorra has had its ups and downs; and the 1980s were a decade of unprecedented growth. While some people may have heard of Totò Riina and Tommaso Buscetta, very few people outside Italy have heard of Carmine Alfieri or Pasquale Galasso. Yet in a report by the Anti-Mafia Commission (a permanent government committee established to investigate organised crime and make recommendations to Parliament), Alfieri's gang is described as: 'a phenomenon that has taken on a stronger form of oppression and corruption than the Mafia', and when he was arrested in September 1992 Alfieri's personal assets were estimated at $1.2 billion, making him the richest criminal in Italy.

Alfieri's gang was not based in Sicily but in the town of Nola, 15 miles north-east of Naples, and became the most powerful Camorra gang of the 1980s and 1990s. In terms of violence, while the Mafia sometimes engages in spectacular assassinations, the Camorra is perhaps an even more efficient killing machine, as proved by the admission of Carmine Alfieri's main hit man, Domenico Cuomo, who confessed to 'about' ninety murders in the 1983–93 period. Indeed the police estimate that Alfieri's killers alone may have been responsible for 500 murders.[12]

Outside Italy, even the British *Sun* had heard of the Camorra nearly twenty years ago, referring to it in typically lurid but inaccurate tones as, 'the Camorra, the Mafia's most evil branch'.[13] Ten years ago, without making any distinction between the Camorra and the Mafia, the *Daily Mail* published a list of Italy's top ten organised crime bosses – the top two were Carmine Alfieri and Lorenzo Nuvoletta, both members of the Camorra.[14]

During the 1990s reporting in the more serious newspapers became more accurate, particularly thanks to *The Guardian*'s former Italian correspondent Ed Vulliamy, who once gave this vivid picture of the city:

Naples is a Third World city with Third World politics, it's super-rich surrounded by a miserable hinterland sprawling back from the volcano and the bay, a dilapidated jungle of violence, half-finished buildings, motorways that lead nowhere, cocaine, primitive Catholicism and stinking, dumped rubbish.

Its legal economy is based only on lavish state aid, money procured by its political leaders and distributed at their discretion and pleasure ...

There is vast private wealth in the city – at night the downtown streets are crammed with new cars, mobile phones and fur coats – but this is illegal wealth, the result of the most important ingredient of the Neapolitan scandal: the Camorra ...

Hundreds of thousands of people in Naples owe their jobs and livelihoods to either Byzantine political patronage or to the Camorra – or both. In southern Italy there are no rights – only privileges – and for those you pay a politician, either in cash or with your vote – or both.[15]

What has become truly shocking over the last decade is that the Camorra is hardly mentioned within its home country. While there is frequent discussion about the Mafia there is almost a conspiracy of silence over the Camorra, in the sense that for the last ten years, from a whole range of official sources, the reality which has been emerging is that the Camorra has more money and more members than the Mafia. Even more serious is the fact that, although the regions of Sicily and Campania have almost identical populations, there have been many more councillors debarred for illegal acts in Campania than in Sicily; the same goes for councils disbanded for organised crime infiltration, and for MPs, Senators and investigating magistrates being investigated or convicted for having links with organised crime (see Table 1).

But the disbanding of these councils is not the result of just a few individuals wielding an unacceptable level of influence. In a report published in late 1993, the Anti-Mafia Commission stated: 'In the disbanded councils of Campania, rather than speaking of the Camorra's infiltration, penetration or influence, one can speak of the Camorra's merging with local administration.'[16]

Seven years later, in October 2000, another Anti-Mafia report reached similar if not more alarming conclusions. The merging of local councils with *camorristi* allows local politicians: 'to ensure for themselves, through the Camorra, the systematic control of voting patterns over a wide area'. Whereas the Camorra receives: 'huge financial resources, complete dominance of economic activities in the area under their control, and through the possibility of providing jobs and a trickle-down effect from their profitable economic operations, they create social consensus and exert massive electoral influence'.[17]

Providing jobs is the key to understanding the Camorra's popularity. The current EU unemployment rate is 7.6%; in the Campania region it is 23.3% and in Naples 28% – far higher than unemployment levels in areas such as the West Bank and Gaza Strip.[18] At this point it is not surprising to learn that in one opinion poll amongst young people the Camorra received an approval rating of 14.6% and political parties just 13.7%.[19]

Arresting suspected criminals is a very difficult thing to do in many towns and areas of Naples because mass spontaneous revolts break out against the police. One police patrol car is never enough because people will surround it or barricade its exit route: a simple arrest often turns into a major police operation. Here is just one example from September 1999: in Naples' *piazza Mercato*, twelve policemen were injured in running battles during a failed attempt to arrest somebody for selling contraband cigarettes.[20]

A parish priest in the Spanish Quarters, one of the poorest areas of Naples, once recounted that following the arrest of local gang leaders, his parishioners 'tell me that things were better when the Camorra was in control, when people were under the protection of people who mattered'.[21] Indeed when young people were asked what they would do following a theft, 97% said they would not report it to the police, but instead contact the local Camorra boss in the hope of getting their goods back.[22] It should now be clear why, in another opinion poll in which people were asked the question whether the Camorra controlled certain areas of the city rather than the government, 11% disagreed, but 70% agreed.[23]

The aim of this book to tell the story of the Camorra and explain how it works. In many ways this tale is long overdue. Because while much media and government attention, both nationally and internationally, has been focused on Sicily and the Mafia, a separate and distinct organisation, arguably even more difficult to eradicate, has been consolidating itself in the shadow of Vesuvius.

CHAPTER ONE

The origins of the Camorra and the Mafia

Death is only a possibility, but hunger is certain.

Victor Serge

The origins of a Neapolitan criminal organisation called the Camorra are far from clear. Some writers have claimed a history which goes back as far as the sixteenth century, arguing that it is the direct descendant of a Spanish secret society, the *Garduna*, founded in 1417. Officials of the Spanish Bourbon monarchy would have then introduced it to Naples during their rule over southern Italy, 'the kingdom of the Two Sicilies'.[1]

Another possibility is that the members of a criminal organisation called Camorra were a new type of *lazzaroni*, a word which had been used to describe a very poor common thief. But as Naples grew both in size and wealth, criminality began to change. Whereas the *lazzaroni* had been individuals, *camorristi* were part of an organisation.

A far more likely explanation is that the Camorra grew out of Neapolitan society during the period of the French revolution, between the end of the

eighteenth century and the beginning of the nineteenth century.

What is beyond doubt is that throughout the
centuries there is evidence of small criminal gangs
operating in Naples. All of these gangs arose amongst
the city's poor – people who never kept written
records due to their illiteracy; hence the difficulty in
establishing any categorical evidence about what kind
of organisation, if any, the Camorra grew out of.

It is therefore not surprising that there are also
differing opinions on the origin of the word itself. The
first official use of the term 'Camorra' occurred in
1735, when a Royal circular authorised the establishment of eight gaming houses in Naples, including the
'Camorra avanti palazzo' (the 'Camorra in front of the
Palace'), the Royal Palace in today's *Piazza del Plebiscito*,
where a gaming house had existed for many centuries. In this case the word is almost certainly an
amalgamation of *capo* (boss) and the Neapolitan street
game, the *morra*. The *morra* is one of Italy's oldest
street games, in which two players open their fists
varying the numbers of fingers on display. The player
who guesses the right number, which he must shout
out as the fists are opened, is the winner.[2]

Others argue that 'Camorra' was the word used to
describe the rake-off earned by *camorristi* from goods
being delivered or transported around the city. In any
event, it was a word used to describe extortion.

Despite the disputes surrounding the precise origins
of the Camorra, what is certainly beyond doubt is
that:

When the Camorra emerges into the life of
Naples it does not seem a totally new fact, it is
rather the point of arrival, or the result, of the

city's long history, and it almost seems the most natural expression of the history of the Neapolitan popular classes.[3]

This is not to say that ordinary Neapolitans had some inbuilt biological instinct which led them to create a large criminal organisation; rather a combination of political ignorance and autocratic repression probably left them incapable of creating any other form of organisation.

Indeed it is the history of Naples itself which explains why such an organisation arose here and not elsewhere, and why organised crime has remained such a dominant feature of the city during the last two hundred years.

The city of Naples had been Europe's third largest city for three centuries, from around 1500 to the early 1800s. With a population of approximately 350,000 throughout the sixteenth century, it often vied with Paris for the title of Europe's second largest city.

But towards the end of the seventeenth century it began to experience economic difficulties due to a fall in its exports of silk, wheat, oil and wine, caused in turn by an international economic recession and the rise of new competitors. Furthermore, the plague of 1656 led to 60% of the city's population either dying or leaving the city.

Despite such calamities, throughout this period many thousands of people migrated from the countryside to Naples because the city offered the possibility of work; furthermore the ruling aristocracy had decreed that taxes were not to be paid within the city walls. However work was often scarce, so for the aristocracy the city's key problem was the existence of masses of impoverished and unemployed people desperate for money and some kind of solution to their misery. The authorities needed a repressive network able to control a volatile and unpredictable population which could suddenly break out into violent revolt, such as the popular rebellion led by Masaniello in 1647–48.

Three-quarters of southern Italian trade passed through Naples, with large numbers of people being employed in the port, the warehouses and in the distribution of commodities; the servicing of the aristocracy and the middle classes also employed many people. As the eighteenth century came to an end the rest of Europe and northern Italy were experiencing huge economic expansion during the industrial revolution, while Naples was stuck in a virtually feudal system, run by a monarchy terrified of any innovation. The city's role as a capital also meant it had a large number of non-productive inhabitants: it has been estimated that in 1792, over a third of the entire population was made up of clerics and aristocrats.[4]

As the decades and centuries went by, it became clear that population growth was not being matched by an increase in production. Indeed, by 1871 35,000 people, out of an active population of 220,000, were still employed as cooks, chambermaids and gardeners, the same percentage as in the first half of the seventeenth century.[5]

Another related problem which affected the city at the time, and which is arguably still important today, was the absence of a dynamic entrepreneurial spirit amongst the middle classes. Up until the French Revolution, Naples had been a residential centre for the ruling classes of the South, as well as a bureaucratic and administrative capital. Most of the middle classes lived off government monopolies and commodity production, which were protected by tariff barriers, and therefore had no interest in innovation. Although only 1,356 'merchants' were recorded in the 1845 census (out of a population of 400,000), most of these were shopowners. Very few were engaged in investment and manufacture; and most decisions were made within the immediate family circle.[6]

It is likely that the Camorra emerged in this period as a result of the failure of the Neapolitan Republic, proclaimed in 1799 on the wave of the French Revolution ten years earlier. If the Masaniello revolt 150 years earlier had been a revolution made by the people without leaders, the 1799 revolt was carried through by liberal leaders without the people. This allowed the whole experiment to be quickly destroyed by an alliance of the Bourbons, the Church and the British navy under Horatio Nelson. Although the Bourbon dynasty was not fully restored until 1815, the Camorra first emerged during the chaotic vacuum of power in the years 1799–1815.

In the following period, the middle classes organised themselves into secret societies such as the Freemasons and the Carboneria, and entered into negotiations with the Bourbons. But for the vast majority of Neapolitans the Camorra became their only voice, the only way in which their presence could be felt: 'In this fashion the Camorra was a mass class-based phenomenon, one of the most popular illegal manifestations of nineteenth century European history.'[7]

At this time northern Italy and the rest of Europe were enjoying a period of intense economic development: trade was blossoming between states and with overseas territories, industrialisation had begun, along with the widespread building of railways. Yet in

the early part of the nineteenth century the only railways built in southern Italy linked up the three Royal
Palaces of Naples, Caserta and Portici.

In many areas of his kingdom Ferdinand II was
known as 'King Bomba', because during the 1848
revolutions he ordered the bombardment of Palermo
and Messina. He reigned for thirty years (1830–59) as
a total autocrat, and was highly distrustful of any
innovations, at one point even banning the introduction of the first cameras into the city. Marco Monnier,
a Swiss academic living in Naples during this period,
describes the king's attitude towards the ordinary
people thus:

> He never considered for a moment raising the
> people up from their level of degradation; on the
> contrary, he wanted to keep them there until the
> end of time as he knew very well that, given the
> nature of the period we live in, an absolute
> monarchy is only possible if it rules over a
> degraded and exhausted populace.[8]

The first official news of the Camorra as an organisation dates back to 1820, when police records detailed a
disciplinary meeting of the Camorra. Such an event
indicates a qualitative change: the Camorra and
camorristi were no longer simply local gangs living off
theft and extortion, they now had a fixed structure
and some kind of hierarchy. The first written Statute
of a Camorra organisation was also discovered in
1820, once again indicating a stable organisational
structure amongst the underworld, and the second
Statute was discovered in 1842.[9] There were initiation
rites, and funds set aside for the families of those
imprisoned.

In the early part of the nineteenth century Naples was both economically and politically stagnant. The general level of poverty is illustrated by the outbreak of cholera – a water-borne disease primarily caused by contaminated water and lack of public and personal hygiene – which occurred in 1836–37, killing 20,000 people.[10] This mass poverty, together with the lack of any political outlet, made for a chaotic and ungovernable city, and under these conditions the ability to unleash a widespread reign of terror is an important consideration for those in power. The control of the impoverished and alienated masses was a service which the Camorra could offer local rulers. And for many of the Neapolitan poor, the use of violence was the only way out of their miserable existence; the static economic climate blocked any other solution.

One of the Camorra's first strongholds developed within the prison system. This is how Marco Monnier described an inmate's relationship with the Camorra:

> He wasn't allowed to eat, drink, smoke or gamble without a *camorrista*'s permission. He had to give him a tenth of all the money he was sent, and had to pay for the right to buy and sell, as well as paying for both essential and non-essential things. He even paid to get legal advice, as if he were getting a privilege: he even paid when he was poorer and more naked than the walls of his cell, he was forced to deprive himself of everything. Those who refused to accept such impositions ran the risk of being clubbed to death.[11]

Camorristi also took money from the prison authorities, as they effectively guaranteed order. Interestingly, however, they generally left the few aristocratic and middle class prisoners alone; even though some *camorristi* had considerable wealth, they still felt some deference towards those in a higher social position.

The revolution of 1848 appeared to offer new political hope to the city, with Ferdinand II initially granting a liberal constitution. But the key weakness of the revolt was its lack of mass popular support, as the same writer noted a few years afterwards:

> That revolution, if it can be called such, took the form of a simple demonstration of gentlemen, without even one sword being drawn. The common people supported the absolute monarchy. In the insurrection of 15 May the barricades were defended by heroic young men, who were all from good families.[12]

Conscious that ordinary people 'cared little about whether they were a citizen or a subject',[13] the king was soon able to clamp down again, suspending the new constitution and imprisoning leading liberals. But he was not only spurred on by the inherent weakness of the Neapolitan revolt, he was also worried because liberals had taken power in cities such as Milan and Venice. Both Ferdinand and the Pope were strongly opposed to liberalism; indeed Pope Pius IX sheltered in Naples during the Roman republic of 1848–49, and Neapolitan forces contributed to the overthrow of the Roman republic led by Garibaldi and Mazzini.

Hopes of any immediate change were dashed, and communication with the outside world became very difficult:

> You found yourself living with a people who were isolated from the rest of Europe, extraneous to all

the issues which interested the two Worlds, imprisoned in its beautiful cell where neither ideas, beliefs, nor the material discoveries of our century could penetrate ... Foreign newspapers could only be obtained through foreign legations, booksellers hid forbidden books under their beds and then sold them at exorbitant prices: people then dug out holes in the walls of their rooms to hide their illicit and forbidden fruits.[14]

This repression not only affected liberals and the educated middle classes, it also conditioned people in the business world, both Neapolitan and foreign: 'I have seen highly respected foreign merchants and industrialists buying portraits, chalk busts, or little bronze and terracotta statues of the king and queen. They then placed them around their premises so they wouldn't be suspected of liberalism.'[15]

The effect on ordinary people, and the consequences, were even more serious:

Any social, political or religious links had been destroyed through terror. As with the intelligentsia, the healthy forces in the country are directionless and worn out because they are too isolated and dispersed. No cohesion whatsoever was possible: the authorities even banned groups of people who met to play chess ... What emerges from this is that in all the popular classes no association could be created to counteract the dominance of the wicked.[16]

Despite the liberals' ineptitude, their lack of popular support, and the strict rule of Ferdinand II, demands for change continued throughout the 1850s. The southern economy continued to grow slowly, with the vast majority of goods passing through Naples. Between 1838–52 grain exports increased sixfold, with fruit exports also doubling during 1832–59. Naples' dock was now handling a huge amount in trade; in 1855–59 alone the port doubled its activity.[17]

The Camorra was involved in all these activities. Not only was it earning money from gambling and theft, it also earned rake-offs from goods which arrived at the port and passed through the city's gates; indeed the amount they took could often reach 10% of the value of the goods themselves. According to a popular saying, they could 'squeeze gold out of fleas'.

Alongside this economic growth, the Camorra may have also enjoyed a degree of political protection. In some circumstances they effectively replaced the police: 'The police had no need to intervene in those dangerous places; they entrusted the members of the sect [the Camorra], which was then tolerated.'[18]

Not only had trade increased, a degree of industrial-isation had also started; for example the Naples' cigarette factory was probably the largest in the entire South, employing 1,220 women.

Yet most of this was taking place *despite* the king and his administration; most of the capital invested came from Germany, France or Switzerland. Tariff barriers discouraged new investment and new methods of production; and many members of the middle class depended on the old system for jobs within the administration.

Throughout Ferdinand II's reign Neapolitan society had been highly unstable: masses of poor were forced to eke out a living doing whatever came to hand, which obviously included criminal activities, whilst the middle classes were frustrated by economic and political restrictions. What changed things was Giuseppe Garibaldi's landing in Sicily in May 1860 and the beginning of his campaign to unite Italy.

The other catalyst was the liberals coming to an agreement with the Camorra. Following their defeat in 1848, liberal oppositionists had realised that they needed the support of the masses to overthrow the king. And it is an indication of the Camorra's strength that the liberals turned to them, and paid them, in order to build links with ordinary people.

A meeting was arranged behind the *Albergo de' Poveri*, during which the *camorristi*:

> told them off for their gentlemanly revolution in 1848. They told them what I had already noted, that this revolt had not broken out amongst the people, and neither was it for the people: the well dressed and educated middle classes had only thought about themselves, leaving the poor people aside. If any changes were to occur the rabble did not intend to give all the advantages to those who already had money; at the end of the day the art of launching an uprising needed money, lots of money, and to start with every local leader, that is every Camorra boss, demanded payment of ten thousand ducats.[19]

The liberals had very little alternative; Ferdinand II's ferocious repression had meant that the masses had no other organisation but the Camorra – in reality the *camorristi* were the leaders of the city's poor. The Camorra had clearly come a long way in just a few decades, effectively becoming power brokers. It is important to note however that their attitude was mercenary; there is no evidence of the organisation

consistently expressing any kind of political belief or
following a strategy of its own, independently of
others.

So as Garibaldi defeated the Bourbons in Sicily and
crossed over onto the Italian mainland, the old regime
was about to come to an end.

'na bestemmia pe' sta' libertà.[20] Unification and the stabilisation of the Camorra

As Garibaldi's expeditionary force advanced up the
peninsula from Sicily the government of Piedmont,
which had organised his trip without really intending
to unite the whole of Italy, became severely alarmed.
The Prime Minister, Cavour, tried to engineer a conservative revolt in Naples in favour of Victor Emmanuel,
the Piedmont king and future king of Italy, but it failed
due to an almost total lack of support.

On 24 June 1860 Francis II, the new Bourbon king
in Naples, was forced to finally implement the Constitution agreed upon in 1848; he also released many
camorristi who had been arrested the previous year
accused of spying for the liberals. Francis was desperately trying to head off the enthusiasm for Garibaldi's
victories in Sicily and his successes in Calabria, as he
feared that the revolutionary enthusiasm of poor
peasants would jeopardise his own rule. But he had
moved far too late: two days later attacks began on
police patrols and on numerous police barracks, probably the work of *camorristi* taking revenge for their
imprisonment. The old order was rapidly collapsing;
the police soon began taking off their uniforms and
melting into the crowds, whilst senior members of the

old regime tried to convert their banknotes into gold, aware that the old regime could quickly be completely overthrown. Finally, on the evening of the 26th a state of siege was declared.

Italian Unification, as the Italian Marxist Antonio Gramsci argued, can be seen as a 'passive revolution', with little involvement by the masses. In effect the change of government in Naples was the result of *trasformismo* – incorporation of the opposition into the ruling circle – with ordinary people being deprived of any important or long-term role.

In the chaos of a disintegrating dynasty a new Prefect of Police had been appointed, Liborio Romano, who turned to the Camorra to maintain 'law and order'. This attitude of managing the level of illegality is still a characteristic of the Neapolitan ruling class, and it is therefore worth quoting from his memoirs at length:

How could the city be saved in the midst of so many disruptive elements and imminent dangers? Amongst all the possibilities which passed through my anxious mind, rendered such by the seriousness of the situation, only one appeared to me to offer probable, although not certain, success, so I tried it. I thought of making use of the evil skills of *camorristi*, offering the most influential leaders a means to rehabilitate themselves. It appeared to me that this would drag them away from the mob, and at least paralyse their most evil intentions, it also meant that there would be no attempt to repress or contain them, as this was a moment in which I lacked any kind of strength …

It was my intention to draw a veil over their past and ask the best of them to join a new police force, which would no longer be made up of wicked assassins and vile spies, but of honest people who, well paid for their important services, would have soon gained the respect of their fellow citizens.

The man [a Camorra leader invited to Romano's house] who initially appeared to be doubtful and uncertain, after I had spoken threw away all suspicion and wanted to kiss my hand; he also promised more than what I had asked for, and added that in an hour he would have returned to see me at the Prefettura. Even before the hour was up he had returned with a colleague, and they assured me that they had passed on my instructions to their friends, and that they would lay down their lives for me.[21]

The fact that one of the Camorra leaders who ran this new police force, Salvatore De Crescenzo, had already been convicted on six separate occasions, once for murder, did not seem to concern the Prefect of Police. The most important thing was keeping 'order', or in other words stopping the masses from taking control; any considerations of a moral or legal nature came a very poor second.

Romano's manoeuvres worked. The king withdrew from Naples on September 6 and Garibaldi arrived by train from Salerno the following day.[22]   The changeover was so smooth that Garibaldi arrived with just thirty men to take over the running of a city of half a million people, the largest city in the new Italian state.

The need first by the liberals, and then by Romano, to make an alliance with the Camorra was a clear indication of the Camorra's strength. However,

Romano's account also illustrates that *camorristi* were very easily manipulated. The Camorra had effectively become mercenaries within the city, acting as secret policemen during the last year of Ferdinand II's reign, as liberal oppositionists during the last year of Bourbon rule, and then as official policemen in the first few months following Unification. The Camorra had played all of these roles for money; there is no evidence of *camorristi* having had any consistent political opinions.

But the fact that leading *camorristi* were now moving quite regularly in the corridors of power obviously increased their political awareness and self-confidence. Their position as policemen naturally gave them greater freedom of manoeuvre and they quickly moved into the contraband industry, not only extorting money from those already smuggling goods, but also forcing shopkeepers and merchants to take smuggled instead of official goods. Once they had paid off the Camorra, traders found that they were still paying far less than the official price.

This clearly meant a huge drop in revenue for the new administration. But traders were very unwilling to change their habits:

> They chose the lesser of two evils. If they paid a tax to the sect [the Camorra] they only ran the risk of being discovered by tax inspectors and receiving a minor conviction; but if they paid the tax inspectors then they were certain of being caught by *camorristi* and given a good beating. So they paid a tax to the sect.[23]

The new administration soon realised that its income was being severely reduced, and that using the

Camorra as a police force had created a whole range of problems. So they set up a new police force and brought in soldiers from outside Naples, and in December 1860 turned on the Camorra, arresting ninety people. The Camorra responded with demonstrations against the new Chief of Police, Silvio Spaventa, with attacks on both his house and office.

Marco Monnier commented on the growing power and self-confidence of some Camorra leaders:

> All those swaggering men from the market squares of Naples were no longer satisfied with stealing small amounts from ordinary people: they had become politicians. During the elections they barred certain candidates, comforting the conscience and the beliefs of voters with their weapons.[24]

However it is important not to exaggerate this tendency towards some kind of intervention in politics. Although some Camorra leaders began to make statements in favour of the deposed Bourbon regime, these were never part of any independent political ideology or strategy. Such manoeuvres were limited in scope, and were probably aimed at influencing politicians over a small number of specific issues. For example in the first years of Unification, if (in the Camorra's eyes) a deputy had behaved badly in the new Parliament in Turin, demonstrations were organised in front of his house – but the Camorra never tried to stand its own candidates.

In reality the Camorra could only apply pressure under certain circumstances as it did not have either the ability or the knowhow to stand its own candidates. Economically it still relied mainly on extortion;

and the ruling authorities did not depend on their investments to keep the economy ticking over.

These political and economic weaknesses made it possible to curb the Camorra's growth, although by now it was too strong to be totally destroyed. A state of siege was declared in July 1862, and in the next three months 500 *camorristi* were rounded up. The special legislation passed to defeat the banditry which was sweeping remote southern areas, requiring the stationing of 100,000 northern troops throughout the South, was also applied to Naples, with the Camorra being defined as 'urban banditry'. So in this period the authorities clearly re-established their dominance, as 1,200 convicted *camorristi* were sentenced to house arrest during 1863–64.[25]

Most economic indicators for this period showed that Naples and the South began to fall even further behind the rest of Italy. The highest tariff barriers in Europe (80%), set up to contain competition from France and Britain, were suddenly removed; the sudden influx of cheap foreign goods devastated local producers whose goods were priced artificially high. Taxation also doubled; but the majority of taxes collected and capital accumulated were destined for investment in the mushrooming industry of the North.[26] Poverty still remained widespread, and surfaced in a particularly virulent form in another outbreak of cholera in 1884. (Cholera is endemic to the city, which last suffered an outbreak in 1973.)

The Camorra began to make inroads into new economic areas, becoming directly involved in commerce for the first time through the buying and selling of bran and horses. The city's economy became increasingly dominated by council contracts, as well as the rebuilding of many of the city's oldest areas.

The change in the Camorra's manner of dress also indicated some kind of transformation. In the period from their emergence up until 1860, it was important for them to be recognised as *camorristi* to be able to intimidate people. So many of them adopted a kind of uniform, which included tight jackets and wide trousers, often with a beret, tattoos and several rings on their fingers. But as some now aspired to enter the middle classes, their dress became more respectable and inconspicuous. In essence there was very little mystery surrounding their identity, as the local Prefect wrote to the Ministry of Interior in 1874: 'Their activities and behaviour ... are etched into the memory of all the inhabitants of their local areas, more so than Christian doctrine is taught to the faithful of the parish.'[27]

The extension in suffrage in 1882 and 1889 also led them to gain more influence in politics for the very same reason as thirty years before: the liberal politicians had very little contact with the vast majority of the population, and were therefore obliged to look to the Camorra to guarantee them votes. It is in this period that the Camorra began to gain political protection, and in exchange for this led street protests in 1893 against the massacre of Italian workers at Aigues-Mortes in France. They also led the demonstrations in support of the Liberal politician Francesco Crispi becoming Prime Minister.

The Camorra's predominantly mercenary attitude towards politics emerged once again when an eleven year old boy was killed by the police during a demonstration. Tram and carriage drivers went on strike in protest, and following the precedent set during the 1860 crisis, the Prefect asked Ciccio Cappuccio, leader of the Camorra at that time, to bring the strike to an end, which was swiftly done.

Although full democracy had still not been created, a political space was now available for challenges to be made against the collusion which existed between the local political system and the Camorra. In 1879 the Republican Party made the following accusation in its newspaper (although its distribution was banned by the Questura, the Police Headquarters):

> We have heard that Questura policemen are being subsidised by gaming houses, and that the average daily amount is the tidy sum of ten lire! One could say that the Camorra are always around, all that changes is the uniform of the lazy bourgeois and that of the idle police official.[28]

This political dispute was one of the first signs of various changes which were soon to take effect, leading to the long-term decline of the Camorra, a decline which was to last until about 1970.

The next major street demonstrations occurred in 1898, in protest against a massacre of workers in Milan. One contemporary account described the events:

> Ordinary people left their work and started to move through the streets where large factories were, calling their brothers out. As the crowd got bigger, it moved to the richer areas where the government building was, and kept on chanting: 'Long live the Republic, long live socialism, long live our brothers in Milan.'[29]

The fact that Neapolitans were demonstrating in solidarity with people in a faraway northern city was an

important event in itself; the provincialism of Neapolitan society, nurtured under the Bourbons, was being
whittled away.

The people behind the demonstration were
members of the Socialist Party (PSI) and trade unionists; the gradual industrialisation of the city meant
that ordinary people finally had a new ideology of a
better future, that of socialism. Although most people
were still highly religious they had remained indif-
ferent to the Liberals; the socialists were offering a
new society in which working people would finally be
able to take control of their own lives. The socialist
tradition in Naples goes back as far as December 1868,
when a branch of Karl Marx's First International was
founded, with a reported membership in August 1872
of 800–1,000.[30]

The Camorra was absent from these demonstrations; their lack of political understanding meant that
their control of the streets and the working masses
was usurped for the first time. Socialists also began to
attack the collusion between the city council and the
Camorra, with a campaign that led to the conviction
of a councillor for corruption, and eventually to the
resignation of the entire city council in November
1900. Campaigns such as this made the whole country
aware of the links between politicians and the
Camorra, and led to a huge public inquiry conducted
by Giuseppe Saredo, instituted in November 1900 and
eventually reporting with 2,000 pages of evidence in
September 1901.

Saredo's conclusions should be quoted at length
because they constitute a damning indictment of
Neapolitan society in the forty years since Unification.
Politicians had been more concerned with jockeying
for position in order to maintain power, rather than

solving any of the city's problems. The result of their lack of mass support and the desperation engendered by mass poverty was that the Camorra had thrived:

Together with the original 'low level' Camorra, which had ruled over the poor with various forms of bullying in periods of abjection and servitude, a 'high level' Camorra has arisen, which is made up of the more audacious and cunning members of the bourgeoisie. These people, taking advantage of the indolence of their own class and its lack of resolve, mainly the result of economic difficulties, also used the confident and ignorant multitudes to impose themselves. They managed to feed off commerce and council contracts, as well as public demonstrations, clubs and the press ... With the development of the Camorra, there also arose a new electoral organisation based on patronage; services were exchanged and rendered in return for votes, and this took the form of protection, help, advice, recommendation; which also permitted the growth of a strata of go-betweens and fixers, who in the period before 1860 were already an essential element in the business cycle ... The addition of electoral corruption not only made all this possible, but even made the presence of an intermediary essential in all corners of general social and administrative practice ...

From the rich industrialist who wants a clear road into politics or administration to the small shopowner who wants to ask for a reduction in his taxes; from the businessman trying to win a contract to a worker looking for a job in a factory; from a professional who wants more clients or greater recognition to somebody looking for an office job; from somebody from the Provinces who has come to Naples to buy some goods to somebody who wants to emigrate in America; they all find somebody stepping into their path, and nearly all make use of them.[31]

Although such a picture is clearly alarming, the Camorra was nevertheless already entering a period of decline. Even so, its influence did not disappear overnight. In 1904 the Camorra, led by a priest named Vito Vittozzi, managed to stop the election of socialist deputy Ettore Ciccotti in the Vicaria area. A few years later Ciccotti wrote that the campaign: 'had a clear aim … that of breaking the working class movement and the Trades Council in Naples'.[32]

But overall the Saredo inquiry undoubtedly made a great impact: in 1903 the ex Mayor of the city, Celestino Summonte, was given a three year prison sentence for corruption and abuse of power. And a mass trial in 1911–12 led to long prison sentences for 35 leading *camorristi*, convicted of murdering fellow leader Gennaro Cuocolo a few years earlier.

Mass migration also destabilised the Camorra's power base, the urban poor. Only 3,165 Neapolitans emigrated from the city in 1876, yet this figure rose to 76,000 in 1901 and 90,000 in 1906.[33] This obviously meant that large numbers of the poor physically disappeared from the city, but at the same time many areas were also being transformed as a result of an urban renewal policy.

Those who did remain were living in far worse conditions than their northern counterparts; forty years of Unification had done nothing to solve the perennial 'southern question' of Italian politics, indeed in many ways things were worse. Statistics from the 1901 census showed that 42% of Neapolitan adults were illiterate, compared to 18% in Genoa, 11% in Turin and 4% in Milan.[34]

Nevertheless, the western and eastern edges of the city were now industrialised to quite a significant extent, and there had also been considerable growth of small industries throughout the city. This increase in stable employment, and the consequent rise in trade union and socialist party membership, meant that the Camorra's power to attract the city's poor to a life of crime was for the moment eclipsed. The masses could now find a different voice from that of their traditional spontaneous rebellion.

This is not to say that contemporary lessons cannot be drawn from the first fifty years of Unification in Naples. In short a small secret society of illiterate working class criminals had managed to penetrate the highest levels of Neapolitan society – often as a result of direct encouragement by ruling politicians. A hundred years later the Camorra would not only be more experienced and educated, it would also have far greater economic power, and so from the early 1980s onwards it would prove impossible to deprive them of power and influence.

By the outbreak of the First World War, however, the word 'Camorra' had all but disappeared from normal usage. For example, the new songs about the Neapolitan underworld began to talk about *guappi*, or *guapparia*, more a concept of individual attitude rather than membership of an organisation.[35]

The advent of Fascism in 1922 brought a virtual end to the Camorra within Naples, although small gangs still existed in the countryside. A totalitarian regime such as Mussolini's could not tolerate organised illegal activities and clamped down hard wherever they had any suspicion. Following in the traditions of *trasformismo*, some members of the Camorra were simply invited to join the fascist party, often becoming leading members in the more outlying areas of the city. Many ex-*camorristi* now found themselves supervising the manufacture of tobacco, fruit and vegetable markets, or trading in the port. In other words the few remaining *camorristi* were largely incorporated within the fascist system of power.

In the countryside surrounding the city a more 'Sicilian' situation was allowed to develop. Fascism used the small Camorra gangs to intimidate those peasants who managed to maintain a small degree of organised opposition to the regime. However, any mention of Sicily in this context obviously brings the Mafia to mind, so it is useful at this point to examine the similarities and differences between the Camorra and its Sicilian counterpart.

The differences between the Mafia and the Camorra

The origins of the Camorra lie in the urban poor of Naples at the beginning of the last century. The Mafia, on the other hand, has completely different origins – it appeared later and its origins are rural.

This is not to say that the two organisations had no connections whatsoever in the last century. In its early period the Camorra used the Sicilian word *picciotto* to describe an apprentice member. The same word is still used today to describe a common foot soldier of the Mafia; in this case the common use probably derives from the fact that *camorristi* and *mafiosi* were held together in the same jails.

Even the early use of the word 'Mafia' reveals another difference, as it usually described an attitude, whereas the word 'Camorra' originally referred to an activity and to an organisation.

The first known use of the word 'Mafia' occurred in 1862, over a hundred years after the first use of the word 'Camorra' in Naples, and the first police reference to Mafia occurred in 1865, forty-five years after the first police report on the Camorra.[36]

Although the fact that the Camorra and the Mafia arose in different periods may be interesting in itself, their diverse social origins are far more important in explaining the very real differences which still exist between them today.

The precursor of the *mafioso* can be traced to the figure of the *gabellotto*, which existed in the Sicilian countryside at the beginning of the last century.[37] These men were employed by absentee landowners to supervise the correct functioning of short-term contracts, known as *gabella*, between the landlord and the local peasantry; in other words the *gabellotto* played a key role in checking peasant revolt.

When disputes broke out the landlord often ordered that his interpretation of the contract be enforced using violent means. So as with the Camorra, the offering of violent intimidation as a service was an important first element in the Mafia's growth.

Violence was very frequent in the Sicilian country-side during this period, and had two main sources: banditry was the more common activity, and *gabellotti* were often sworn in as irregular policemen by the Bourbon authorities to fight them. The other source of violence was the continuing resentment of Sicilian peasants towards landowners. The peasants were acutely aware that previously common lands had been effectively stolen from them; in the case of peasant disturbances the *gabellotto* was often the private policeman of large landowners.

Furthermore, in the early part of the nineteenth century many *gabellotti* were already 'upwardly mobile' peasants, in that they often managed *masserie*, or large farms. These farms, which often measured dozens of hectares, were the result of the splitting up of the old feudal landed estates in an effort to increase production. This meant that the *gabellotti* were quite adept at rudimentary administration, using agricultural machinery, dealing with large amounts of cash, all key differences compared to *camorristi*. They also played another important role: ensuring the safe passage of agricultural produce through the countryside to ports on the coast, and in an area without any kind of modern communication, they often were a vital source of information concerning events in the outside world. The *gabellotti* therefore developed a broad range of communication skills and friendships, an important difference compared to the emerging *camorristi*.

A key difference of Sicily compared to Naples was the weakness of the government, whether it be the Bourbon government or the new Italian state. The remoteness of the island and the hostility of its population towards any foreign domination meant that the emerging Mafia sometimes acted as a crude form of government.

In the two decades preceding and following Unification in 1860, the *gabellotto*, or *mafioso*, began to usurp the absentee landowners. This was done either legally, through buying the land in question, or through threats and violence – and the landlords, who had often lived off the rent for these areas for generations, had no real means of opposing this change.

Some *mafiosi* also began to practise extortion on the land; 'Either the owner or the tenant has to pay the *mafioso* if they want to get something useful out of their land, and not see it return to being "a desert".'[38] The landowner also felt obliged to pay because he was normally aware of the collusion between the police and the Mafia; the peasant paid for similar reasons.

The emerging Mafia put this cash to good use, becoming money lenders in the countryside: 'The *mafioso gabellotto* was the only person to have cash and lent it whenever he wanted to; for a wedding, a funeral, an illness, emigration.'[39] The peasant obviously had to pay interest, and if he failed to pay, his goods and animals were seized, or alternatively he was killed. Given the disintegration of the old feudal system and the weakness of absentee landowners, the Mafia quickly diversified into other economic areas, such as the renting and buying of sulphur mines or salt banks, so that they very quickly began to engage in legal activities.

Not only did the Mafia accumulate capital and move into legal economic activities, they also moved into politics – two very stark differences compared to the early Camorra. The Mafia already had a certain sophistication, moving quite adeptly amongst peasants, aristocratic landowners, state officials and emerging businessmen. Not surprisingly, it took them very little time to gain access to important areas of the local political system. Whether it was landowners, politicians or businessmen, they all needed the Mafia, and the Mafia needed political protection.

By 1874 the Prefect of Palermo could write to Rome: 'Up until now there is an opinion that has become firmly established in these Provinces ... that without the Mafia a good police force cannot exist either in the towns or the countryside.'[40] By the end of the century many Sicilian towns had Mafia Mayors.

Furthermore, the Sicilian countryside continued to have far more radical traditions than the rural areas surrounding Naples. During the First World War many southern peasant soldiers had been promised land when they returned home – a promise which Sicilian peasants transformed into reality during a series of land occupations in 1918–20. Sicily also had a strong socialist tradition; in the 1922 Parliament, 20 of the island's 52 deputies were socialists.[41] Faced with such a situation, both the government and land-owners continued to need a force which could terrorise the peasantry, and thus employed the Mafia.

As in Naples, there were both public enquiries and the resignation or conviction of politicians. Sicily also experienced many of the same changes as occurred in Naples around the turn of the century: mass migration, the growth of socialism and a campaign for 'public morality'. But the key difference is that the Mafia had already consolidated itself: diversifying economically and gaining control of legal activities, and inserting its own men into politics, or at least strongly conditioning the behaviour of other local politicians.

Mafiosi had become power brokers – seen as people who got good deals for a local area, as well as being in a position to award favours to those who accepted their authority. Up until the early 1990s membership of the Mafia had involved some association with an honourable way of behaving, a concept totally lacking from popular conceptions of the Camorra in Naples.

Due to their different development, the two organisations have historically behaved in very mutually distinct ways, and are therefore often viewed in a different light by most local people. Because the Camorra has generally been an urban and mass phenomenon, it initially felt the need to 'flaunt' itself by wearing a recognisable uniform. The Mafia, however, still retains many traditionally rural characteristics: total territorial control, discretion, the myth of 'honour', and a close-knit family structure which is normally absent from the Camorra. Camorra gangs are usually 'open' organisations, whilst the Mafia *cosche* are generally based on a family structure.[42]

And, as we have already seen, the political behaviour of the two organisations has been very different. The Mafia sent its own men into politics as soon as possible, whereas it was not until around 1980 that the Camorra began to penetrate the local political system. The Mafia has always been almost totalitarian in its desire for complete control over its own territory, a desire that often leads it to kill any politicians who get in its way; political assassinations are much rarer with the Camorra.

A crucial development for the Mafia was mass emigration to the United States, which took place both before and during the early period of Fascism, a move which was partly prompted by the fact that fascists had effectively taken over the role of the Mafia in many areas. In the 1920s the American Mafia became very powerful through its dealings in illicit alcohol, later moving into gambling and prostitution.

The link with the United States paid huge dividends for the Mafia in 1943, when American forces landed in Sicily. Due to Fascism's twenty year rule, the Allies were to an extent unaware of any pre-fascist or anti-fascist structure in the island, and tended to rely on Italo-American *mafiosi*. Many of these men immediately became mayors of large towns, and quickly made massive use of the Allied presence, often controlling the black market and the sale of stolen Allied goods.

These men were politically convenient individuals because they could not be accused of direct association with Fascism, and furthermore they were willing to repress any signs of peasant radicalism. This murderous knowhow was quickly grafted on to the Mafia's relationship with the new Italian government, and culminated in the massacre of twelve peasants at a May Day celebration at Portella delle Ginestre in 1947.

In the immediate postwar period both the Camorra and the Mafia were revitalised: the Allies' presence in Naples not only meant the end of Fascism, it also provided new criminal opportunities, which were encouraged by the presence of notorious *mafiosi* such as Lucky Luciano in Naples.

The contraband and black market industries which revolved around the port of Naples were one of the key growth areas of the Mafia in the postwar period, and were to constitute the springboard for the Camorra a few decades later.

CHAPTER TWO

The postwar development of the Camorra

Ours is a State founded on labour and theft.

Dario Fo

In the period preceding Fascism certain differences between the North and South of Italy were already pronounced. Although there had been a degree of industrialisation and urbanisation in the South, these processes had occurred to a far greater extent in the northern cities, particularly in Turin, Milan and Genoa.

This had led to the growth of mass trade unions and a large socialist party. Many peasant organisations in rural areas of northern and central Italy had also arisen, partly in response to increased farm mechanisation. Yet the South remained far more rural, and feudal remnants such as large landowners and religious dominance of village life persisted.

Fascism maintained this political and social gap. In the North, Fascism received finance from major industrialists in return for government contracts and favourable policies; whereas in the South, the fascists maintained protectionist policies on agricultural

produce, banned peasants from leaving the countryside to look for work, and suppressed any signs of
rural discontent.

The way in which Fascism ended perpetuated a
fundamental difference between the two ends of the
peninsula. Northern Italy experienced a virtual civil
war in the period 1943–45. By the end of the war in
April 1945 the Resistance movement controlled a
partisan army of 300,000 which sometimes governed
mountain valley communities for several months, and
organised premeditated and successful insurrections
in northern cities shortly before the arrival of Allied
forces.

Events were very different in the South: the Allies
arrived by and large before society became polarised
between fascists, reactionaries and conservatives on
one hand, and communists, socialists and liberals on
the other.

The city of Naples suffered far more damage and
hardship during the war than its northern counterparts. The area around the port was devastated as a
result of over a hundred Allied bombing raids, which
left 200,000 people homeless. The Germans had also
briefly occupied the city in September 1943, following
the signing of an armistice between the Italian
government and the Allies. They immediately
demanded that young men report for compulsory
labour service, and when they refused, the Germans
began to round men up indiscriminately, sparking off
the 'Four Days' of revolt which lasted from 28
September to 1 October, and which forced the
Germans to withdraw from the city.[1]

This was a spontaneous uprising, lacking the political organisation and objectives which later
predominated in the northern cities. This absence of a

developed political consciousness was to continue after the war, with one historian noting:

> the contradictory terms of the clearly fierce insurgency of the 'Four Days' and the moderate outcome as witnessed in the 1946 elections. Between one event and the other, there is the negative effect of the lack of a generalised campaign of Resistance, and the presence of Allied troops of occupation.[2]

While at a national level a small majority of Italians voted against the King and created a Republic in a national referendum held in 1946, in Naples support for the monarchy reached 80%.

If the Unification of 1860 had been a kind of 'passive revolution' throughout the country, then the 'second war of national liberation' of 1943–45 (or the 'second *Risorgimento*' as it was sometimes called), was almost exclusively a northern affair. The traditions of *trasformismo* surfaced once again in the South, with the vast majority of southerners playing no significant or long-term role in their liberation from Fascism.[3]

The legacy of this tradition has been seen ever since during national elections, albeit intermittently. In the five elections between 1948 and 1968 the Monarchist Party vote fluctuated between 26.3% and 9.2% in Naples, compared to a national vote of between 6.9% and 1.4%. And in the five elections from 1972 onwards, the neo-fascist MSI has fluctuated between 26.3% and 11.2%, compared to a national average of between 8.7% and 5.1%. It should also be remembered that votes for the communist party have largely corresponded to the national average.[4]

To a far greater extent than in the North, Naples and southern society witnessed the re-appearance of old politicians and old attitudes; political corruption and patronage quickly reasserted themselves as fundamental elements of southern political life.

The Allies resurrect the Mafia

The Allied invasion of continental Europe began in Sicily on 9 July 1943. In strategic terms it might well have been easier to start the invasion of Italy by attacking Sardinia, which was not as strongly defended as Sicily and only slightly further from the Allies' North African bases. One tactical explanation is that the Americans had close links with Italo-American 'advisers', in other words Sicilian *mafiosi*, who provided them with two vital services: military information about Sicily itself and the ability to guarantee social order once Fascism had collapsed.

In the early months of 1943 several American and English secret agents left Allied headquarters in Algiers and arrived clandestinely in Sicily. They included people such as the British writer Gavin Maxwell, and Colonel Charles Poletti, an American businessman of Italian background, who was to become the senior allied administrator in occupied Italy. Not only did they gather military information, they also encouraged acts of sabotage and met with individuals who would later take control of the island.[5]

It is commonly acknowledged that these agents were able to make contact with 'pro-Allied anti-fascists' through Lucky Luciano, one of America's major gangsters then serving a 30 year sentence in America for running a prostitution ring. Before the Allied invasion many Italo-American *mafiosi* had named Luciano as being indispensable for making the right contacts in Sicily, and there is clear evidence of collaboration between Luciano and US authorities.[6]

Even before the fall of Fascism the Mafia was being consciously resurrected by those responsible for governing Italy. As the veteran anti-Mafia campaigner Michele Pantaleone commented:

> It was no secret that Charles Poletti, governor of Sicily after the occupation, had slipped into Palermo on the quiet at least a year before the end of the war, and had stayed for some time in a villa belonging to a Mafia lawyer.[7]

Poletti went on to use his position as head of Allied administration first in Palermo, then in Naples and all the way up to Milan, 'to trade in foodstuffs with Vito Genovese and Damiano Lumia in Sicily, who was a nephew of Calogero Vizzini, and with Jimmy Hoffa of the Teamsters Union in New York'.[8] The company run by Poletti in Italy collapsed into bankruptcy soon after the Allies' withdrawal, suggesting that his business lifeline was the creaming off of Allied goods for sale on the highly profitable black market. Poletti was also a freemason, a highly secret organisation in Italy, whose activities culminated in the discovery of the P2 Lodge in 1981.[9]

The question of public order is a key factor in understanding the Allies' enlisting of *mafiosi*. The British, under Winston Churchill, were particularly hostile towards communists and socialists. Churchill had first displayed his virulent hatred of trade unionists and socialists as British Home Secretary during the great labour 'unrest' of 1910–14, when he ordered troops to open fire at several towns brought to a standstill by strike activity. And he even went as far as declaring support for Mussolini during a visit to Rome in 1927:

> I could not help being charmed, like so many other people have been, by Signor Mussolini's gentle and simple bearing and by his calm, detached pose, in spite of so many burdens and dangers ... Anyone could see that he thought of nothing but the lasting good, as he understood it, of the Italian people, and that no lesser interest was of the slightest consequence to him.
>
> If I had been an Italian, I am sure that I should have been wholeheartedly with you from start to finish in your triumphant struggle against the bestial appetites and passions of Leninism.[10]

Churchill also supported the Italian monarchists, and throughout the period from 1943 to 1946 he fought a running battle with the Americans, who were more agnostic on the question. But what united both Allied camps was the desire to see Italy transformed from a hostile country seeking to create a self-sufficient economy, into a politically compliant free-market nation, highly dependent on foreign investment, imports and technology. They were willing to enlist any kind of help to ensure that this transformation took place, including the Mafia.

The political legacy of Fascism in Sicilian society was that very little middle ground existed. The Christian Democrat (DC) party had not even been formed, so the Allies enlisted the help of elderly politicians who had been pushed aside by Fascism. These men had enjoyed very little popular support before Fascism, and gained even less now. In other cases, the Allies simply appointed known *mafiosi* mayors of several important Sicilian towns. All the *mafiosi* had to do was to proclaim their 'anti-Fascism' and the Allies thereby acquired trusted partners who were able to police society very effectively.

The most notorious case was that of Don Calogero Vizzini, the head of the Mafia, who was appointed mayor of Villalba a few days after the Americans' arrival in the town. One look at his criminal record during the fascist period illustrated what kind of man he was: he had been tried for four different murders but was acquitted each time, although he was convicted of Mafia membership and spent five years in jail. He had also been charged, but not brought to trial, for: 39 murders, 6 attempted murders, 36 robberies, 37 thefts and 63 extortions.[11] Documents written by US agents at the time clearly show that officials knew who the Mafia leaders were, and had no objection to their being directly involved in politics.[12]

As Raimondo Catanzaro, a leading Italian academic, has noted:

As mayors the *mafiosi* resumed their time-honoured functions as brokers between the Allied government and the population. But it was not only this position through which the *mafiosi* once again began to exercise their traditional function. They acted as interpreters at the military command posts; they held (as Vito Genovese did at Nola) important jobs and performed important tasks that once again gave them the opportunity to place themselves at critical junctures of the relations between political authorities and the population.[13]

Genovese had fled from New York in 1936 to escape several charges of murder. In Italy he was praised by Mussolini in an official meeting in 1937, where his 'Italian work carried out in Brooklyn' was recognised with the granting of the highest civilian decoration; furthermore he was given important banking responsibilities.[14] Genovese later returned the favour by giving $290,000 towards the construction of a fascist party headquarters.[15]

Despite such a record, Genovese was employed as Colonel Poletti's personal interpreter, but the relationship was far from that of a senior officer giving orders to his lowly batman. Poletti would often drive about in a 1938 Packard, which the FBI later discovered had been a gift from Genovese.[16]

It is therefore beyond doubt that the Allies occupied southern Italy with the help of the Mafia, and in early October 1943, three months after their landing in Sicily, the Allies reached Naples and its highly prized port.

The Mafia resurrects the Camorra

A major command post was set up in the town of Nola, to the east of Naples, where both Charles Poletti and Vito Genovese were based; for Genovese it was a return to the town where he had been born in 1897. Looting, particularly from American stores, was already widespread; the Mafia also began to defraud the Allies' supplies of Italian foodstuffs. Some studies estimate that 60% of the merchandise unloaded in Naples during this period ended up on the black market.[17]

Genovese and his men were clearly moving fast and making huge profits: grain legally bought from official sources at between $1.60 and $2 a ton was being sold on the black market for up to $12.[18]

Genovese's greed however finally led to his demise. The FBI had already reached the conclusion that he stole trucks full of sugar, oil, flour and other highly-prized goods from the American army, and then went on to sell them in the markets of nearby towns.[19] During the summer of 1944 American police stopped Canadian soldiers driving two trucks full of oil on their way from the port of Naples to Nola. When questioned, the soldiers admitted that the trucks had been stolen from the port and would be destroyed once their load had been disposed of at Nola – indeed at the rendezvous investigators found the remains of twenty burnt out trucks. Genovese was subsequently arrested on 27 August, charged with both theft and passing on military information, and eventually sent back to the US.[20]

Yet individuals such as Genovese were just the tip of a very large iceberg. Once he was removed there were many other *mafiosi* more than willing to take his place, and it quickly became 'business as usual' again.

The strategic importance of the port of Naples, with the Allies stuck south of Rome in the winter and spring of 1943–44, remained vital. Goods for the Allied forces, as well as those destined for the much larger civilian population, continued to pour ashore.

The fact that the Mafia enjoyed a monopoly of Allied 'protection' meant that they were able to consolidate their position in the coming years, and obviously had no interest in favouring the creation of a rival organisation. As Michele Pantaleone perceptively commented as far back as 1962:

> From 1943 to 1946 the entire Sicilian Mafia dedicated itself to this black market traffic which made large fortunes for its chiefs. And during the same years the foundations were laid for the drug traffic which, as we shall see, had one of its major distribution centres in Sicily.[21]

Even though there was as yet no real Camorra in the city of Naples itself, the seeds were being sown. Large sums of money could be made working for the Mafia, which needed a wide variety of skills and services.

Both the Allied administration and the Italian police had become aware of the Mafia's resurgence, and so they often kept watch on known leaders, concentrating on Sicily itself. Naples meanwhile became a convenient staging post for Mafia activities, and whilst the contraband trade disappeared from other areas of Italy very quickly after 1945, it became rooted in Naples, constituting one of the city's principal economic activities: food dominated the trade during the war period, then various Allied goods, then clothes and textiles, then cigarettes and electrical appliances, and finally hard drugs from the 1970s onwards.

The gap left by Vito Genovese's departure was partly filled by Lucky Luciano two years later. In 1946 the head of the American Navy's secret service wrote that Luciano 'had been a great help to the armed forces', a testimonial which spurred his release on parole from a thirty year minimum jail sentence handed down in 1936. As he had never taken American citizenship, he could conveniently be deported. He arrived in Naples in the summer of 1946 and was to live there until his death in 1962.[22]

Luciano was arguably one of the Mafia's most influential bosses during the late Forties and Fifties. The intelligence chief of the New York Police publicly admitted after his death: 'There is no question that [Luciano's] power was so great that even in Europe he could exercise it.' Biographers of Luciano have also written that, 'No important decision that might affect the future of organised crime in the United States … was made without his consultation and advice.'[23]

Although it is impossible to verify the precise accuracy of these statements, what is beyond doubt is that Luciano decided to base his operations in Naples. Luciano's notoriety in the United States meant that Naples became a port of call for *mafiosi* in transit. The veteran American journalist Claire Sterling once estimated that there were 'some five hundred Italian-born racketeers, dope traffickers, and all-purpose mobsters shipped back from New York in the wake of Senator Kefauver's 1951 hearings. Half of them were in Naples, desperate and broke.'[24] And according to Luciano, many of them would come to him for help.

The contraband industry was not the work of a few dozen modern-day pirates. Large amounts of money were needed to keep it running, and considerable investment in transport and wages was required. The Mafia employed Neapolitans very much as junior partners, but over a period of many years those Neapolitans who were to later become Camorra leaders progressed from activities such as casual thefts of Allied goods to working in a highly organised, professional operation, involving large amounts of money. Organised crime was starting to evolve from small-time extortion and racketeering into international business syndicates, and the Camorra was eventually to follow the Mafia's lead.

Two Neapolitan groups slowly began to emerge within the Mafia-run contraband industry. The main one centred on the town of Giugliano, to the north of the city, and extended up to Mondragone and as far as the Garigliano river. This was initially led by Alfredo Maisto, with Luigi Sciorio, Raffaele Ferrara and the Nuvoletta brothers all joining later. The other was based to the south of the city, in the towns of San Giovanni a Teduccio and Portici.

Top *mafiosi* were active in Naples throughout the 1950s; Tommaso Buscetta has admitted to working with Lucky Luciano immediately after the war, and Tommaso Spadaro was amongst many *mafiosi* sent into 'internal exile' to Naples.[25] Many of them happily continued their activities, including Spadaro, who went to live in via Pallonetto a Santa Lucia, the heart of the contraband industry.[26]

Yet at the same time as the Mafia was consolidating its position in Naples and nurturing a new generation of Neapolitan criminals, separate developments were taking place in Campania, the region surrounding Naples. Over a period of two decades these developments would lead to the rise of Camorra groups totally distinct from the Mafia.

In the aftermath of the Second World War, most areas of the southern Italian countryside were swept by a wave of land occupations by peasants. In many cases they were taking advantage of government indecision concerning the return of common lands which had been stolen from them in the previous century.

But Campania was different. Under Fascism it had lacked an organised and long-term Resistance movement, and now land occupations were similarly scarce. Consequently, its social structure remained largely unchanged. The main reason for this was that Campania had fewer large estates than other Italian regions, with only 12.4% of the region being made up of estates larger than 100 hectares, compared to a national average of 26%.[27] Despite the fact that it contained 4.5% of the nation's cultivated land, Campania only received 2.2% of land redistributed as a result of postwar agricultural reforms. This low level of land redistribution, and its concomitant dislocation, was perhaps the main reason behind Campania reaching pre-war levels of agricultural production by 1949–51, one of the few Italian regions to achieve this.[28]

This is not to say that there was no industry in Campania, according to the 1911 census the region was fifth out of twenty in terms of industrial development. But as Table 2 shows, it was mainly concentrated in Naples. Coastal towns and towns with easy access to the coast had been industrialised to a significant extent, whereas the more mountainous areas of the interior remained predominantly agricultural.

Evidence of Camorra activity in the provinces of Campania is scarce; in any case virtually all criminal activity was likely to be the work of isolated local gangs rather than an urban organisation as in Naples. Nevertheless, it appears that in the period preceding the First World War local provincial criminals had played a key role in getting politicians elected.[29]

In the twenty years of fascist rule social relations largely remained static; local criminal gangs were

probably tolerated to some extent as they could occa-
sionally be employed as convenient shock troops
against peasant unrest, or as assassins of individual
political enemies, but by and large nothing much
changed in these areas between 1922 and 1943.

The end of Fascism and the arrival of the Allies, and
particularly individuals such as Vito Genovese in Nola,
meant however that both social relations and the local
economy suddenly experienced rapid changes.

With the withdrawal of the Allies the main activity
of these criminal gangs became control over agricultural produce. Their influence was particularly strong
in rural areas to the north and east of Naples, particularly in the rich cattle area around Nola. Sometimes
gangs would shoot it out for dominance in a given
market; for example 61 murders were committed in
the Nola area during 1954–56 alone.[30] They also intim-
idated farmers who refused their services or
protection, normally by burning their crops.

Although Nola itself was not a large town, *camorristi*
acted as parasitical mediators between cattle farmers
and butchers because the town was the main centre
for sending meat to Naples, a market of a million
people. Compared to the entire city of Naples, in a
town such as Nola Camorra gangs must have been far
stronger and enjoyed greater political protection,
which in turn enabled them to take a cut of any meat
sales.

However, there was no reason to stop at meat, so
the Camorra quickly moved into other areas of agricultural produce. And by the mid-1950s,

in the fruit and vegetables sector, the underworld
exercises control above all over the San Giuseppe
Vesuviano market, but in all cases it always

makes its presence felt before goods reach
Naples; as for milk, the supervising of inspections
and all other concerns has been moved from the
Central Dairy in Naples to the Castellammare
Consortiums, which are controlled by *camorristi*.[31]

Just as there was no reason for *camorristi* to limit
themselves to control over the meat market, there was
also no reason to physically limit themselves to small
agricultural towns. A third of all Italian fruit exports
passed through Naples in this period, amounting to
$23 million of produce annually, and from the early
1950s many rural gangsters moved to the city to
supervise this trade. The prices imposed between
buyers and sellers, according to one trader, 'are not
imposed through violence, but through convincing
arguments', with the *guappi* then taking a percentage
of the sale price.[32]

This was a business which was carried out without
offices, in the open air, and was based only on verbal
agreements. The Camorra, both in the provinces and
within Naples, was therefore still characterised by
rather small-scale intimidation and extortion. *Camorristi* had yet to amass enough money to think about
where to invest it; their horizons were limited and
decisions therefore remained tactical rather than strategic. This is a crucial difference compared to Palermo,
where Mafia activities already involved widespread
participation in postwar building speculation and
control over council contracts, a process which led to
the intermeshing of criminal and political power in
the Sicilian capital.

Nevertheless, the Camorra's operations were
already sizeable, and as in the preceding century, they
could not have developed without some political

protection. A good example of this was the funeral in 1955 of a major Camorra leader, Pascalone 'e Nola, to which twelve MPs sent wreaths.

One of these MPs was Giovanni Leone, who began his career as a lawyer and Christian Democrat politician in the town of Pomigliano, and had later to resign as President of Italy in 1978 as a result of his involvement in a corruption scandal concerning the Lockheed aircraft corporation. Leone defended many people accused of belonging to Camorra gangs throughout the 1950s, including Pascalone 'e Nola, who dictated prices at the main fruit and vegetable market. Indeed their relationship had been so close that Leone was best man at his marriage to Pupetta Maresca in 1955, yet there was a political as well as a personal element to their association: Pascalone was also DC deputy mayor of Nola, and managed to do his lawyer a good turn by getting 2,000 first preference votes for Leone at every election during this period.[33]

As early as 1957 one observer began to outline the reasons behind the police's failure to stop Camorra activity in Nola: 'It is not difficult to work out the reasons for the police's difficulties: they lie in the political protection which is normally granted out of electoral interests, and which allows the underworld to prosper and to impede the fight against crime.'[34]

A similar complaint was made in 1961:

The work of people whose responsibility it was to apply the law was being hindered by the political protection provided by those who personally benefit from certain ramifications of the Camorra, in exchange for the electoral preferences which the Camorra is able to ensure.[35]

Although the Camorra was slowly gaining in power and influence in the provinces during this period, it was in Naples and Campania's coastal towns, i.e. in the Mafia-dominated contraband industry, that Camorra gangs were destined to take their next major step forward.

The contraband industry

Throughout the 1950s several important *mafiosi* had been sent into internal exile in Naples and the surrounding area. The main activity of the Mafia during this period was cigarette smuggling, which in the Mediterranean area was centred on the free port of Tangiers. The profit margins involved were enormous: in 1959 a case of Chesterfield, Camel or Pall Mall could be bought for $23 and sold on the streets of Europe for $170.

Most of this trade was run by a Corsican named Paolo Molinelli, who also carried morphine base from the Lebanon to Marseilles, where it was refined into heroin and sent to Sicily for forwarding to the United States.[36] Both the scale of cigarette smuggling, and the profits to be made from heroin meant that Italian police were keeping the Sicilian coastline under very close observation.

The free port of Tangiers was closed in 1961, and the warehouses of companies selling cigarettes moved to the Yugoslavian and Albanian coasts. This move was to turn Naples into the cigarette smuggling capital of the world. Not only did the Mafia increase its activity in the port and along the Campania coast, the Neapolitans began to carve out a niche for themselves too. One writer has commented of this transformation: 'It gave a reason to firm up those business relationships which had been sporadic and connected with personal situations before; they now had to become complex linkages of an associational and commercial nature.'[37]

Delivery was no longer made in ports, but outside territorial waters on the high seas. The terms of trade were also modified; suppliers now wanted to be paid 50% upon placement of the order, and 50% when the speedboats came to pick up the goods. The need for capital and large investment in transport necessitated a big commitment by the Mafia both in terms of smuggling and in the use of Naples as a base. This also meant that some Neapolitans had to be taken on as equal members of the Mafia:

If a Mafia organisation severely exposed itself in terms of capital expenditure (in foreign currency) and taking on great risks, in exchange it had to be sure that it was operating with a cast-iron structure, in which every member carried out his duty blindly.[38]

Given that Naples' contraband industry was undoubtedly enjoying rapid expansion throughout the 1960s we shall shortly return to this point. However, in social terms the interior regions of Campania were undergoing huge and traumatic changes, which were subsequently to give rise to a new type of Camorra, different from the previously dominant rural model.

The whole of Italy was on the move during the 1950s and 60s. Most of the movement was from the South to the North, from the southern countryside to either the industrial cities of Genoa, Milan and Turin, or even further north to Germany or Belgium.

Although the population born in the South rose by 5 million during 1951–71, emigration took 4.1 million away, leaving an effective increase of 900,000. The key change within the South itself was urbanisation, as people moved from the countryside to large towns and cities. During the same twenty year period, there was an increase of about 1 million people living in towns and cities of over 100,000. This was due to existing towns either growing in size through a high local birth rate, or internal migration within the South.

In any case, the changes were very rapid, particularly after the war. While at the start of the century only 12% of southerners lived in towns of 100,000, this figure rose to 16% in 1951 and 23.4% in 1971.[39]

Yet in the city of Naples in the period between 1950 and 1980 the population rose by only 1%, with three-quarters of this increase taking place in the 1950s alone. Compared to Naples' stagnation, most towns in Campania recorded huge population increases during this 30-year period. Small towns close to Naples registered a population increase of between 60% (Torre del Greco) and 200% (San Giorgio a Cremano). The area around Vesuvius too saw increases ranging from a minimum of 60% (Grumo Nevano) to a maximum of 150% (San Sebastiano). And to the north of the city, the lowest increase was recorded in Frattamaggiore (60%) and the highest in Casoria, with over 200%.[40]

These population increases had two main reasons; industrialisation and its concomitant increase in employment, and the overcrowding of Naples, which forced people to live outside the city and commute in for work. One of the consequences was the creation of an urban sprawl, with the towns closest to Naples effectively becoming part of the city.

Although Naples had first experienced industrial development soon after Unification, one of the first major industrial developments in the provinces was the arrival of the aeronautical industry in Pomigliano d'Arco during the 1930s. Pozzuoli had a significant engineering industry, which increased in size between the wars, while at nearby Baia a torpedo factory was built.[41]

Most of these industries were linked to war production. After their reconstruction and conversion in the immediate postwar period, industrialisation began anew in the second half of the 1950s with both Olivetti and Pirelli building factories in Pozzuoli. The first new factories to be built inland were set up in Casoria, with Rhodiatrice producing synthetic fibres and Resia synthetic resins.[42]

Until the mid-1960s population increase in the province of Naples was clearly differentiated:

> For the towns situated to the north and west of Naples, demographic increases could mainly be linked to the establishment of ... new productive activities ... while for the towns at the foot of Vesuvius, the increase derived from becoming a residential appendix of the provincial capital.[43]

These developments – population increase, urbanisation, industrialisation – all led to a change in the characteristics of organised crime. Although agricultural produce continued to be important for Camorra gangs, whole new areas were beginning to open up: extortion from small and medium industries, as well as from local shopowners, and the awarding of local public sector contracts and development grants. Agricultural products may still have been important, but people and therefore money were moving away from the land; in 1951 46% of the active population in Campania worked in agriculture, by 1971 this figure had fallen to 24%.[44]

One of the main reasons for this was government intervention in the South. It is widely accepted that this intervention has passed through three main phases: 1950–57, 1957–73 and 1974 to the early 1990s. The first phase involved the creation of a basic infrastructure rather than real industrialisation. During the second period, when public enterprises were obliged to invest at least 40% of their profits in the South, problems began to arise. Local authority consortia were set up in an attempt to create 'poles of development', but politicians were more concerned with guaranteeing their re-election through the clientelist use of public funds and jobs, and so more often than not *cattedrali nel deserto*, 'cathedrals in the desert', were built. The most famous example of this is the Alfa Romeo factory at Pomigliano d'Arco, a 'cathedral' whose construction was intended to lead to the development of a local component industry centred on the factory. This project failed abysmally, and the area consequently retained many aspects of a 'desert'.

A grasp of political concepts such as patronage and *clientela* is essential for understanding not only local politics, but also how these mechanisms favour the influence and involvement of organised crime. As the political scientist Percy Allum noted in 1973:

The key to a successful parliamentary career in Naples is having a following or a *clientela*. The building of a *clientela* requires economic resources or patronage. In consequence, the politician with parliamentary ambitions is obliged to join an organisation to win resources.[45]

Through control over public expenditure and the favours which can be granted, a politician will slowly build up 'clients' who will then return the favour granted, usually in the form of votes.

Although political patronage exists throughout Italy and in most other advanced countries, in Naples it was grafted on to an already weak tradition of democracy and political honesty. In addition, the endemic poverty of the area has led to the problem becoming far more entrenched and widespread than elsewhere:

Where Naples differs from the North is in the placing of people in strategic positions at the middle and lower levels of society ... In Naples, patronage appointment has been extended to all levels of society. The reasons are simple: Naples is a society of limited resources and unemployment is still rife. In these circumstances, the state provides the chief source of employment, not only through the extension of the public administration, but also through the introduction of modern industry ... The intelligentsia aspire 'for a job in the municipality' or 'for stable employment with the chance of a career ... probably in the public administration', while the workers dream of 'a job with a regular income'.[46]

This tradition encourages Camorra influence within the political system, as they can often act either as brokers for people looking for jobs or as election agents for politicians seeking election. As for economic development, it has meant that the public sector was dominated by corruption and was therefore haphazard and uncoordinated.

The economic crisis of the 1970s and 1980s changed this situation considerably. In the private sector the crisis hit Campania just as hard as other areas, and by the end of the 1970s one of the new two companies set up in Casoria had closed down, while the second one had relocated elsewhere.

Due to the rapid, chaotic and often illegal nature of economic development, according to the 1971 census almost half of the houses registered in Campania had been built after 1951.[47] Many towns had been thrown up in 15 or 20 years; and planners had been either unable or unwilling to create any sense of social cohesion. Since the War Campania has suffered the highest population density in Italy, with an average of 422 people per square kilometre in 1988. This figure rises to far higher levels within individual provinces such as the Salerno plain, which has an average of 810 people per square kilometre, the Naples' plain with 1,318, the Avellino hill areas with 2,629 and the hills of the Province of Naples with 3,065, one of the highest population densities in Europe.[48]

Public transport, schools, street lighting, cultural amenities had all been severely lacking throughout the years of development; and public hygiene is still so bad that many towns suffer outbreaks of contagious hepatitis during the summer, whilst the city of Naples even experienced a small outbreak of cholera in 1973.

By the mid-1970s economic development had largely come to a halt in Campania. The rise in industrial unemployment, however, was largely camouflaged by the use of government-financed redundancy schemes, which guaranteed 75% of wages to those laid off. For example the total amount of lay-off hours financed in Campania rose from 7 million in 1972 to 20 million in 1980 and 63 million in 1982.[49]

Until the advent of this economic crisis, many people had been willing to accept high levels of unemployment and low levels of public services, as they had generally believed that there would be some future economic development. With the onset of a long-term and seemingly intractable economic crisis, a 'life of crime' became more appealing.

The new Camorra gangs which arose in the 1970s did not need to assert their power over the old Camorra through violence. The huge economic changes ushered in by State and local authority activities, and the effects of urbanisation and emigration had severely, if not terminally, affected the pre-war and postwar gangs. The predominance of urban areas over rural areas, of industry and the service sector over agriculture, led to their rapid and painless demise. However, it is now time to turn our attention away from the towns of the hinterland and examine further changes within the contraband industry.

Contraband: from cigarettes to drugs

Until the late 1960s the European contraband trade was run by a complex mix of Corsicans, Genoese, *Marsigliesi* and Sicilians. Naples was the centre of the cigarette trade, and in the main provided merely the manpower for the unloading and transportation of goods, although the urban area of Naples and Campania also constituted a large market in themselves. The fact that port costs as a whole were reportedly inflated by 35% due to gangs demanding protection money also indicates a high level of lawlessness.[50]

George Bush senior was not the first American President to declare 'war on drugs'. Soon after his inauguration in 1969, Richard Nixon promised a war on drug traffickers, setting up 'Task Force One' under Henry Kissinger. Its only real success was the smashing of the 'French Connection' run by the *Marsigliesi* and Corsicans in France's second city. Not only did France close down eight heroin refineries, probably the world's biggest, the Corsicans' operations in Brazil were also stopped.[51]

But the problem simply moved on, partially to Naples but also to Sicily and elsewhere; the *Marsigliesi* decided to diversify more into tobacco contraband and saw Naples as an excellent territory to move into. In the meantime the Mafia had been reorganising its activities, sending top *mafioso* Gerlando Alberti to the town of San Sebastiano al Vesuvio at the beginning of 1971. He set to work organising the contraband industry on a far greater scale, but his work was interrupted by his arrest in December 1971.

At the same time the *Marsigliesi* were trying to move into the port and were enticing local *camorristi* into becoming their partners by loaning them some of their boats. The French were well organised, with their own container ship and fast motorboats, compared to the Neapolitans' slow fishing boats. However, the French also limited their offers of integration as they didn't fully trust the Neapolitans, believing them to be far too close to the Mafia.[52]

Estimates of the number of people directly involved in contraband rose from 3,420 in 1970, to 4,672 in

1971 and 4,885 in 1973; roughly 50,000 people now depended on smuggling to survive.[53] By 1975 40% of arrests for contraband in Italy were made in the Campania region alone, and in the following year 528,044 kilograms of foreign cigarettes were seized by police in Campania.[54]

The growth in the drug trade inevitably increased the tension among the emerging criminal gangs. One notorious example was the killing of Gennaro Ferrigno by Antonio Spavone in 1971; Ferrigno was a drug trafficker importing cocaine from Peru, whilst Spavone was a major Camorra boss of the postwar period who had received a Presidential pardon from a life sentence four years earlier. The following year a major Mafia summit, also involving Camorra gangs, was broken up by the police at the Hotel Commodore in Naples, causing more suspicion. Another turning point was the murder of an ambiguous cigarette smuggler and ex-policeman, Emilio Palamara, in late 1972.[55]

A bloody gang war then erupted between the Sicilians and the *Marsigliesi*, with the defeated French leaving the port in 1973–74. The Camorra was still weak, playing a very minor role in the gang warfare between the Mafia and the *Marsigliesi*, but the huge profits to be made from drugs soon led to a swift growth in its importance.

According to estimates of the Italian Customs & Excise Police, 1% of contraband cigarette cargoes in 1970 were in fact made up of hashish; a percentage which rose to between 5–10% by 1975.[56] Because neither politicians nor police yet perceived the Camorra as a serious threat in Naples, and with Sicily and the Mafia subject to a significant degree of police attention, the quantity of hard drugs coming into Naples under Camorra control also increased sharply.

By 1979 a total of 400 speedboats had been seized by customs police, and it is estimated that 105 had been in operation throughout that year alone. With the price per boat at around $24–$29,000, a total of approximately $13,500,000 had been invested in the primary means of transport alone.[57]

Michele Zaza was one of the first *camorristi* to emerge as a powerful figure in the contraband industry. The son of a fisherman from Portici, Zaza was known as *Michele 'o pazzo*, or Mad Mike, for his outspoken and improbable public pronouncements. His rise to power however was achieved through his connections with the Mafia rather than his supposedly unbalanced mind. He was first arrested for criminal association in 1974, along with top *mafiosi* Gerardo Alberti, Stefano Bontate and Rosario Riccobono. Soon after that he was arrested in Palermo together with Alfredo Bono for illegal possession of firearms. According to the Mafia 'supergrass' Tommaso Buscetta, from the mid 1970s Zaza, along with the Nuvoletta and Bardellino gangs, were already part of Michele Greco's *cupola*, the supreme body of the Sicilian Mafia.

Twice in 1977 Zaza was discovered in the company of senior *mafiosi*, first at a restaurant with Vincenzo Spadaro and Filippo Messina, and again at a Social Democrat Party branch in Naples, with Bernardo Brusca and Francesco Messina.[58] According to documents found in his possession, he was already selling 5,000 tons of cigarettes per year.

Zaza is prepared to admit that he made large amounts of money smuggling cigarettes. This is how he once described his activities during questioning by an investigating magistrate:

First I'd sell five cases of Philip Morris, then ten, then a thousand, then three thousand, then I bought myself six or seven ships that you took away from me ...

I used to load fifty thousand cases a month ... I could load a hundred thousand cases, $10 million on trust, all I had to do was make a phone call ...

I'd buy $24 million worth of Philip Morris in three months, my lawyer will show you the receipts. I'm proud of that – $24 million![59]

It would appear that Zaza's success was due to the fact that he was less interested in traditional activities such as extortion – concentrating far more on smuggling first cigarettes and then drugs. From there he quickly moved to investing in more 'legitimate' areas such as real estate, construction companies and restaurants, but as most of these developments were part of the 'new Camorra' which emerged in the late 1970s, they will be explained in detail in a subsequent chapter.

However, this is not to say that the Mafia totally controlled the emergence of the 'new Camorra'. Indeed, the strongest Camorra organisation for most of the 1970s was distinctly hostile to the Mafia.

The 'Mass Camorra' of Raffaele Cutolo's *Nuova Camorra Organizzata*

The origins of Raffaele Cutolo's *nuova camorra organizzata*, (i.e. New Organised Camorra, or NCO) in some ways recall the Camorra of the last century.

Apart from eighteen months on the run, Cutolo has lived inside maximum security jails or psychiatric prisons since 1963, and it was from there that he built up his organisation. He began by befriending young inmates unfamiliar with jail, giving them a sense of identity and worth, so much so that when they were released they would send Cutolo 'flowers' (i.e. money), which enabled him to widen his network.[60]

Another more direct method was to help poorer prisoners by buying food for them from the jail store, or arranging for food to be sent in from outside. In such ways Cutolo created many 'debts' or 'rain cheques' which he would cash at the opportune moment.[61] Another key bond Cutolo created was regular payments to the families of NCO members sent to prison, thereby guaranteeing the allegiance of both prisoners and their families.[62] As his following grew, he also began to exercise a monopoly of violence within a number of prisons, thus increasing his power. Indeed, it seems that during the 1970s Cutolo was able to decide which of his followers would be moved to which jails, use a prison governor's telephone to make calls anywhere in the world, and on one occasion he claims to have slapped the governor of Naples' jail for daring to search his cell.[63]

What is unusual about Cutolo is that he had a kind of ideology, another factor which appealed to rootless and badly educated youths. He founded the NCO in his home town of Ottaviano on 24 October 1970 (the day of Cutolo's patron saint, San Raffaele); and the organisation deliberately used a statute and rules, often purely notional, but deliberately harking back to the Camorra of the last century.

The NCO's strongholds were the towns to the east of Naples, such as Ottaviano, and Cutolo appealed to a Campanian rather than Neapolitan sense of identity, perhaps a result of his peasant background: 'The day when the people of Campania understand that it is better to eat a slice of bread as free men rather than eat a steak as slaves is the day that Campania will win.'[64]

This approach naturally made the NCO hostile to the Sicilian Mafia and its Neapolitan allies, and Cutolo consequently forged an alliance with Calabrian gangs, who had no designs on Naples or Campania whatsoever.[65] He also played a key role in the formation of an essentially new criminal organisation in the southeastern region of Apulia, the 'Holy United Crown'.[66]

Through his book of 'Thoughts and Poems', together with his many interviews with journalists, Cutolo was able to create a strong sense of identity amongst his members. Even though his book was impounded by magistrates within days of its publication, many prisoners, alienated from society both 'inside' and 'outside' jail, wrote to Cutolo and other NCO leaders asking for a copy.[67]

Cutolo's organisation was unique in the history of the Camorra, in that it was highly centralised and possessed a rudimentary form of ideology. For example, he publicly declared that children were not to be kidnapped or mistreated, and allegedly arranged the assassination of at least one child kidnapper.

Perhaps the most potent ideological weapon was the cult of violence, which sometimes bordered on a kind of death wish, as Cutolo once wrote:

The value of a life doesn't consist of its length but in the use made of it; often people live a long time without living very much. Consider this, my friends, as long as you are on this earth everything depends on your will-power, not on the number of years you have lived.[68]

Although such opinions would appear bizarre to most people, they began to gain a hearing amongst considerable numbers of young people – a depressing but accurate testimony to the lack of future or purpose which so many of them felt in these towns. This is how one NCO member once looked back on how he got involved:

> I was in Novara jail, and my relatives had come to see me ... when I went back to my cell and sat down on my bed I started to think that everything I had done in my life had been wrong 'cause I had never done anything which was important to me personally. Every single thing I've done was somebody else's idea. I ain't done nothing in my life. I was a peasant, and in 1978 I got arrested for extortion by mistake, but I was innocent. I went to the old Avellino jail, where I got to know certain *camorristi*. I thought that the Camorra was just, was only ... at most, I thought, I would have broken into houses or robbed a bank, that sort of stuff.[69]

For these feelings to be fully understood, they need to be analysed in the wider context of the poverty and alienation which are experienced in these towns. It is no coincidence that the strength of organised crime in Italy largely corresponds to levels of poverty. For example, government statistics from 1978 show that Campania, out of Italy's twenty regions, had the next to lowest average share of wealth. Using the figure 100 as the average per capita share of Gross National Product, Calabria had the lowest share at 53.1, followed by Campania at 64.8 and Sicily with 65.3[70] – and it is no coincidence that these are the

three Italian regions where organised crime is at its
most powerful.

Official figures for unemployment amongst 14–24
year olds in 1979 again illustrate why organised crime
is so dominant in the South (see Table 3). Statistics
from the town of Secondigliano, just to the north of
Naples, show the same tendency on a smaller scale.
One measure of its widely acknowledged poverty is
that it has the highest percentage of council houses in
Campania; it also has the sad record of the highest
percentage of murders committed using firearms.
Before they even reach adulthood, 3% of children
from Secondigliano will have spent some time behind
bars.[71]

In 1983 the journalist Luca Rossi recorded this
tragic statement from a Secondigliano youth:

> The life of a man is worth nothing here. I have seen
> enough in my twenty-three years and I already feel
> dead. Now I am living another year, and it feels like
> an extra life. If they want to kill me then let them
> go ahead, I've already seen enough.[72]

Of the 148 deaths caused by firearms which occurred
in Naples and its province during 1980, and the 235 in
1981 (80% of which are estimated to be Camorra
murders), almost half were under 30, and a third were
under 25.[73] The attention which Cutolo paid to young
inmates inside prison, and the sense of identity which
he attempted to give them on the outside, often
provided the only occasions when these youths felt
valued and cared for. However, people such as Cutolo
can only prosper if those who are responsible for
providing employment, housing and social services
fail in their task.

The NCO spread like wildfire in the crisis-ridden Campanian towns of the late 1970s, offering alienated youths an alternative to a lifetime of unemployment or badly paid jobs. Initially the main specialisation of NCO gangs was extorting money through protection rackets against local businesses; they later moved on to cocaine, partly because it was subject to less police investigation than heroin, but also because the Mafia were less involved in the cocaine trade.

Two different types of Camorra gangs were now beginning to emerge: the NCO-type gangs which dealt mainly in cocaine and protection rackets, preserving a strong regional sense of identity; and the business-orientated gangs linked to the Mafia, who dealt in cigarettes and heroin, but soon moved on to invest in real estate and construction firms.

However, a brief comparison with the Mafia and its stronghold of Palermo shows that clear differences still remain. The Mafia faces no other external criminal competition in Sicily, and over several decades has often enjoyed a stable hierarchy and division of spoils. The Camorra was resurrected largely thanks to the Sicilian Mafia, which had its own agenda, and pursued its own particular interests. Crucially, no hierarchy between Camorra gangs or stable spheres of influence have been created, and no gang leader was likely to agree to taking a back seat without making a fight of it.

And this is just what happened towards the end of 1979. The previous year Michele Zaza had formed the 'honourable brotherhood' in an attempt to get the Mafia-aligned Camorra gangs to oppose Cutolo and his NCO, although without much success. It was in this period, before the outbreak of the gang war and during the NCO's highest point of expansion, that

Michele Zaza paid Cutolo's organisation $400,000 for the right to carry on operating in contraband cigarettes.[74]

The gang war between the NCO and the 'New Family'

The NCO was expanding rapidly during this period and moving into new territories and operations. The turning point came when the NCO took on the Giuliano gang, who had traditionally controlled the Forcella or 'casbah' area in the centre of Naples. Up until the first half of 1979 Giuliano's men had been friendly with the *cutoliani* (members of Cutolo's NCO), indeed it appears that the Giuliano gang were on bad enough terms with Zaza to launch an attack against his nephew Pasquale in December 1979.[75]

Another gang leader named Luigi Vollaro had first raised the idea of an anti-Cutolo alliance with Luigi Giuliano in 1979, following Cutolo's demand to receive a cut from his illegal gambling centres and lottery system in his base of Portici.[76] A provisional 'death squad' was set up, which contributed to the dozens of gangland deaths in 1979, but this was on a small scale when one considers the resources of the various gangs which had mushroomed during the 1970s. Indeed the fact that more than 1,500 people were murdered in the Campania region in the years 1977–83, and the fact that over 10,000 people were accused of membership of a Mafia-type organisation,[77] are clear evidence of the Camorra's growth.

The situation reached breaking point when the *cutoliani* tried to move into the Giulianos' strongholds of

Forcella, Piazza Mercato and Via Duomo, in the heart of the old city.[78] A few days before Christmas 1980 two *cutoliani* presented themselves at an unloading of contraband cigarettes at Santa Lucia and demanded immediate payment to their organisation of $400,000, as well as insisting on future payment of $25 for every crate of cigarettes brought ashore.[79] They then shot and wounded one of the men unloading the cigarettes, a member of the Giuliano gang. Events then moved quickly with their leader, Luigi Giuliano, being wounded in an attack on Christmas Eve.

This clash, which had obviously occurred in a period of growing tension, led to the formation of the *nuova famiglia*, or New Family (NF), an alliance of all the major Camorra gangs against Cutolo's predominant NCO.

Attacks continued over the next month, until a summit meeting was called at the end of January 1981 in a top Roman hotel, under the mediation of Antonio Spavone.[80] A shaky peace was established, only to be broken on 14 February when, during the confusion caused by a strong earth tremor, *cutoliani* in Naples' Poggioreale prison killed three adversaries.

A more serious episode occurred in May, when the NCO bombed houses in Portici owned by men working in the contraband cigarette trade for the Zaza brothers. Retaliation followed two weeks later, with the two men who had tried to encroach on the Zazas' patch being shot, and with a car bomb being left outside Cutolo's family home in Ottaviano.[81]

The gang war was far from being the result of individual psychological derailments which suddenly pushed the structure of organised crime off the tracks. In short, the war was caused by two main factors: the rapid growth of two distinct types of Camorra gangs, and the profound political and financial instability created by the November 1980 earthquake.

The war rapidly became a straightforward battle for power which was fuelled by the billions coming down from Rome for earthquake reconstruction. Table 4 illustrates the cycle of violence. The highest number of deaths occurred during 1981–82, when most reconstruction contracts were being awarded. Indeed during this period some Neapolitans placed illegal and macabre bets, in a system run by the Camorra itself, on whether there would be more gangland murders than days over the coming year.

As regards the balance of forces between the two groups, not only was Cutolo more exposed in terms of notoriety, he had not expected such a strong reaction from his adversaries. His hostility to the Mafia also gave his opponents another tactical advantage as they were able to call on Sicilian help. Yet it was as a result of his intervention in the Cirillo kidnapping (see Chapter 5) that Cutolo was fundamentally weakened.

Cutolo's demise became starkly evident in the first of a series of 'maxi-blitzes' between 1983 and 1984. In the first round-up, on 17 June 1983, 800 people were arrested in a single day of coordinated operations carried out by 8,000 police and *carabinieri*. Of those arrested in that series of raids, 300 were convicted very quickly and another 630 committed for trial.[82] Perhaps because of their youth and their fairly unsophisticated criminal activities, NCO members also had a tendency to kill fellow members they suspected of treachery, further reducing their numbers. Important NCO members such as Pasquale Barra and Giovanni Pandico began to co-operate with investigators, probably aware that the NCO was heading for defeat. Cutolo's influence was also reduced as a result of

President Sandro Pertini's insistence that he be removed from a mainland jail to a maximum security prison on a small island near Sardinia.

Speculation about the importance of the Cirillo affair aside, Cutolo's defeat was clearly the result of several factors. The first was simply his impatience and arrogance, which caused the birth of the NF; had he moved at a slower pace and sought greater consensus, he might have eventually succeeded in becoming the undisputed gang leader of the Naples area. The second factor was the youth and rawness of many of the NCO's 'foot-soldiers' compared to the more experienced members of the NF gangs, as one supergrass recalled: 'The *cutoliani* committed arrogant acts, killing people for no reason.'[83] The third reason was strategic: Cutolo had made a crucial error in concentrating on labour-intensive activities such as protection rackets, avoiding heroin trafficking almost entirely. As an investigating magistrate commented in 1985: 'It can be said that most of the organisation's energies were employed in this sector [protection rackets], which is more demanding and less profitable than the former [drug trafficking].'[84] In other words, the most financially sophisticated organisations won the day.

Yet another key advantage was that the individual gangs of the NF alliance were less notorious than Cutolo's NCO, and were initially less affected by police operations and therefore able to carry the attack to the NCO, although the NF suffered its own 'maxi-blitz' in 1984.

But with Cutolo and the NCO out of the picture, the NF alliance quickly fell apart, with a war breaking out between the Bardellino and Nuvoletta gangs towards the end of 1983.[85] Once again we can see a difference between the Mafia and the Camorra: the Mafia can often experience long periods of internal harmony, but Camorra gangs have never been unable to set aside their mistrust and agree on spheres of influence to any significant extent.

These gang wars also had an important lasting effect within Naples and Campania: that of intimidating the local population. Until then the Camorra had been a fairly sporadic if worrying phenomenon in the eyes of the public, but the continual news of mass murders and shoot-outs obviously created a climate of fear and conditioned Neapolitans to accept permanently high levels of Camorra activity.

However an event which has so far only been mentioned in passing came to dominate the Naples area in the 1980s: the earthquake of November 1980 and its consequences.

CHAPTER THREE

The 'administrative economy' and the 1980 earthquake

The Christian Democrats were truly democratic, they divided power up. You could come to an arrangement, you could … cheat a lot more.

Mafia supergrass Antonino Calderone

The San Carlo theatre clock showed 7.35pm and I was in the Mayor's box with my wife and some friends. We were applauding the last piece that Gazzelloni had played and at that point naturally I was standing up. I had the sensation of feeling ill, it seemed like my head was spinning and I barely had the time to say 'I don't feel well, what's happening to me?' The entire theatre was moving in waves. Only after a few seconds did we realise what was happening.[1]

The earthquake struck at 7.35 in the evening of Sunday 23 November 1980. According to government figures, it caused 2,735 deaths, 8,848 injuries and made 300,000 people homeless. Many more people however found themselves living in buildings which were either unsafe or in urgent need of repair. Commercial premises were

also destroyed or damaged, as were public offices, telephone lines, electricity, gas and water supplies, as well
as many major roads and railways.

A huge programme of reconstruction would clearly
be needed, and the Camorra was already in a position
to win major contracts and siphon off large amounts
of money. Furthermore, reconstruction was to provide
an excellent opportunity for gangs to diversify:
moving away from drug trafficking and into the
construction industry, as well as providing them with
an area within which they could recycle their 'dirty
money'.

Indeed, the earthquake represents a turning point
in the development of the Camorra. Yet it is only if the
surreptitious growth of the Camorra during the 1970s
is borne in mind that the qualitative and quantitative
leap which the organisation took in the 1980s can be
understood. As Isaia Sales, a local centre-left politician, comments: 'Italy discovered the Camorra after
the earthquake, but it is not the case that the earthquake signalled the beginning of the Camorra as a
business phenomenon.'[2]

By 1980 the Camorra had already become a serious
economic power. Yet to fully understand the earthquake bonanza, it is vital to analyse the success they
had already achieved in obtaining public sector
contracts and influencing local politicians.

The changing climate within the ruling political
class was embodied in the decline of the Monarchist
Party Mayor of Naples during most of the 1950s,
Achille Lauro. His localised power base was slowly
eroded by the emergence of nationally-orientated
Christian Democrat politicians such as Silvio Gava
and his son Antonio during the 1960s.

Silvio Gava was a Catholic activist under Fascism, quickly becoming linked to the Catholic trade union association ACLI (Associazione Cattolica dei Lavoratori Italiani) in the postwar period. His arrival on the national political stage did not stop him from developing a series of 'patron-client' relationships within the Naples area. His contacts were concentrated within state-controlled economic enterprises, such as ISVE-IMER (Istituto per lo Sviluppo Economico dell'Italia Meridionale) and SMF (Società Meridionale Finanziaria), the control of which enabled him to slowly eat away at the foundations of Lauro's political support, and persuade his backers to change their allegiance.[3]

Although the Gavas represented economic dynamism when compared to Lauro, they were not averse to having connections with the Camorra. During election campaigns in the 1950s, Silvio Gava, who was a lawyer as well as a Christian Democrat (DC) candidate, made a point of walking round his constituency of Castellammare arm in arm with Catiello Di Somma, the local Camorra boss – even though Di Somma had two or three arrest warrants out for him.[4]

Despite connections such as these, the Gavas were nevertheless new faces compared to many leading Christian Democrats of this period. Most DC politicians, in the South at least, were 'notables' – ex landowners who had recently sold off their landed estates and were now investing in building speculation in major southern cities.

In other words, the old system of 'notables' was slowly being replaced by a series of technocratic managers, although this process only became significant at the end of the 1950s. The postwar period therefore saw a fundamental change in the ruling group of southern Italian society:

In the South a new social bloc was taking shape; no longer based on the countryside and land ownership, it depended on the control of the huge flows of public expenditure that were mainly channelled through the Southern Development Fund. The progressive emptying of the countryside and inland regions caused population increases in towns; especially along the coast, which were dominated by public administration and the service sector, i.e. by activities that were largely parasitical and speculative. So southern cities did not become modern urban centres of rationalist neo-capitalism; in the 1960s they took on the form of nerve centres of a new social bloc based on the urban middle classes, largely unproductive and linked to a system of political control over the sharing out of resources.[5]

Many of these changes were also occurring because of the policy instituted by the Christian Democrats' new Party Secretary, Amintore Fanfani, elected in 1954; faced with very effective communist competition in all walks of life, Fanfani galvanised his rather complacent party into creating more structures on the ground, as well as setting up better patronage networks.

However, over the postwar decades each Christian Democrat faction, reliant on its own local leader for national influence and resources, fought an increasingly bitter internal battle to defend its own position within the party's national pecking order, with the definition of victory being the control of greater and greater financial resources and client networks. In the South, by the 1970s, these internal Christian Democrat battles became translated into public political slogans, such as the call for 'special intervention' or 'extraordinary intervention' in the South. The existence of real problems was constantly referred to in political debate, yet there was little serious commitment to providing solutions, indeed the solving of problems would actually reduce the justification for resources, and therefore the power-base of the local ruling group.

Once the major economic crisis of the early 1970s began to make its presence felt, the whole gravy train was thrown into confusion and traditional southern politics fell into crisis. Disquiet began to spread within the DC and the Gavas' predominance in Campania was challenged by Ciriaco De Mita in Avellino. Nominally on the left of the party, De Mita succeeded in forcing the Gavas to share power with him. Writing prophetically in 1973, the political scientist Percy Allum commented:

> The fall of the Gavas, when it comes, in no way implies the fall of the power system they incarnated. The De Mita group centred in the Province of Avellino is built substantially on the same clientelistic foundations, even if it has different ideological orientations.[6]

Much the same can be said twenty years later: the fall from grace of Antonio Gava, Paolo Cirino Pomicino and other leading Neapolitan politicians during 1993 in no way implies the end of the clientelistic tradition of mainstream Neapolitan politics.

Indeed clientelism and illegality have become so ingrained in Neapolitan society that they can sometimes reach the level of the absurd. In an attempt to reduce the number of re-offenders, a scheme was established in the late 1970s to provide public sector jobs for those who had recently been released from prison. As a public sector job at that time was widely seen as a job for life, some unemployed people created false criminal records for themselves in the hope of getting one of these vacancies.[7]

With a relative reduction in funding as a result of economic crisis, many of the established notables could no longer guarantee favours and jobs, leading on one hand to the growth of the left, epitomised in the election of a PCI council in Naples in 1975, and on the other to the rise of the illegal economy and organised crime.

The growth of illegality and the entrance of organised crime into positions of influence were generally overseen by a new generation of ambitious middle-ranking politicians. The administrative system was soon to be further decentralised, giving local councils greater economic influence in the context of a 'deindustrialisation linked to the crisis of large industries and large cities, and the reindustrialisation of the region's whole area with a new industrial structure linked to small and medium businesses and provincial centres'.[8] One historian has described this period as:

> a process involving the faster circulation and replacement of local political leaders in favour of younger and more ambitious elements, who emerged from a more modest social situation and who were less well-educated. These were small businessmen, shopowners and professional politicians, people who would be the protagonists of the breakup of the monopoly of political representation which had been previously held by the liberal professions.[9]

Although these new groups were younger, more ambitious and technocratic than their predecessors, they nevertheless maintained and updated a system of patronage and clientilism which was enhanced by changes to local administration.

The creation of fifteen new regional units of government throughout Italy in 1970 played a crucial role in the development of the relationship between organised crime and the political structure.

From the following year the billions set aside for agricultural and industrial development in the South began to pass through a regional rather than a national government structure. And in 1975–77 the Socialist and Communist parties, in return for not voting against Giulio Andreotti's weak Christian Democrat government, insisted on even greater devolution of powers, so much so that by 1980 the regions were spending 18% of the national budget.[10]

From the early 1970s and the creation of regional government the pendulum of political power began to swing back in favour of local politicians and their control of a local system of patronage. No major political party held back from developing a series of client networks which depended on them for influence and favours; communist politicians were to invite senior trade unionists to play an important role in their administrations, while Christian Democrats tended to absorb local businessmen. Local councillors also nominated themselves to the Board of local health authorities, which controlled huge financial resources.

The onset of economic crisis in Italy during the early 1970s meant that the widespread industrial development which had been planned earlier did not take place. The level of industrial development in the South, as a percentage of the whole nation, charts the decline in the South's industrialisation. From a low point of 16% during the 1950s, the South's share of national industrial investment rose to 37% in the 1969–73 period, before falling back to 31% in 1975 and 27% in 1978.[11]

Local government therefore came to play a more and more important role as both private industry and national authorities scaled down their activities in the area. An official report has calculated that in the 1976–82 period local expenditure increased by 26%, whilst inflation rose by an average of 16% a year, and GNP by 22% a year.[12]

So in areas of low industrialisation such as Campania, local authorities were often the only economic agent able to carry out large investments. Isaia Sales, who has termed this an 'administrative economy', writes: 'In this fashion political power becomes the absolute regulator of social and economic life.'[13] Although Sales may be guilty of ignoring a degree of investment by private industry and national government, as well as the service and tourism sectors, he nevertheless has a point. And in a wider context, northern industrialists must also take their share of the blame for the closer relationship which developed between local politicians and organised crime, as their withdrawal from the area only exacerbated the dangers of this kind of development.

Nevertheless, it is important to acknowledge the consequences of decentralisation and development under these conditions, given that it is still proposed as a solution. This point was really brought home by Giovanni Falcone, the main anti-Mafia investigator of the 1980s, who argued shortly before his murder in 1992:

It is useless to take refuge in the generous illusion that development will wipe out the Mafia as if by magic. We have reached the point where any economic intervention on the part of the state only runs the risk of offering the Mafia further opportunities for speculation, and of widening the economic gap between North and South. The same is true of state subsidies ... It is all too clear that investment initiatives are driven by politically motivated choices with short-term, typically pre-electoral aims.[14]

There is another important argument which shows the failure of decentralisation: in economic terms southern administration is more inefficient. Once accountability is largely avoided, and politics becomes a battle for the control of resources rather than the solution of common problems, the achievement of financial rigour becomes impossible.

This can be seen for example in the maintenance of public parks and spaces: in the North 2 lire are spent per m^2, whilst in the South the figure is 11 lire per m^2. Similarly rubbish collection costs $11 per tonne in the North as against $16 in the South.[15]

Once organised crime takes hold in an area, financial mismanagement becomes even more serious. A good example of this is the Marano council, the stronghold of the Nuvoletta gang discussed in the next chapter:

The Marano council pays the Naples Water Board $4 million annually for its consumption, yet it only manages to obtain payment amounting to $1,840,000 because $2,160,000 worth of water is consumed by people who have made illegal connections to the water system.[16]

Political corruption

Although Camorra bosses had obtained votes for
Monarchist party candidates during the 1950s, closer
political contacts with criminals began with the Christian Democrats at the end of the 1960s; i.e. when
Camorra gangs first began to accumulate significant
amounts of capital.

These 'modern' Camorra gangs now began to diversify alarmingly. They bought large plots of land,
supplied public authorities with fruit and vegetables,
set up food processing plants, ran stud farms, established construction companies and built residential
areas, ran nightclubs and illegal gambling rings, and
kept control of the drug trade. But:

> despite the evolutionary process described here,
> despite the power and economic strength they
> had carved out for themselves, the Camorra, up
> until the eve of the 1980 earthquake, had not
> surfaced in terms of national public opinion.[17]

Local politicians however became increasingly aware
of the Camorra during the 1970s; and the nature of
the political system itself meant that it was relatively
easy prey for powerful criminal gangs.

By the mid-1970s politics in the Naples area had
largely been a Christian Democrat fiefdom for over
twenty years. The dividing line between the party and
public administration had become increasingly fuzzy
– the decision-making process now revolved far more
around meetings between party officials, their respective factions, and various powerful lobbies, rather
than being conducted through the official institutional channels. The infiltration and intimidation of

such a system was particularly easy for an organisation such as the Camorra.

The danger signal of widespread 'a-legality' or illegality within public administration was already becoming clear by the mid-1970s. Southern regions only make up 36% of the population, yet according to official statistics, southern politicians are rather over represented among those Italian officials charged with 'neglect of public duty' (see Table 5). It should always be remembered that such statistics indicate a general trend during that period; yet this trend has been confirmed by the explosion of charges since 1992.

During the period of surreptitious Camorra growth, i.e. during the 1970s, the local political system was itself passing through a transitional phase. This relative weakness of the political structure, coupled with the semi-democratic traditions of the structure itself, allowed the Camorra to begin to influence local politicians, and to effectively penetrate the 'first level' of politics.

By this period the Camorra was making huge drug profits, which it urgently needed to recycle and protect, and the old-style politicians who were unable or unwilling to accept this new state of affairs began to suffer both from Camorra threats and pressure applied by their younger colleagues. Furthermore, the tension between these rapidly-growing criminal organisations and a new and semi-corrupt political elite also led to 'the breakup of another monopoly, that of political control over public spending in the South, through the emergence of a fearful competitor in this area, that of a Camorra elite'.[18]

The beginning of a series of political murders carried out by Camorra gangs is clear evidence of organised crime's growing power and its relative autonomy from the political structure, in comparison to the preceding period when it had been subordinate. Although there were many woundings and attempted murders during the late 1970s, the first significant political murder was that of Socialist Party councillor Pasquale Cappuccio, killed in Cutolo's stronghold of Ottaviano in September 1978. The reason for the murder clearly illustrates the degeneration of local politics: an ex-Mayor from the Social Democratic Party wanted to join the Socialist Party, probably because it offered better business opportunities, but Cappuccio refused him membership due to his links with the Camorra.[19] Another councillor, a communist called Domenico Beneventano, was killed in the same month as the earthquake, November 1980. The following month the Mayor of Pagani, Marcello Torre (an independent Christian Democrat), was gunned down.[20]

So even before the earthquake struck, the Camorra had begun to act independently of their political protectors, in some cases killing local politicians who either did not keep their promises or would not give in to their demands. This tendency was to worsen tragically following the 1980 earthquake.

The consequences of the earthquake

The most disturbing aspect of the reconstruction scandal following the earthquake is that so much of the money allocated to the disaster fund was siphoned off legally. This situation was deliberately facilitated by an avalanche of 32 separate laws which were passed in relation to funding and rebuilding. Therefore, while evidence of shady deals is widespread, for various reasons it has been hard to gain criminal convictions. Nevertheless, the billions which have disappeared remain, at the time of writing, Europe's largest financial scandal.

A good part of this money vanished without direct Camorra involvement, revealing a corrupt ethos which has become an undisputed fact since the emergence of the *Tangentopoli* scandal in early 1992. It has been estimated that 25–30% of the total expenditure was pocketed by architects, building surveyors and civil engineers (who often doubled-up as mayors or local councillors). On average, these people legally 'earned' $950,000 from the various contracts they were awarded.[21]

One of the first moves made by local authorities was to overstate the extent of the damage caused by the earthquake. Table 6 illustrates a sudden increase in the number of councils defined as damaged six months after the earthquake.

As the months passed, it became clear that reconstruction was proceeding at a very slow pace. Consequently, in October 1982, two decrees extended the right of private individuals to obtain advances from bank accounts set up by local councils for reconstruction,

> as long as they showed a document stamped by the Mayor and the Secretary of the Council, in which the following phrase had to be written: 'Following verification of entitlement and the correct nature of the documentation presented, pay Mr X the sum of Y lire.'[22]

Never before had local mayors wielded such powers, or controlled such large amounts of money; banks were now flooded with deposits set aside for reconstruction.

Months of delay turned into years, and these delays also gave time to increase the size of projects, and consequently their total cost. For example, the cost of repairs to the ring road around Lago di Patria was originally estimated at $102 million in February 1985, rising to $136 million in October 1985, $272 million in 1986, and $370 million in 1988. The Conte Sarno canal was first estimated at $37 million, rising to $82 million in 1987 and $400 million in 1988.[23]

One of the myths surrounding the earthquake is that it was a strictly southern affair. In reality, 28 of the 50 companies which were awarded the largest contracts were based in central or northern Italy.[24] These big consortia quickly realised that they could make huge profits from delaying the start of building work, as they were allowed to take an advance of between 20–37% of the project's total cost once it had been officially approved. Even though work was frequently started months or even years later, companies could potentially make use of these large sums of money to finance other operations in the meantime.[25]

These consortia then often sub-contracted the work to local construction companies, normally at prices 40–70% below what had been agreed between the consortia and public authorities, thus creating another huge source of profit. Indeed just 11% of the construction companies which actually engaged in reconstruction were part of the original consortia that had won the contracts. And many of these local companies were controlled by the Camorra, as we shall see below.

The important point to remember is that this system benefited both the Camorra and major construction consortia. The mechanics of the system are outlined in the following hypothetical scenario published by the then major opposition party, the Partito Comunista Italiano (PCI):

How to earn $80 million without setting foot on a building site

Let's imagine a contract worth $80 million, with a construction company receiving an advance of $28 million, an amount which is only subtracted once the builder has spent $40 million. Let's suppose that it takes three years to complete half the project (18 months to actually start work, and another 18 months to complete half the work). For three years a builder has earned interest worth over 40%, taking into account the interest rates of the early 1980s.

What can therefore happen is that from an initial projected cost of $80 million a firm receives $28 million immediately (twenty days after signing the contract), $11 million in interest from the bank, another $32 million due to rising prices, and if the project is then sub-contracted at half price, another $40 million. In net terms, a firm can therefore make over $80 million without ever having set foot on a building site.[26]

While the national government was favouring a 'carpetbagger' mentality, the local political structure lacked a tradition of openness and decision-making based on an applicant's merit. This had not escaped the notice of the local police, and on 10 October 1982 the prefect of Avellino, the main town within the area most affected by the earthquake and reconstruction:

convened the representatives of the 119 councils of the province in order to agree upon common action to be taken against the Camorra and organised crime. During the meeting it was established that there had to be a full council meeting once a month, that greater space should be given to smaller opposition parties, and that the council must become a 'glasshouse' in terms of its general administrative management.[27]

Speaking to the assembled politicians, the prefect's warnings were prophetic:

The mobilisation of councils cannot and must not end up a ritual, similar to a religious litany, because it is in the badly-lit areas of certain administrations that the Camorra makes headway. In many councils the opposition is well and truly ghettoized, council meetings are only held in exceptional cases, often everything is decided without ordinary people being aware of anything.[28]

Two years later the Neapolitan sociologist Amato Lamberti, who had researched twenty of these councils in detail, assessed the outcome of the meeting:

The most important decisions, those on the contracts to be awarded, are only made in meetings of the ruling group. It has become a fixed rule that there is no monitoring of the subcontracting firm at all, whilst there are large gaps in checking up on the firms which have actually won contracts.[29]

This sequence of events illustrates two facts: contracts were being awarded to companies without any checks being made on them: decisions made behind closed doors were far more likely to be influenced by the Camorra and to lack the accountability which would characterise full and public council meetings. What it also illustrates, crucially, is the unwillingness of local politicians to make themselves accountable.

Fourteen Inspection Committees were instituted to monitor the progress of building work, although they had very little technical expertise:

Operations of a purely technical nature, such as an inspection on the progress of building work, or projects of primary or secondary urbanisation, motorway link roads, the re-routing of rivers and streams, the restructuring of railway lines, etc, were all entrusted to commissions which lacked any technical support. On the contrary, they were led by and made up of magistrates, state attorneys, prefects, bureaucrats of the regional council, academics, magistrates of the regional court and the state finance commission, MPs, ex-regional councillors, mayors, etc. What is impossible to understand is how such committees were able to ascertain and verify anything from a technical point of view, given their composition.[30]

Indeed, of the original 143 members of these committees, 30 were ordinary magistrates.[31]

Yet it would be wrong to think that the judiciary was the only high-level institution involved. Most sectors of the legal and state bureaucracy also played a role:

When the names of the other inspectors are scrutinised one finds even more surprises: three prefects, including those of Naples and Salerno (the prefect of Naples resigned in 1987, whilst his counterpart in Salerno never did, even though he was also employed at the Special Office for Reconstruction in the 'earthquake crater'), seven deputy prefects, the president of the Campania regional court together with other members both of the Latium regional court and the Campania regional court, four magistrates from the state finance commission, including the president of the Campania section, Silvino Covelli. He was also an inspector at Monteruscello, and apart from being an inspector, also managed to see that his daughter was employed within the commission's bureaucracy. The chief registrar of the Naples Law Court was also an inspector, as was the head of personnel.

Furthermore, members and officials of the control commission of the Campania Region were inspectors, as were ordinary employees of the same commission who effectively carried out regulatory checks. This is not to forget ex-regional councillors, office staff employed by particular Ministers, officials of the regional council, and a local director of education, and so on.[32]

Inspectors were paid 1% of the value of the projects they inspected.

Senior public servants were therefore legitimising the whole reconstruction, but many of them would also be called upon to make judgements if any legal controversies or accusations arose concerning the legitimacy and legality of such a huge programme of works.

And conflicts of interest did arise. For example, Neapolitan magistrates began an investigation into Camorra involvement in the building of thousands of houses at Monteruscello, and the fact that the new flats were already showing serious signs of damage. Yet the people who had previously inspected the flats were their colleagues at the Naples law courts.[33] A similar conflict of interests also arose concerning water infiltration in new houses built in Casoria and Casalnuovo.

Apart from these conflicts of interest, there is another very good reason why magistrates should not be involved in work such as this – it takes them away from their duties within the legal system. The Campania region has one of Italy's highest crime rates, yet its magistrates are also at the top of the table as regards time spent on extra-judicial activities.

Perhaps the most telling fact from this scandal is that many local politicians became millionaires as a result of the earthquake. In addition to being elected as mayors and councillors, as private individuals they were also allowed to win contracts as practising architects, construction engineers or consultants. Of the eighteen mayors in the Province of Avellino in the 1982–90 period, fifteen won a total of 1,334 reconstruction contracts, an average of 89 contracts per mayor. These figures need to be roughly quadrupled to include all the councillors who also won reconstruction contracts.[34] Other influential people have also gained advantages. The town church in Sant'Arcangelo has never been repaired, but the house of the Archbishop of Naples has been completely rebuilt, even though it was never damaged by the earthquake in the first place.[35]

Yet there was a perfectly viable alternative:

Instead of building useless roads one could have
created tens of thousands of jobs by activating
productive sectors. Yet elevated sections were as
useless as they were expensive, and therefore
extremely profitable for builders and the politicians associated with them. But directing these
huge amounts of public expenditure towards
productive investments would have given rise to
a real process of development; which would have
meant the collapse of that unhealthy link
between power politics and the parasitic
economic interests of the public, private and
criminal sectors.[36]

The inescapable conclusion from the fiasco of earthquake reconstruction is that the greatest beneficiaries
have been local politicians, senior members of the
judiciary and the state bureaucracy, and the Camorra.
Another important point to bear in mind is that *all* the
major political parties were involved. The political
affiliations of those Avellino councillors who had won
reconstruction contracts closely mirrored their political strength within local councils: 44 Christian
Democrat councillors had won contracts, 24 socialists
and 12 communists.[37]

Although vast amounts of money were earned
legally by individual politicians, the huge *Tangentopoli*
scandal of 1992–93 led to the discovery of an illegal
system of financing political parties. Over the years a
widespread system of kickbacks had developed, in
which politicians demanded a fixed percentage of
contracts be siphoned off into party coffers. One of the
reasons this particular system emerged in 1992 was

that demands became too high, as one local businessman explained: 'In recent years kickbacks increased from 3 to 7%. Extortion had become even worse, businesses were being strangled.'[38]

But if we step back just for a moment from the activities of leading politicians and business people, we should not forget that the earthquake has also been a traumatic experience for many ordinary people. For example in early 1994, more than thirteen years after the earthquake, at least 700 families – 4,000 people – were still living in steel containers of 12 m². It is also fitting, in terms of his political traditions, that over a hundred of these families live in Castellammare di Stabia, Antonio Gava's home town.[39]

As the years go by, the protests continue. On one hand, 50 people started a protest camp outside the Afragola town hall in September 1995, given that they were still forced, after 15 years, to live in steel containers which were frequently flooded by liquid sewage.[40] And on the other, after 20 years local mayors are still complaining that reconstruction is only 80% complete, and are demanding more funding.[41]

The sad but inescapable conclusion is this: 'The billions which were set aside for reconstruction work stopped, rather than encouraged, any prospect of a real expansion of production and employment in the South.'[42] There are now many 'ghost towns' in the earthquake crater, as young people move away in search of work – indeed unemployment levels in Campania are higher than twenty years ago; similarly, the standard of living in relative terms is still amongst the lowest in the country. In many areas the only real innovation has been the growth of organised crime.

CHAPTER FOUR

The 'business camorra' of the Nuvoletta gang

The Jolly Roger is the banner of competitive business.

Sean O'Casey

The Nuvoletta gang and the earthquake

When Lorenzo Nuvoletta was finally arrested in December 1990, it was widely believed that he was the leader of the Camorra's second most powerful gang, second only to the one led by Carmine Alfieri. The rapid rise of his gang was largely due to its intervention in earthquake reconstruction, which involved relaundering money and winning contracts. The well-documented rise of this gang, based around four brothers – Angelo, Ciro, Gaetano and Lorenzo – is an excellent case study in the transformation of an insignificant family from the provinces into multi-millionaires.[1]

The Nuvolettas were born into a local farming family, who also had other agricultural interests near Florence, and were probably intimidating local peasants into selling them land in Marano in the late 1950s.[2] In the early 1960s one of the Camorra gangs operating to the north of Naples, dealing mainly in contraband cigarettes, was led by Antonio Maisto. However, when he had to go into hiding in 1971–72 the reins were taken over by his sons, Luigi and Enrico.

The Nuvolettas initially joined this gang as minor members, with Angelo earning one of his first convictions as a 21 year old in 1963, for illegal possession of a firearm and for using it to make threats.[3] Stefano Bontade was another member during this period, son of the old Mafioso Francesco Paolo Bontade, a member of Michele Greco's Mafia gang. In a disastrous government policy Bontade, along with many other Mafiosi suspected but not convicted of serious crimes, was obliged to live in 'external exile' in the Naples area, where he naturally continued his criminal activities. This quickly brought the Nuvolettas into contact with the Sicilian Mafia, a link which was to prove crucial in their rise to power. During the early 1970s Bontade, along with Salvatore Riina and Gaetano Badalamenti, began to set up a new Mafia Commission, or *cupola*.[4]

The Nuvolettas are from Marano, a town of nearly 60,000 just to the north of Naples. After their early exploits in the Maisto gang, they made their first independent move which came to characterise them: in the mid-1960s they diversified and became significant landowners; using state funds set aside to establish small agricultural landholdings, they bought up a total of some 100 ha of land from various smallholders. A company called 'Viticola Nova', founded in July 1966 and run by Giuseppe Iacolare, had the function of paying their farm labourers. The first loan to

the Nuvolettas, in this case Angelo, was received in
1969 from the Bank of Naples: $40,000 repayable over
forty years.[5] This was the start of a fifteen year relationship between the Nuvoletta gang and the South's
major bank.

They were soon supplying many military and
civilian establishments with various foodstuffs, and
were not surprisingly implicated in swindles against
the Italian government and the EEC, 'for the non-
delivery of fruit and vegetables'.[6]

During this period the Nuvolettas made large
amounts of money through intimidating insurance
officials as a result of a variety of claims made, and
much of their power within local agriculture derived
from intimidating local farmers. Two *carabinieri*
reports from 1976 detail the threats made against two
local farmers by the Nuvoletta gang; in one case they
demanded to become co-owners of their business and
in the other to become sole suppliers.[7] But it was not
only brute force which led them to wield such influence – many farmers took out loans from finance
companies managed by the Nuvolettas, thus
becoming more and more dependent on them.

And it was not long before they moved into an even
more lucrative sector, that of hard drugs. It was here
that they made much of their illegal money from then
on.[8] Aniello and Antonio Nuvoletta, both sons of
Gaetano, are believed to have been involved in a large
cocaine trade with another major Camorra leader,
Umberto Ammaturo; indeed Antonio was convicted of
cocaine trafficking in March 1977.

In the same period arrest warrants were issued for
the Nuvolettas, charging them with importing a
consignment of cocaine worth $208,000. Part of the
charge also concerned phone calls made by Aniello

Nuvoletta to Germany about the purchase of Leopard and Centurion tanks, the cost of which apparently ranged between $800,000 and $1,600,000, although the German police found no evidence of this.[9]

So by the mid-1970s the Nuvoletta brothers were well known to the police, having been arrested on a variety of charges. What is particularly significant is that according to the Mafia supergrasses Tommaso Buscetta, Antonino Calderone and Salvatore Contorno, the Nuvolettas had very close links with Sicily, normally arranged through Angelo Nuvoletta.

Before he was murdered, the Mafioso Giuseppe Di Cristina confirmed the Nuvolettas' links with Luciano Liggio's gang, stating that somewhere between Naples and Caserta there was a large fruit production factory, which also contained a drugs deposit and possibly a heroin refinery, owned by Liggio himself. The Nuvolettas managed the whole enterprise on his behalf.[10] According to police reports the Nuvolettas were allowing Mafia men on the run to stay in their houses as early as 1971, one of the most important Mafia bosses being Liggio himself. When Liggio was finally arrested, the police found a cheque stub detailing a payment made to the Nuvolettas' bank account.[11]

With hindsight, it is now clear that the murder of an ambiguous underworld figure named Emilio Palamara in December 1972 marked the beginning of a close alliance between the Nuvolettas and the Mafia. Lorenzo Nuvoletta committed the murder along with Rosario Riccobono, one of the leading members of the Mafia at the time. What is significant is that the Mafia would never have asked the Nuvolettas to become involved in the murder if they did not consider them very close allies. Supergrasses have subsequently confirmed that: 'This murder was interpreted amongst the criminal fraternity as the first clear sign of the strength which local criminal groups in alliance with the Sicilians had gained.'[12]

These links with top Mafiosi were one of the main reasons behind the Nuvolettas' rapid rise. Apparently the first meetings between the Nuvolettas and the Greco family from Palermo were held in Marano in 1974. Crucially, it is widely believed that at this time Michele Greco was the leader of the Sicilian Mafia's *cupola*, the Mafia's supreme decision-making body. Furthermore, other Mafia supergrasses have detailed two top Mafia-Camorra summits held in Marano in 1978 and 1979, involving the Nuvoletta and Zaza brothers from Naples, Salvatore Riina and other top Mafiosi.[13] Other meetings would also take place, during which Angelo Nuvoletta would initiate the Zaza brothers and members of the Gionta clan into the Mafia.[14]

This is how the Mafia supergrass Antonino Calderone recalls the links:

In 1974, during one of my visits to Naples, an old man of honour originally from Palermo, who lived in a building in the Santa Lucia area, told me of the family, (i.e. the Mafia) which went back to the 1930s. The most important members of the family in Naples were the Mazzarella, Nuvoletta and Zaza brothers. Then there were other people such as Nunzio Barbarossa, the Sciorio brothers, and others. The entire Naples family was controlled by Michele Greco, but within it the Nuvoletta gang had about ten members, with an even closer and more direct relationship with Michele Greco, who could direct them without the mediation of the family itself.[15]

A major Camorra supergrass, Pasquale Galasso, has revealed details of further meetings held at one of Nuvoletta's villas in 1981. What was remarkable about these meetings is that they frequently involved representatives of all the major Camorra families, and so there were often a hundred people present, many of them on the run, as well as dozens of cars. But as he explains:

Our worries arose from the possibility that the police would arrive during our meetings and cause a bloodbath, yet Nuvoletta always managed to calm us down. Sometimes when Carmine Alfieri and I looked out at his farmhouse when leaving Vallesana, we saw some police cars parked outside Nuvoletta's house. That proved to us he was well protected ... in the course of these meetings we had to sort out once and for all the tensions Cutolo had created. I can recall that Riina, Provenzano and Bagarella were in Nuvoletta's farmhouse at the same time.[16]

It is generally thought that the influence of the Mafia gave the Nuvolettas a key advantage over their rivals, making them particularly efficient and business-oriented, although they could also engage in cold-blooded acts of violence when necessary. As opposed to the more flamboyant behaviour of many Camorra leaders, the Nuvolettas have followed in the Mafia tradition of extreme discretion and invisibility. Having Mafia support also meant they enjoyed both increased political protection and a relative lack of aggression from other gangs.

With their economic growth through heroin and cocaine activities, the Nuvolettas felt obliged to rapidly diversify their wealth and set about laundering their 'dirty' money by placing it into legal projects. Like many other *camorristi* they chose the construction industry, and in particular cement factories. The reason for this choice has very little to do with the ease of disposing of victims, the main advantage being the low level of technological know-how required. Also, concrete can only be transported for approximately 10 miles once mixed, so major building projects are virtually obliged to use local suppliers.

The Nuvolettas founded their first cement company, SOGEME, in April 1979. This had a capital of $16,000 and a sole director, Luigi Romano, a fruit and vegetable trader. (It is possible that Romano initially acted as a *prestanome*, literally a 'name-lender', as the Nuvolettas' criminal record prevented them from exercising official control of the company – although the fact that Romano was more than he seemed is shown by his purchase of a luxury hotel in 1978 for $2,400,000.) Just two years later, in April 1981, SOGEME's capital had risen to $80,000, an increase of 500% in two years.[17] A year later, in March 1982, capital had reached $1,720,000. Growth rates were clearly phenomenal, with capital increasing by a factor of 25 in the first two years of trading, and in the third year the increase was more than fourfold.

The crucial factor in these developments was the November 1980 earthquake. The Nuvolettas had moved rapidly, renaming the company Bitum Beton the month after the earthquake, restructuring their factory and buying new trucks. Cement is perhaps the most vital raw material in building work, and is normally estimated to make up 30% of the cost of building a house.[18] Bitum Beton's turnover mushroomed alarmingly, from $3.2 million in 1981, to $8.8

million in 1982, $13.4 million in 1983 and $18.4 million in 1984.[19]

According to Judge Mancuso, these huge increases are a classic sign of money laundering. As regards the 1981–84 period, 'Not one piece of evidence has been provided concerning the legal origin of the approximately $2 million difference which existed between financial resources and actual investments.'[20] It appears that sometimes the Nuvolettas made up this difference through an ingenious if rather crude method: with shareholders providing 'loans' to the company.

Control of the company moved back and forth between Luigi Romano and his cousin, Vincenzo Agizza, who in turn was the major shareholder of a cleaning company which held the contracts for Naples University, Naples Central Station and other major public buildings. Neither Romano nor Agizza had anything to do with the building trade by profession. Their staggering success, as Mancuso laconically comments: 'was achieved by a company led by a fruit and vegetable trader and the owner of a cleaning firm, without any real experience in this area'.[21]

Judge Mancuso has defined Vincenzo Simonelli, unknown to the authorities until December 1983, as the *éminence grise* of the Nuvolettas, their effective intermediary with the local and national business world.[22] According to his tax declaration he appeared to be virtually destitute, with an income of just $2,560 in 1980 and $1,360 in 1981. Indeed his desperation was such that he was twice convicted in 1983 of writing uncreditworthy cheques. Yet in December 1982 he bought a plot of land for $72,000 upon which a factory would be built, and spent another $290,000 on another piece of real estate.[23] And even earlier, in

March 1981, he had written a valid cheque for
$41,000.[24] Simonelli is believed to have been the
Nuvolettas' main *prestanome*, and when they realised
that much of their property was due to be seized, they
gave him dozens of thoroughbred racehorses, so much
so that Simonelli came to own 60 during the summer
of 1985, although he never convincingly explained
how he had come into possession of them.[25]

Not only do the business inexperience of these individuals and their inexplicable financial operations
arouse suspicion, their associates and connections
give rise to further concern. During 1983 Romano had
asked Giovanni Napolitano, a convicted heroin trafficker who had already received a nine year sentence,
to become a shareholder. Indeed Mancuso has documentary evidence to suggest that Romano exchanged
many cheques with the Napolitano brothers, visiting
their house in Canada at least once a year. They in
turn are suspected of involvement in illegal gold
trading and drug trafficking, and were also said to be
on close terms with Sebastiano Aloi, reputedly the
head of the Italo-American Mafia in Miami, who is
connected with the Columbo and Gambino families of
New York. This particular connection was apparently
useful in setting up facilities for heroin refining in
Canada.

Vincenzo Agizza's role appears to have been that of
providing financial services. He was the head of a
huge cleaning company, which in 1984 provided
services worth over $16 million to a variety of institu-
tions: state railways, the Alfa Romeo/Nissan factory
just outside Naples, the state electricity company and
Venice council. What is particularly disturbing in this
context, given the widespread use which the Camorra
makes of minors who cannot be brought to trial, is the

contract to clean Naples' two main borstals, Filangieri and Nisida. Not to speak of the contract to clean the flat of the Prefect of Naples, the major representative of the government in the city.[26] Furthermore, Agizza's cousin owned a company which won the cleaning contract for one of the major Law Courts in Campania, at Santa Maria Capua Vetere.[27]

In this particular case it is clear that the company concerned was very successful, but it is important to understand in detail how that success was achieved, chiefly because this gives an indication of how difficult it is to defeat the Camorra.

Compared to their competitors, Camorra companies have an advantage due to the following three reasons: intimidation of workers, potential clients and politicians; varying degrees of political collusion and protection; and financial advantages obtained as a result of their economic success.

There is no direct evidence of intimidation of workers in the Bitum Beton case. Yet intimidating workers is a vital component in keeping down labour costs, and not surprisingly there have been many Camorra attacks on local trade union activists. Given the unifying nature of large workplaces, it is not surprising that one of the first demonstrations against the 'modern Camorra' in Campania occurred in the shipbuilding town of Castellammare in summer 1980. Workers at the naval shipyards felt that the arrival of the Camorra, with its demands for protection money, would significantly raise costs in comparison with rival northern and central Italian shipyards. In 1983, for example, Castellammare workers claimed that a ship built by them, identical to one built in Genoa, cost $800,000 more due to the infiltration of the Camorra.[28]

This is not to say that workers are not affected by fear
or by their own historical and cultural traditions,
which could often lead them to believe that the
Camorra only bothers those with power and money.
Nevertheless, as one trade union leader from Caserta
has stated:

> In this area [the Camorra] has only one antago-
> nist, trade unionists: we are the only social
> aggregation which fights for control over the
> economy and the openness of political institu-
> tions, and we are the only ones able to mobilise
> large numbers of people.[29]

Apart from direct intimidation, the Camorra has also
practised a more insidious strategy: that of long-term
infiltration of trade unions, and in Naples, the infiltration of the organised unemployed movement.

The Bitum Beton case provides more detail of
intimidation in the world of business. In 1982 a
building co-operative called CMC won a contract to
build 1,000 houses, and due to their long-term
connections, considered Calcestruzzi Ltd as their
natural suppliers of concrete.

Yet, as the CMC Supplies manager recounts, things
went rather differently:

> As early as 1982 I sent one of my technicians to
> the Naples area to ascertain who were the biggest
> and most reliable cement companies …. Bitum
> Beton offered us a price which was about 80
> cents lower per cubic metre than the others. At
> that point, the common practice is to contact all
> the other companies and try to obtain further
> reductions, but in this case we received

information from our orders manager, Marco
Abbondanza, who stated that it was best to leave
things with Bitum Beton both in technical terms
and for reasons concerning the 'social peace'
which this kind of supplier could guarantee us.[30]

Indeed he later stated that CMC were extremely
happy with Bitum Beton's performance, particularly
their guarantee to provide 'social peace' in a very
turbulent area. And in terms of competitive business,
CMC's choice also appears to have been the most
rational.

A Mr Rambaldi, a witness from the firm which lost
the contract, Calcestruzzi Ltd (part of the giant
Gardini group), has made a fascinating deposition.
Writing before the company's involvement in *Tangentopoli*, Mancuso described Rambaldi as a 'witness
above suspicion, the Naples representative of one of
the largest European business groups':

Following the setting up of Bitum Beton's factory
I soon noticed something that went against all
my expectations – i.e. that the firm concerned,
given the owners' total lack of experience, would
have had just as much trouble as we had had, or
as any other company had had, to launch themselves on the market. Yet reality completely
overturned this expectation: the reality was that
Bitum Beton acquired important market sectors
in a rapid and completely unexpected fashion.[31]

The ultimate consequence of Bitum Beton's swift rise
was the creation of a cement consortium in 1983, the
Consorzio Campania Costruzioni. For Bitum Beton's
competitors, it was a case of 'if you can't beat 'em, join

'em'; stability was finally achieved by a common agreement on market share. Given the dynamic growth of Bitum Beton, it might seem strange that they should call a halt to a competition they had been winning, but the creation of a consortium meant that Bitum Beton gained credibility, legitimacy and also expertise. Mancuso is extremely perceptive on Bitum Beton's motivation: 'One should repeat that the objective here is civil society, and not simply profit, and this has now been reached.'[32]

One last area of intimidation concerns politicians, although discussion of this point will be brief as this subject will be dealt with in greater depth in a later chapter. For now I will again concentrate on the Nuvolettas' activities in a very specific field – their battle for building contracts in Quarto, a town next to their stronghold of Marano.

This occurred in 1982–83, and revolved around the Nuvolettas' desire to obtain building contracts before the passing of a new town development plan. Due to the reputation of the Nuvolettas and their empire, there was resistance within the council to granting them the contract. At one point the council even prevented the building committee from meeting, in order to block the awarding of the contract. The Nuvolettas allegedly responded by blowing up the car of the Mayor, Carendente Giarusso Castrese, and that of Russo, another senior council official.

These bombs had their desired effect: the council resigned and the new administration installed in January 1983 agreed to the Nuvolettas' demands. As a result of police phone tapping, it appears that Lorenzo Nuvoletta and others were even in close contact with Quarto councillors just before the approval of the Quarto town development plan. Other council officials, the government's Extraordinary Commissioner for Quarto, and individuals who were selling land were also involved. Mancuso laments the fact that the relevant documentation concerning these contracts has disappeared from council files.

In any event, just a few months later council planners discovered that three quarters of the projected 10,000 rooms had already been built, essentially without authorisation or a contract.

A 1988 *carabinieri* report states that as regards their wider political contacts, the gang 'is definitely in a position to control and deliver a huge amount of votes in favour of a given local political candidate'.

The Nuvolettas were certainly well connected: Vincenzo Agizza, who is reputed to have committed serious crimes as a member of the Nuvoletta gang, was a Christian Democrat councillor from 1980–83 in the inner city area of Poggioreale. A 1990 report from the Naples police headquarters also reveals that all members of the 1984 ruling group on the Marano council had been committed for trial on charges of forgery and promoting private business interests.[33] Furthermore, according to a June 1990 *carabinieri* report, two Christian Democrat councillors elected in May 1990 were close relations of leading members of the Nuvoletta gang; and another DC councillor at Marano has been arrested by finance police for illegally exporting currency.[34] Carlo Di Lanno, Mayor in 1991, was recently convicted of membership of a Camorra gang.[35] Not surprisingly, the council was disbanded by government decree in September 1991 and a special commissioner appointed to run local administration.

It appears that famous Camorra names are often a guarantee of a high number of votes. One of the candidates elected for the first time in the May 1990 council elections was Carmine Romano, nephew of Luigi Romano, elected as a Socialist Party candidate in the nearby town of Brusciano with 1,164 personal preferences.[36]

The percentage swings in the May 1990 local elections also gave rise to suspicion. In a country where until 1992 even a 2 or 3% swing had been seen as being very important, the swing in Marano compared to previous elections was 6.3% in the elections for the Regional Parliament, and a massive 18.5% in the council elections.[37] The concern expressed in the 1988 *carabinieri* report appears to be fully justified: it is very unlikely that the percentage swing was caused by mass attraction towards the political programmes of the respective parties or some local political issue. The most likely explanation is that the Camorra, in this case the Nuvoletta gang, had delivered the vote to its own candidates, or to candidates it had come to an agreement with. Indeed in towns such as Marano political parties no longer match up to the normal stereotype, according to the then Special Commissioner: 'One does not identify with the national party. Here there are councillors who change party every year.'[38]

Political 'networking' was engaged in to a vast extent. Antonio Saracino was a Republican Party councillor in Marano during the 1980s, and from 1983–85 was the personal secretary of Giuseppe Galasso during his period as Under-Secretary for the Ministry of Culture; Galasso's importance is that he is probably the major living historian of the city of Naples and perhaps the leading intellectual based in the city. In December 1984 Saracino phoned the Director of the Naples National Library to enquire about a cleaning contract for Agizza Ltd, and openly used his political influence: 'The Under-Secretary is asking for news, haven't you got any for him? I don't get it?'[39]

Then there are also classic examples of 'friendship', such as that of Nicola Di Muro, who attended the 1987 wedding of Luigi Romano's daughter, Leonilde; Di Muro was Christian Democrat Deputy Mayor in the town of Santa Maria Capua Vetere.[40]

Furthermore, when he was arrested for membership of the Nuvoletta gang, Luigi Romano's address book contained many private phone numbers or direct office numbers of important government Ministers. He had a particularly close relationship with Christian Democrat politician Vincenzo Scotti during his period as Minister of the Interior – Scotti also came to the opening of the Castelsandra Hotel. Furthermore, Romano admitted at his trial that he had met another important Christian Democrat Minister, Paolo Cirino Pomicino; 'I met him twice in the company of Scotti, and then never again.' But Romano was obviously being economical with the truth as it also emerged that he had four different numbers for Cirino Pomicino, Budget Minister during this period.

He also had the phone number of Caserta Christian Democrat MP Gaetano Vairo, who after his re-election in April 1991 became President of the Parliamentary Committee responsible for revoking MPs parliamentary immunity from prosecution.[41] Yet there was perhaps nothing surprising in this, in the sense that up until 1987, over a period of many years, Vairo had been Romano's lawyer.

Once Luigi Romano and Vincenzo Agizza had been convicted of several crimes (although not of belonging to a criminal association) their power and credibility were seriously undermined. Hence the later revelation of their apparent links with Vairo – allegedly the supplying of free cement for the building of Vairo's villa in Maddaloni and providing him with $100,000 for his 1987 election campaign – has been interpreted as being a personal vendetta of Romano and Agizza.[42]

Even a few of these details provide irrefutable proof of close links between organised crime and major politicians; yet it is simply unavoidable that major businessmen such as Romano and Agizza regularly meet and discuss a whole series of issues with politicians, whether they be broad discussions of policy or illegal arrangements.

It is also important to deal with finance, because it illustrates very well how the dividing line between legality and illegality can become virtually indistinguishable, and criminal activity therefore almost unstoppable.

According to Amato Lamberti, an academic specialised in the Camorra and currently President of the Province of Naples,

> When the Camorra invests in residential house building or tourism, or in other words in 'clean' business activities, it must have its own experts on tax, finance, commercial law, indeed its own legal office; there has to be a 'brains' which advises on what kinds of investments to make. Today, the professionals of the Camorra are still anonymous figures.[43]

However, it is not only academic observers who are of this opinion, as Judge Mancuso also recognises that the Camorra enjoys:

comprehensive relationships with the world of finance, and with the most knowledgeable experts of financial and commercial companies, where the dividing line between legality and illegality seems to dissolve, making the ascertainment of individual responsibilities extremely difficult.[44]

Indeed it is in the world of finance that the Nuvolettas have been at their most innovative, as outlined in the March 1988 conviction of Marano businessman Domenico Di Maro, found guilty of criminal association:

> The infiltration of capital into the business world from illegal activities permitted, on one hand, extremely advantageous re-investment (thanks to financial liquidity and the ease in obtaining clients through the use of intimidation), and on the other hand it allowed entry into the less risky area of civil society (the world of finance, politics, public administration). These are the typical methods adopted by the Sicilian Mafia, and they strongly influenced the innovative decisions made by the Nuvolettas, who then introduced these ideas within the Camorra as a whole.[45]

Di Maro had been involved in suspicious financial dealings for many years, as in the case of easy loans from his property company to a Sicilian Mafioso as far back as April 1979,[46] as well as writing cheques payable to various members of the Nuvoletta family from as early as 1976.[47]

The huge liquidity enjoyed by Camorra companies allows them to engage in massive investment, thus quickly outstripping their rivals. For example, Agizza Ltd increased its capital from $1,200,000 in 1981 to $3,500,000 in 1982, but this occurred without an increase in the firm's turnover, i.e. in the volume of its activities.[48] 'Legal' Camorra companies can quickly create large operating profits, and are able to outbid rival established companies for public contracts. Once credit institutions hear of their performance, the rules of the market dictate the creation of a close relationship:

> All the offers made by Camorra firms are 20–25% below the real costs. In order to compete for a contract, a healthy firm knows it has to estimate costs and the amount of advances it receives from banks. Yet the Camorra enjoys such a financial liquidity that it always wins the tender, and in many cases the banks are making a profit from this situation.[49]

The result is a vicious circle. Camorra firms become excellent investments in free market terms: as far as banks are concerned, only the most successful companies will be offered the most enticing repayment schemes on loans, thus creating for the Camorra a further advantage over their fully legal rivals. For example in 1981–82 Bitum Beton received 'easy-term financing' of more than $800,000 from ISVEIMER, the Institute for the Economic Development of the South.[50] And during their 1990 trial the prosecuting judge declared that Nuvoletta's gang 'enjoyed very strong and important alliances within the Bank of Naples.' Contacts can extend down to a very low level; one piece of evidence presented to the trial detailed a telephone conversation between the clerk of a local bank, who empathised with Vincenzo Agizza about the manager of the local bank in question, and thanked Agizza for the Christmas present his wife had received.[51]

Once these major companies develop close relationships with large banks, many peculiar details are likely to be ignored, as Judge Mancuso reveals in the Monte dei Paschi di Siena bank report dated 10 March 1983, which expressed concern about 'the inexplicable concentration of enormous liquidity in a very short period of time, for no reason and without any apparent cause'.[52]

The most prominent case of the 'legitimate' business world's involvement with the Nuvolettas concerns the South's largest credit institution, the Bank of Naples. The general manager of the Bank from 1980–83, Raffaele Di Somma, has been convicted of providing illegal credit to a whole series of companies owned by an associate of the Nuvoletta gang, Domenico Di Maro. That Di Maro was even allowed any credit in this period was surprising, as the *carabinieri* had been making investigations within the bank during 1982, making it clear he was suspected of involvement with the Camorra.[53] Nevertheless, Di Maro was allowed credit for $7.2 million.

Given his background it is not surprising to discover that Di Maro took full advantage of his special relationship with the bank, illegally obtaining a further $3.2 million in credit, causing severe financial problems for the bank.[54] Di Somma however gained an immediate personal benefit from all this, in the shape of two silver plates worth $800 given to him by Di Maro every Easter and Christmas.[55]

But this was not simply a case of a hardened criminal corrupting a mild-mannered banker. Independently of any Camorra involvement, Di Somma was also convicted of forcing ninety-one companies indebted to the Bank of Naples to take out loan insurance policies with his son's insurance company.[56] Indeed the power of intimidation of such a major financial institution is likely to be very extensive indeed; businesses on the verge of bankruptcy are clearly likely to remain silent even if they believe that the bank is involved in sharp or illegal practice, as they would risk having vital credit immediately denied.

Even more alarming is that 'crossovers' now occur in an unexpected direction. The classic business figure has always been that of the *mafioso imprenditore*, i.e. the gangster who moves into legitimate business. Today, given the power of the Camorra in some areas, one can see the emergence of an *imprenditore mafioso* – an individual who previously worked within the law by and large, acting as a banker or consultant to a firm known to have Camorra connections, advising on areas of investment, profit distribution and a whole host of legitimate financial issues. Once this *imprenditore mafioso* learns the tricks of the criminal trade, he or she is in an excellent position to strike out independently, as appears to be the case with Di Somma.

The strengths and weaknesses of the Nuvoletta gang

During the 1980s the Nuvoletta gang transformed itself into a huge international holding company; investing in agriculture, cleaning contracts, construction, drugs, fraud and stud farming. And like any major conglomerate, they also diversified into the leisure industry, with Luigi Romano buying a huge luxury hotel on the coast south of Salerno, worth approximately $8 million before its seizure. The Castelsandra Hotel has 124 rooms, 8 suites, 30 villas, tennis courts and even a small zoo, during the construction of which a hill containing rare wildlife was destroyed.[57]

The value of the real estate seized when the judiciary acted against the Nuvolettas' empire in 1988 gives some kind of idea of their wealth, although this is very probably just the tip of the iceberg. Luigi Romano and the Agizza brothers had the following properties seized: two flats in Brusciano worth $320,000, a villa near Paestum worth $240,000, a block of flats in Naples worth $1,050,000 as well as other minor properties. Land, buildings, flats, villas, machinery and vehicles worth $16 million were seized from the Bitum Beton company, whilst Agizza Ltd had $20 million of property seized.[58] The finance police have calculated their 'legal' investments to have been worth $280 million at that point.[59] The final order to seize the gang's assets in October 1992 involved holdings valued at $240 million.[60]

But despite this huge growth, the Nuvolettas were unable to immerse themselves completely into 'civil society'; although they had created a huge 'legal' empire, their illegal activities were still central to their operations. The fact that a war broke out between the Nuvolettas and the Bardellinos at the end of 1983, both previously part of the New Family alliance against Cutolo, is proof that as yet the Camorra has failed to create a lasting peace within its own ranks.

A turning point in the battle occurred with the killing of Ciro Nuvoletta in his Marano 'bunker' in June 1984. Two months later a massive attack was

launched against some of the Nuvolettas' allies at
Torre Annunziata, which saw eight people killed and
twenty four wounded – Italy's worst ever gangland
massacre. But bloodletting was not the decisive factor
in this war. Bardellino was now in alliance with
Carmine Alfieri's gang, destined to become the most
powerful Camorra organisation of the 1990s. The key
strength of this alliance was its close relationship with
the Christian Democrats, which provided greater legal
protection and more financial strength through the
awarding of public sector contracts. In the long run,
the Nuvolettas could not win against such a strong
combination of military, economic and political power.

So by the end of 1984 the Nuvolettas' sphere of influence had been restricted to Marano and its immediate
surroundings,[61] yet the organisation was soon to enjoy
a new lease of life. A man named Giuseppe Polverino
was introduced by his uncle to the Nuvolettas, and
joined their organisation in 1985–86, becoming head of
their military wing in the late 1980s.[62]

But Polverino was far from being just a violent
thug: alongside his explicitly criminal activities, he
was managing construction companies. And once
again, it was public sector tenders which provided
opportunities for Polverino's grouping, in this case
building work for improving the *Cumana* metropolitan
railway line. In just a few years this gang had
extended its operations considerably:

This Camorra organisation did not limit itself to
obtaining rake-offs through *ad hoc* invoicing for the
supply of cement. They took a qualitative leap in
the direction of becoming a so-called 'second
generation business', by making use of a system of
imposing various firms, such as those specialised in

excavation, fixed plant machinery, worked steel, in such a way as to profit directly from the contract.[63]

The scale of profits could be quite staggering. The turnover of Polverino's Zingara Express cement company rose from $16,321 in 1987, to $1.8 million in 1992 and $3.8 million in 1993,[64] until it was shut down by the authorities.

When compared to all the other major Camorra gangs of the 1980s and 1990s, what made the Nuvolettas almost unique was their lack of high-level supergrasses, an indication of the continued dominance of the old Mafia code of silence, 'omertà'. As Judge Giuseppe Borrelli explains, they were also able to protect themselves by adopting the cellular structure dominant within the Sicilian Mafia:

They have a system of *decine* and *capodecine*. So the few supergrasses we've had from their ranks haven't been in a position to tell us very much. This is the main reason they have been able to resist investigative work. Each *decina* doesn't know anybody outside of their own *decina*, they don't know anything about the activities of other *decine*. Only the *capodecine* have a larger picture. Angelo Nuvoletta doesn't get involved at all in the day to day running of these activities, he only intervenes when capital needs to be invested – or when disputes arise. This system of operating is a real anomaly for a Camorra gang.[65]

Spring 2001 saw the definitive decline of the Nuvolettas, beginning with the arrest of senior gang member Gaetano Iacolare on 26 March, and then with the capture of Angelo Nuvoletta on 16 May. However the Polverinos, who according to Judge Borrelli have been the dominant element within the alliance for many years, are still organisationally intact. Yet one of the long-term problems for the Polverinos is the exist-ence of a reforming left-wing council in Marano, elected for the third time in May 2001.[66]

But despite the council's best efforts mass unemploy-ment, the underlying lifeblood of the Camorra, is still at very high levels. This is why some local people reacted so strongly to Angelo Nuvoletta's arrest – after all the Nuvolettas and Polverinos are the biggest employers in the area. 'Leave him alone, you bastards. Let him go, he hasn't done a thing,' people shouted when the police launched their raid. A local journalist wrote: 'An exit poll taken after the raid gave more support to the anti-state than for the state.' A television crew was greeted with spitting, the throwing of eggs, whilst one woman threw a flowerpot at a cameraman.[67]

The rise of the Nuvoletta gang is a good example of the combination of 'old' and 'new' elements of crimi-nality that characterises the Camorra – the continuing importance of the use of violence combined with sophisticated financial manoeuvres. Yet the Nuvo-lettas were ultimately unable to resolve a central contradiction, as outlined by a senior investigator: 'If they become respectable people there is the free market law of competition, which could see them end up as losers.'[68]

Although the Nuvolettas' operations were distinc-tive for their entrepreneurial nature, they could never have been successful without strong political connec-tions. And the best overall example in the modern era of the links between politics and the Camorra is undoubtedly the kidnapping and release of Christian Democrat politician Ciro Cirillo in 1981.

CHAPTER FIVE

The Cirillo affair

Whether 'tis nobler in the mind to suffer
the slings and arrows of outrageous fortune,
Or to take arms against a sea of troubles,
and by opposing end them?

Shakespeare

On the evening of 27 April 1981 the Red Brigades kidnapped a senior Christian Democrat named Ciro Cirillo in a town just outside Naples; in order to take him away they killed two bodyguards as well as wounding his secretary. Almost three months later, on 25 July, Cirillo was released unharmed.

The kidnapping and eventual release of Cirillo saw the involvement of three major players: the Red Brigades (BR), the Christian Democrat party machine and the various secret service groups linked to it, and the Camorra – principally Raffaele Cutolo's NCO, then at the height of its powers. The Cirillo affair undoubtedly reveals the DC's duplicity and lack of morals, but it also clearly illustrates the power the Camorra had now come to wield in Neapolitan society and politics.

Not only were the highest levels of the state machinery mobilised on behalf of the Christian Democrats – fully accepting negotiations and payments to both the Camorra and the Red Brigades during the kidnapping – the subsequent seven year judicial investigation was frequently obstructed and vilified. When the verdict was finally announced in 1988, Christian Democrat Prime Minister Ciriaco De Mita described the investigating magistrate, Carlo Alemi, in the following terms: 'A Judge who acts outside of procedures, and who abuses procedures as a vehicle for his own suspicions, places himself outside the institutional network,'[1] and called for disciplinary measures to be taken against him. These were subsequently set in motion although no disciplinary steps were ever taken. Vincenzo Scotti, one of the Christian Democrat Ministers mentioned in the final verdict, also attempted to sue Judge Alemi for libel but without success.

The main Naples daily, *Il Mattino*, faithfully echoed its Christian Democrat owners, with the editor Pasquale Nonno writing that Alemi was only looking for:

> a negotiation between the Christian Democrats and the Red Brigades through the Camorra ... everything objectively takes on the shape of support for communist propaganda, which has an entirely political proposition: the Christian Democrats' negotiation ... Public opinion is convinced that Judges believe they are above the law.[2]

The general climate of institutional hostility surrounding the whole affair also emerged in an unusual fashion in 1986, when the first film directed by Giuseppe Tornatore (who later won an Oscar for his *Cinema Paradiso*), was withdrawn after just two months following threats by Cirillo to take out a lawsuit.[3]

Why was Cirillo kidnapped?

The minor player in this affair is dealt with relatively easily. If the NCO was at the height of its powers in 1981, the Red Brigades' star was starting to wane. They had achieved their greatest success in 1978, with the kidnapping and subsequent murder of senior Christian Democrat politician Aldo Moro.

One of the weaknesses of the BR was that they had been a largely northern grouping. Broadly speaking, they had been an offshoot of the student movement which had erupted in Italy in 1968, followed by a wave of militant workers' struggles in the 'Hot Autumn' of 1969.

The founding leadership of the BR was made up of revolutionary students who had become frustrated with the meagre gains won by such a mass radical movement of students and workers. They sought to speed up events by 'carrying the attack to the heart of the state' through selective assassinations and kidnappings of leading politicians, trade unionists, journalists and company managers. This would in turn force a repressive reaction from the state which could, in theory, provoke a revolutionary counter-reaction by the masses.

Through such a strategy the Red Brigades sought to effectively substitute themselves for a mass revolutionary working class, in the sense that throughout their existence they never had more than 500 members.[4] But during the 1970s elements within the

government's secret services began to view the BR as
a useful tool. It has subsequently emerged that the BR
were penetrated during the 1970s by secret service
agents, who would sometimes 'pilot' them into
certain actions which would be convenient for a given
faction with the Christian Democrat party. It does not
appear that the Cirillo kidnapping was a 'piloted'
operation, although the secret services did play a
significant role in the negotiations.

For the 'genuine' BR, the Cirillo kidnapping represented an opportunity to recruit members in the
South's capital. Hundreds of thousands of people had
been made homeless or were living in accommodation
made unsafe by the earthquake. Many families had
been placed in huge hotels along the coast which were
closed down for the winter, and were effectively
isolated from their original place of work, as they were
far away from the main lines of public transport.

Many of those living in the city were housed in
either old or dangerous accommodation, and in the
months following the earthquake there were almost
daily demonstrations of people demanding to be
rehoused. The 12,000 homeless before the earthquake
had now risen to 150,000. Roads were often blocked
by demonstrators, and sometimes buses were seized
and burnt in order to make temporary barricades;
indeed in one afternoon alone fifteen buses were
seized and destroyed.

At the same time, however, there were thousands of
unrented flats within the city and its immediate
outskirts, which were the 'second' or 'third' homes of
the wealthy. In such an emergency, it would clearly
make sense to house homeless families temporarily in
these flats. Many schools had been immediately occupied by 'earthquaked' families as they were often

modern and low level buildings. But this obviously created chaos, as the number of available schools was drastically reduced, often requiring a three-shift system in the primary sector.

For the BR the existence of a Communist Party council in Naples was a highly significant factor. The council's refusal to requisition these second homes was concrete proof of the Communists' conservatism and accommodation to bourgeois society, one of the key arguments in the Red Brigades' political analysis.

The kidnapping of Cirillo, combined with the demand to requisition second homes, enabled the BR to present themselves as the defenders of the city's poor, in the hope of creating a stable base in one of Italy's major cities. But the choice of Cirillo was far from random, as the BR explained in the first communiqué they released after his kidnapping:

It is easy to explain who Ciro Cirillo is: this murderer represents the continuity of power of the Christian Democrat party-regime in the Campania area. If yesterday, together with his friend and godfather [Antonio] Gava, he was the man of unbridled building speculation, today he is in the front line of imperialist restructuring in the urban area of Naples.

His strong and numerous links with all the economic and political forces of regional government have given him both the role of guide and strategist of restructuring and reconstruction on a regional level.[5]

Cirillo was first elected as a Senator in 1948, in Antonio Gava's home town of Castellammare, and in many subsequent years he was appointed by the

Gavas' faction at Christian Democrat congresses as President of the electoral commission. Effectively Cirillo was one of the party's main power brokers in Naples, and therefore the custodian of many secrets. Having been president of the regional council in the past, in 1981 he became president of the regional council committee for urban planning. His most important role in this period was that of vice-president of the regional committee for reconstruction, a position which in practice meant control of the committee. In other words, Cirillo was the politician who made the most important day-to-day decisions concerning the massive earthquake reconstruction programme.

It is also likely that Cirillo, like all powerful Neapolitan politicians, had had links with the Camorra before his kidnapping. For example in one trial against the NCO, evidence emerged of a letter from Michele Gaglione to Andrea Quintosegno, both members of the New Family alliance, written almost a year before the kidnapping, in May 1980. Gaglione urged Quintosegno to become active in Cirillo's re-election campaign, 'because if he gets re-elected, there is a good chance that he will help me to get out on parole'.[6]

One of the dangers was that if Cirillo were to talk to the BR it would not only be the DC that would suffer. The general political destabilisation, and the possible revelation of DC links with the Camorra, would also have harmed both wings of the Camorra, currently engaged in a massive gang war.

It would appear that the BR's strategy during the Cirillo kidnapping differed markedly from that of Aldo Moro's kidnapping three years earlier. In 1978 the main BR objective had been to gain open political recognition through negotiations for the release of Moro, including the release of some jailed BR members. On this occasion it appears that their main objective was to gain a following in Naples by demanding urgent government measures to help the homeless, and to stop widespread profiteering from the reconstruction.

The different nature of their demands compared to the Moro kidnapping eventually led the BR to decide to release Cirillo; however, perhaps more important than this was the DC's immediate willingness to negotiate for Cirillo's release. The existence of this channel of communication did not emerge publicly during the kidnapping itself, as it coincided with three other, more newsworthy, events: the attempted murder of the Pope, the publication of the membership list of the secret P2 Freemason lodge and the subsequent resignation of the government.

Negotiations only took place because the secret services requested them: they moved with astonishing speed – asking the National Prisons Office for permission to visit Cutolo the day after Cirillo's kidnapping, and actually seeing Cutolo within just sixteen hours of the abduction.[7] The early meetings were attended by a delegation of two secret service agents, two senior NCO members and Giuliano Granata, Christian Democrat Mayor of Giugliano. The action of the secret service was in no way opposed by government ministers; in fact, on the very same day that the secret services first met Cutolo, the Minister of the Interior Virginio Rognoni declared: 'The Camorra could have an interest in helping to free councillor Cirillo. Sometimes the relations between organised crime and terrorism are intertwined, other times they are separate. All possible channels must therefore be opened.'[8]

One of the main reasons the Camorra was willing to intervene in the kidnapping was that the massive police presence in urban areas – principally in the form of road blocks and searches of houses and buildings – got in the way of many of their activities, such as smuggling, extortion and the distribution of drugs. The drop in the number of murders gives a chilling indication of the Camorra's reduced room for manoeuvre during this period: both before and after Cirillo's kidnapping, the number of gangland deaths reached almost one a day – yet during his three months in captivity this number fell to just over one a month.

This is how one leading NCO member, Giovanni Pandico, recalled the period and Cutolo's response:

> This situation had practically paralysed all our activities: from murders to bank robberies, from theft to picking up money due from protection rackets, it also prevented the unloading of contraband cigarettes and drugs as the coast was under surveillance.
>
> Cutolo was immediately informed of the situation and decided to intervene, getting the word outside that he was prepared to get involved in the problem.[9]

The initial messenger between Cutolo and the BR was Luigi Bosso, an ordinary inmate who had declared himself a left-wing 'political' prisoner while serving a sentence for a series of common crimes. In another trial Bosso stated: 'Cutolo asked me to contact the Red Brigades' members in Palmi prison and give them the following message: "The Christian Democrats are willing to negotiate at any level, using Cutolo as a middleman."'[10]

Pandico, a leading NCO member held in the same jail as Cutolo, has stated that on 5 May he and Cutolo met with Silvio Gava, secret service agents, and NCO members Vincenzo Casillo and Corrado Iacolare. (Casillo was a notorious *camorrista*, widely considered to be the number two in the NCO chain of command, and although he was not on the run at that time, Iacolare was.) At the end of the meeting it was agreed that Cutolo would use his influence within jails to persuade the BR to release Cirillo.[11] It is important to remember that in all these meetings there is no evidence whatsoever of any desire by the secret service or the DC to discover Cirillo's whereabouts. From the first day negotiations were based on Cutolo's NCO acting as go-between with a view to obtaining the safe release of Cirillo. Subtle details such as this show clearly the DC's toleration of illegality.

Several other meetings followed between the negotiators, some of them held at the high security Ascoli Piceno jail where Cutolo was imprisoned – an incredible venue considering the fact that notorious criminals who were wanted for serious crimes also took part in meetings inside the jail, and were apparently given *carabinieri* uniforms and identity passes.[12] Not only was Silvio Gava probably a frequent visitor to Cutolo's jail, along with DC Senator Francesco Patriarca, but according to many other witnesses interviewed during the investigation, DC Ministers Antonio Gava and Vincenzo Scotti also attended meetings in the jail.

Indeed Cutolo has stated that Scotti arranged for the NCO to receive a consignment of machine guns as evidence of his willingness to negotiate.[13] If true, Cutolo has also provided a more long-term and directly political explanation for Scotti's behaviour. Apparently Cutolo's 'spiritual father', Alfonso Ferrara Rosanova, told him: 'Look, we've got Scotti in our pocket now. Thanks to our intervention, he got 10,000 more votes than he expected at the election. If we get Cirillo free for him, who knows how important he'll become. He can't escape, he's one of us now.'[14]

Although he has given different versions on different occasions, Francesco Pazienza, one of the key secret service agents involved in these meetings, has also stated that he met Vincenzo Casillo, and that he negotiated directly on behalf of DC National Secretary Flaminio Piccoli.[15]

In the short term, Cutolo wanted an end to the intense police activity; in the medium term he hoped to be released early or transferred to a more relaxed prison environment; and in the long term he hoped to gain large numbers of important reconstruction contracts and perhaps one day be released on parole earlier than he might have expected prior to the kidnapping.

Meetings continued at a frenetic pace both inside and outside the jail. The deputy director of the secret services has admitted that one of his men had frequent meetings with Vincenzo Casillo during the kidnapping,[16] and added: 'The presence of Casillo was also essential, inasmuch as without an introduction which vouched for the visitors, Cutolo would have never accepted to give out information.'[17] He also specified that three official meetings, authorised by the Ministry of Justice, took place between Cutolo and the secret services in Ascoli Piceno jail.

Eventually an agreement was reached amongst the three parties: it was absolutely clear that a large sum of money would be paid to the BR, and there were many other details which to this day have never been clarified.

None of the BR's political demands were met (an end to the 'deportation' of the homeless from the city, the requisitioning of empty flats, and the closure of a huge 'caravan city' rapidly erected to house hundreds of families), but in the end they accepted that a ransom was enough for them to release Cirillo. It appears that the BR kidnappers managing the operation were less 'principled' than those who had kidnapped Moro, in the sense that they were quite willing to use the Camorra as mediators, thus deflecting the crucial impact which any direct BR-DC communication would have had. Indeed the failure of the BR to achieve any of their political demands, and Cirillo's subsequent release, might suggest either a successful intervention by the secret services within the BR or just sheer political ineptitude. However, a far more likely explanation is the potential for NCO gangsters to attack BR members inside jails, one of the factors that probably led the secret service to contact Cutolo in the first place.

At any rate, once an agreement was reached, a collection was held amongst the managers of the large construction firms who supported the Christian Democrats. A ransom of at least $1,200,000 was then paid to the BR, and the NCO also received a minimum of $720,000.[18] It is also likely that the same firms agreed to subcontract many reconstruction projects to NCO-controlled firms.

Although these major construction companies may have eventually sub-contracted work to the NCO, these companies probably gained many contracts from the DC, given that they had paid the ransom to get the DC's man out of the hands of the BR. One example of this was the $70 million contract for the building of 1,000 prefabricated houses in the Avellino

area.[19] In a pattern typical of earthquake reconstruction contracts, the company which received the initial
contract, Volani, based near Venice, then sub-
contracted it to another central Italian company based
in Bologna, with the final sub-contract involving a
company linked to Cutolo's son Roberto.

In its fantasy world, the BR apparently saw no
contradiction in claiming to be an organisation of the
working class while financing itself through donations from the highest levels of capitalism. In their
last communiqué before Cirillo's release they wrote:
'The Red Brigades have expropriated from Cirillo the
murderer, from his family of speculators, his party of
bloodsuckers, and his social class of exploiters, the
sum of $1,200,000.' And they continued, 'The Cirillo
campaign, through the dialectic of revolutionary
initiative and the struggles of the marginalised prole-
tariat, has built and reinforced the linkage between
the party and the masses.' The release of Cirillo had
suddenly become irrelevant, 'purely a problem for the
regime'.[20]

This last assessment was absolutely correct – ever
since his release, the Cirillo kidnapping continues to
haunt all those involved. Cirillo was freed after nearly
three months of imprisonment, early on the morning
of 24 July, and found by a traffic police patrol car. The
traffic police telephoned their superiors who told
them to take him to police headquarters for the
customary debriefing. Two hundred yards down the
road, however, their car was surrounded and stopped
by four state police cars and Cirillo was 'kidnapped' a
second time – given that he was bundled out of the
traffic police patrol car. This second group was led by
Biagio Ciliberti, a face Cirillo recognised as '[he was]
the son of Bettino, an old party comrade'.[21]

Cirillo was bundled out of the patrol car and taken instead to his home, where his doctors refused access to investigating magistrates for three days, saying he was 'unable to make any statement' because of the 'trauma' he had suffered. The primary motive of investigators at this point was not to unearth the truth surrounding the negotiations, but to locate the terrorists while the trail was still hot.

Despite Cirillo's alleged nervous exhaustion he immediately received visits from leading Christian Democrat politicians, such as Antonio Gava and the party's National Secretary Flaminio Piccoli. During subsequent questioning Piccoli has admitted that the day after Cirillo's release 'we were left on our own to chat and Cirillo outlined his beliefs on the current situation of terrorism in Italy, which he had deduced from the ideas he heard Senzani and others outline during the period of his imprisonment'.[22] In other words, Cirillo was lucid enough to talk to leading Christian Democrats for two days, during which it is presumed they established a common version of events. Only then did he agree to be questioned by investigating magistrates.

During the kidnapping, and immediately afterwards, there were rumours about negotiations. It has to be said that these rumours were caused by an obvious puzzle – the Red Brigades would have never released Cirillo without getting something in return, and for this to have happened some form of negotiation must have taken place. Less than three weeks after Cirillo's release even magazines sympathetic to the DC were writing: 'It was the Camorra that saved Cirillo – Don Raffaele Cutolo, boss of the Neapolitan underworld, was the intermediary with the terrorists, who received $2.4 million.'[23]

A cover-up would clearly be necessary, and the first 'deviation' from the truth concerned a document published in the PCI daily *l'Unità* the following year, which named the leading Christian Democrats who went to see Cutolo in jail. A few days later it emerged that the document was a forgery organised by Cutolo; it was apparently designed to remind the politicians who had negotiated that they ran the risk of exposure if they didn't keep their side of the bargain.

More important than this isolated example is a long series of facts, events and statements which, taken as a whole, can only lead to the conclusion that there has been a cover-up. For example, many of the pages covering the time of the Cirillo kidnapping have been ripped out of the visitors' book at the high-security prison where Cutolo was held; on others the names of visitors had been cancelled out. Tape recordings of Cutolo's telephone calls during this period were inexplicably erased on order of the appropriate Ministry; similarly, Cutolo's normally copious correspondence appears to have trickled down to virtually nothing during these three months. Furthermore, recordings of telephone conversations between the Red Brigades and the person due to bring them the ransom were tampered with in an attempt to present a completely different version of events, while the tapes of Cirillo's revelations to the BR whilst imprisoned have never been found.

Even more disturbing is the number of 'illustrious corpses' linked to the kidnapping – the two main victims being Antonio Ammaturo in 1982 and Vincenzo Casillo in 1983.

Ammaturo, the head of the Naples Flying Squad, was murdered on 15 July 1982. Although the official version of events places sole responsibility on the BR, the car used in the attack was provided by two *camor-risti* with whom the BR were in contact.[24] Furthermore, one of terrorists wounded in the attack was hidden and nursed back to health in the house of a known *camorrista*.[25]

Ammaturo's position obviously made him an enemy of both the Red Brigades and the NCO, but the fact that he appears to have been investigating the Cirillo kidnapping inevitably leads to the suspicion that the same 'unholy trinity' of terrorists, *camorristi* and politicians conspired to silence him. His brother Grazio recalls that just a few days before his death Antonio told him: 'I've finished, it's really big – all of Naples will tremble, I've sent everything to the Ministry,'[26] but no trace has ever been found of his report. His sister has testified that the last time she saw him, two weeks before his murder, he told her that he had been working on the Cirillo case: 'If they don't rub me out first, many important heads will roll.'[27] Ten days before his death, he told one of his police team that he was finishing a report on the Cirillo affair.[28]

The murder of Vincenzo Casillo, Cutolo's main nego-tiator during the kidnapping, is even more important, as it represents a turning point in the relationship between the Camorra and local politicians. Although there are some rumours claiming that Cutolo had Casillo killed because he had stolen Cutolo's share of the Cirillo ransom, Cutolo has stated that he was worried by the untrustworthiness of politicians, and claims to have warned Casillo after the kidnapping:

> It was me who told Casillo to keep documentary evidence of the meetings he had with these people, whom I didn't trust because all they do is

sell hope by the ton to poor people and then, when
things don't work out as they expected or when
they've got what they wanted, *they cast you adrift*.[29]

The whole question of the murder is further compli-
cated by the fact that a secret service card that could
have been used by Casillo was found in his burnt-out
car.

But Ammaturo's and Casillo's are far from being
the only deaths linked to the Cirillo kidnapping.
Casillo's partner disappeared a few weeks after his
death, and her body was eventually found in a ditch
under a motorway in December 1983, while
Ammaturo's brother Grazio died in an unusual
hunting accident in the same year. Another clearly
related murder was that of criminologist Aldo
Semerari, often employed to give psychological
profiles of Cutolo and other Camorra leaders, who was
found decapitated in 1982.

Nicola Nuzzo, a key NCO member involved in the
negotiations, was battered to death in the ward of a
Roman hospital in 1986, soon after a meeting with
investigating magistrate Carlo Alemi. Salvatore Impera-
trice, Casillo's bodyguard and also a member of the
NCO negotiating team, died mysteriously in jail in
March 1989. Mario Cuomo, who lost his legs in the
explosion that killed Casillo, was eventually murdered
in October 1990. A secret service agent, Adalberto Titta,
who had several meetings with Cutolo in prison, died of
a sudden heart attack, as did Luigi Bosso at the age of
42. Not only was such a number of deaths highly suspicious, they were clearly harming Cutolo's NCO, and
were therefore likely to be carried out by a rival gang.

A possible explanation for these deaths was given
to Judge Alemi in 1987 by Enrico Madonna, who was

Cutolo's preferred lawyer during the Cirillo kidnapping and probably took part in several meetings:
'Amongst the bearers of [the politicians'] promises
there were Casillo, Iacolare, Giuliano Granata, Nicola
Nuzzo, Semerari.'[30] Madonna was himself murdered
in October 1993, three days after informing a journalist he was willing to tell a parliamentary
commission all he knew about the Cirillo affair.

Indeed the ramifications of the whole affair could
reach as far as London. Vincenzo Casillo once told
Madonna that he had murdered the bankrupt finan-
cier, Roberto Calvi, who was found hanged under
Blackfriars Bridge in 1982.[31] It appears that in an
attempt to avoid imprisonment and further criminal
charges Calvi had intervened in the kidnapping to
help the DC, contacting the Camorra and paying some
of the ransom money. However, as his legal situation
did not improve afterwards, he was apparently threatening to reveal the political connections behind his
corrupt financial operations, and the order was therefore given to eliminate him.

In view of all these events, it is not at all surprising
that a judicial investigation was set up to establish
what had really happened during the kidnapping, and
it is hard not to agree with its conclusion:

> In judgement it seems clear that the evidence
> unequivocally points to an attitude on the part of
> leading Christian Democrats that was markedly
> different from that of the party's 'official line';
> which was that of reacting with firmness to all
> Red Brigade blackmails and refusing all hypoth-
> eses of a negotiation or a compromise. In reality
> there were members of the party who did not
> follow this official line but were active in various

ways to obtain Cirillo's release, turning above all
to the mediation of Raffaele Cutolo and accepting
negotiations with the Red Brigades.[32]

In other words, the truth established in law was that a
group of leading Christian Democrats negotiated with
the Red Brigades through Raffaele Cutolo. Although
no individual politician was named, it was clear who
Judge Alemi was referring to.

But instead of being 'grounded' by the party hierarchy, those politicians involved in freeing Cirillo were
subsequently promoted. Antonio Gava became a
minister for the first time in 1983, which was
followed by the even more incredible decision to make
him Minister of the Interior in 1988. Vincenzo Scotti
also went on to hold a succession of important Minis-
tries throughout the 1980s, and was Minister of the
Interior in 1990–92. Biagio Ciliberti, the man who led
Cirillo's 'second kidnapping', was promoted to a
senior role within the Ministry of the Interior soon
after Gava's appointment and became Italy's youngest
ever police chief when he was put in charge of the city
of Trieste.

The whole issue came up once again in July 1993
when the Court of Appeal turned down the demand
for a reopening of the investigation, regardless of the
fact that important protagonists in the kidnapping
had decided to give new testimony and had been
legally judged to be credible witnesses. While investigating magistrates in the North had brought down
virtually all major politicians in the *Tangentopoli* investigations of 1992–93, it seems that the wind of change
had not yet made such a strong impact in Naples.
Judge Carlo Alemi, leader of the investigation during
the 1980s, was resigned to the decision: 'It doesn't

surprise me, I didn't expect anything else, I had predicted it for a whole series of reasons. Maybe it called for too much courage.'[33]

During this period the hope that the full truth about the Cirillo affair would emerge was based on the revelations of Camorra supergrass Pasquale Galasso, which shed light on the reticence of the legal system to get to the bottom of the affair.[34] The Christian Democrat Senator and lawyer Alfredo Bargi, who defended both Cirillo and his party in various trials linked to the affair, apparently became a senator thanks to a $32,000 contribution by Galasso's gang to his April 1992 election campaign.[35] Galasso also bought him a new office, obviously with the intention of gaining preferential treatment within the legal system. One lowly lawyer, however, would obviously not be enough to guarantee preferential treatment, and Galasso has stated that he also bought an office for Judge Armando Cono Lancuba, and that he let them both have free holidays in a hotel he owned.[36] The involvement of Judge Cono Lancuba is of particular interest here: he was the public prosecutor in the preliminary proceedings of the main Cirillo trial. With hindsight it is easy to understand why press accounts of the trial described his attitude towards those who denied or played down their role in negotiations as that of a goalkeeper rather than a centre-forward – in other words, he did not attack them at all.

Whatever we may think of their methods, it is difficult not to share the analysis of a member of the Red Brigades involved in the kidnapping:

All these elements led us to the historical and political conclusion that all high levels of organised crime and the *Nuova Camorra Organizzata* were nothing but the other side of the coin of the state, in other words the worst and most reactionary elements within the state.[37]

The long-term consequences of the negotiations

However, there was a third party involved in freeing Cirillo – big business – which paid part of the ransom in exchange for reconstruction contracts. This arrangement also committed major contractors to either sub-contract to the Camorra, or alternatively to pay them a fixed percentage per contract. This was later revealed by the boss of what was then the major building company in Avellino, Antonio Sibilia:

> It is a well-known fact amongst building contractors in the province of Avellino that the Camorra was part of such arrangements, particularly Vincenzo Casillo. It is true that a general agreement was reached in which, for every reconstruction contract, contractors had to come up with a double percentage payment: 5% to the Camorra and 3% to the politicians.[38]

In essence, the Cirillo affair reveals the symbiosis which had developed between the Christian Democrat party machine and the top levels of organised crime.[39] The precise nature and consequences of this joint venture began to emerge in greater detail in 1993 as a result of Pasquale Galasso's revelations. Galasso claims that he killed Casillo to free Gava and other Christian Democrats 'from Cutolo's threats'. In a meeting held nine months after the kidnapping, in April 1982, Vincenzo Casillo reportedly told Giuliano Granata, the DC mayor who had taken part with him in the negotiations: 'You did what you wanted and then washed your hands.'[40] This is Galasso's view of the post-kidnapping tension between the two main parties involved in the negotiations:

> The Gavas were feeling the pressure of Raffaele Cutolo's demands, as he expected the agreement to be kept ... and he threatened to unleash a scandal that would have involved the institutional apparatus that had conspired with him for the liberation of Cirillo. So as the Gavas were feeling threatened by Cutolo they turned to, and formed an alliance with, the only person who at that moment could fight Cutolo. That person was Carmine Alfieri.[41]

It appears that the advantages Cutolo hoped to gain from his involvement in freeing Cirillo did not materialise. But if that was the case Cutolo was unlikely to meekly accept the politicians' lack of faith, and he continually threatened to release information showing the direct involvement of DC politicians in negotiations.

If this interpretation of events is correct, the defeat of a powerful organisation such as Cutolo's NCO necessitated the successful coordination of an intricate strategy. To bring about Cutolo's defeat it seems that the DC machine simply turned and provided support and protection to another gang, that led by Carmine Alfieri in Nola.

It was also in Alfieri's interest to destroy Cutolo. It was widely believed that Cutolo had negotiated with leading politicians, and once he had received the advantages he hoped for, he would not have hesitated to annihilate any rival gang. As Galasso has stated:

> When Cirillo was freed we were well aware that his release was due to Cutolo's intervention, and we were afraid that he had strengthened his association with Gava and Scotti ... The murder of Salvatore Alfieri was a signal that Cutolo would never look back, as he felt that he had his back covered by the politicians and the secret service that had been involved in the Cirillo affair.[42]

It was decided to kill Casillo, Cutolo's right-hand man, with a car bomb, one of the first times that the Camorra had used this kind of technique – in logistic terms this is a method that requires far more resources and planning than one man with a gun. According to Galasso, the reasons for this decision were:

> first of all to make it clear to Cutolo that he was finished, and that once and for all he had to stop blackmailing the politicians and the institutions he had dealt with during the Cirillo affair. It is also beyond doubt that through carrying out that action Alfieri wanted to demonstrate to the politicians, mainly the Dorotea faction and perhaps above all to Antonio Gava in particular – that he had to be reckoned with ... The car bomb was therefore intended to demonstrate Alfieri's real importance.[43]

Cutolo's empire collapsed in 1982–84. In April 1982 he was transferred from the mainland to a high security prison off the coast of Sardinia, and the following day his 'spiritual father' and fellow *camorrista* Alfonso Ferrara Rosanova was murdered. Vincenzo Casillo and many other of Cutolo's leading men were either murdered or arrested in a series of 'maxi-blitzes' during 1983–84.

The Cirillo kidnapping and its consequences therefore mark a turning point in the relationship between powerful criminals and corrupt politicians – they were now coming together as a single group which often pursued a common purpose. Just as the DC felt that the best way to respond to the crisis unleashed by Cirillo's kidnapping was to turn to Cutolo for help and thereby legitimise him, it later felt unable to deal with Cutolo's threats without turning to the Alfieri/Galasso gang.

As the Anti-Mafia Commission has written:

> from that moment [Casillo's death in January 1983] until today Alfieri and his men were to stain Campania with blood and obtain large slices of the reconstruction cake; for a long time they would also constitute an undisputed effective government in large areas of the region.[44]

Alfieri and Galasso were also aware of the turning point represented by the murder of Casillo, and as Galasso states: 'As far as I can recall that was the only time we talked about a crime in euphoric terms. Alfieri embraced [here a name has been censored in the original document] and congratulated him for the courage he had shown; I know that he later gave him a Rolex.'[45]

Not only Cutolo, but many other Camorra gangs understood the shift in the balance of power which Casillo's death represented; they subsequently abandoned Cutolo and aligned themselves with Alfieri.

What the Cirillo affair demonstrates is that for leading Christian Democrats in Campania the problem was never one of trying to eradicate organised crime but deciding what arrangements to make with it. In turn, major Camorra gangs have become part of the local political and economic elite, not something outside of it.

The final word goes to Carmine Alfieri, who through his intervention at the end of the Cirillo affair put himself in a position to become the most important Camorra leader over the next fifteen years. What he shows here is not the mind of a criminal, but someone who had been taught 'criminal politics' by the Christian Democrats:

We feared [the NCO's] 'political protection', in that it represented a greater strength than Cutolo's military wing. While – even at the cost of serious losses – we felt able to fight Cutolo's military wing, we could never have neutralised it as long as that 'political protection' remained in place.

At this point I want to outline a concept which I think is important: the majority of politicians in Campania, and certainly those I have identified as belonging to the Dorotea faction, protected Cutolo due to his military control over the territory and his consequent ability to gather in electoral support. Once Cutolo's defeat began, our organisation (with its allies) automatically inherited the very same political protection. To sum up, just as we took control over the territory, we also took on all those relationships with political and big business representatives who had previously had links with Cutolo.[46]

CHAPTER SIX

How the Camorra works

*With adequate profit, capital is very bold. A certain 10%
will ensure its employment anywhere; 20% will produce
eagerness; 50% positive audacity; 100% will make it
ready to trample on all human laws; 300%, and there is
not a crime at which it will scruple.*

Karl Marx

Although most of the activities detailed in this
chapter are clearly illegal, two factors should be borne
in mind: the line between legality and illegality is
often very fuzzy, and there are many other activities
involving the Camorra which are generally run along
legal lines.

Territorial control and Camorra membership

Exercising direct physical control over a given area, as
is the case with the Mafia, is of vital importance for
the growth of Camorra gangs. Once this control is
achieved, criminal gangs can not only extend their
protection rackets, illegal gambling, usury, cigarette
and drug trading, they can begin to become power

brokers, mediating between ordinary people and ruling politicians. Acting as brokers not only increases their general social legitimacy, it also makes them more important in the eyes of corrupt politicians worried about getting elected.

Just as the Mafia evolved over time from guarding rural estates through managing tenant farms to property speculation and public sector contracts in the postwar period, so the Camorra's role and its use of violence, too, have changed. During the last century Camorra violence involved direct acts of intimidation and robbery, without the Camorra playing any sophisticated economic role.

But with the growth of the contraband trade in the postwar period, the role of the Camorra began to change. While many *guappi* had traditionally controlled fairly large and significant sectors, such as fruit, vegetable and meat markets, the growth of the contraband industry required not only a more dynamic attitude and greater financial investment, but also defence against increased police activity. The addition of drugs to contraband cigarettes obviously involved even greater financial investment, higher risks in terms of prison sentences, and more competition from rival gangs. Territorial control has thus become increasingly important to the Camorra in the postwar decades.

It is important to understand the *dynamism* of this process. The growth of the contraband industry meant that the Camorra was no longer simply reacting to what was around it, it was making large investments that needed to be defended. Camorra gangs were therefore beginning to consciously transform the conditions surrounding them rather than simply reacting to them. Easier communication, improvements in transportation and also the competition between rival gangs all led to greater territorial control. The massive increase in profits brought about first by contraband cigarettes and then by the drug trade explains the higher level of violence: just as nation states militarily defend their wealth and privileges against both external and internal threats, Camorra gangs defend their activities through increased militarisation.

The greater frequency of violence between rival Camorra gangs in comparison to the Mafia is explained by the relative lack of mediation between gangs, at least at the lower and medium level of Camorra activity; the Camorra has never had the equivalent of the Mafia's hierarchical *cupola* or 'commission'.

It is not only the level of violence that indicates Camorra control over a given territory; the selling of contraband cigarettes, for example, requires the regular, visible presence of considerable numbers of people. In this respect certain aspects of the Camorra have always been different from the Mafia – the difference in environment between rural Sicily and urban Campania, and the different activities taken on, have always made the Camorra far more visible than its Sicilian counterpart.

However, one important similarity is that organised crime in both these areas has come to take the shape of an alternative form of power, described by many as an 'anti-state'. The Camorra is actually much more of a 'parallel state' than an organisation committed to destroying or taking over governmental power. But once systematic criminal influence within the political structure, with its consequent protection from legal sanctions and harassment becomes generally accepted, territorial control can take on a literal meaning: Camorra control becomes a widely known fact, conditioning both the local population and the political structure. When this position of power is reached, all manner of criminal activities can flourish, privately sanctioned by local political leaders.

No less a figure than the Federal Prosecutor of Naples, Agostino Cordova, once outlined the fundamental importance of territorial control:

> Recent investigations have allowed us to ascertain that it is through complete control over an area, and in particular control of elections and financial activities, that the leaders of the Camorra – Carmine Alfieri in the Province of Naples, Gennaro Licciardi in the city and Francesco Schiavone in the area of Caserta, have been able to dominate the politicians and businessmen with whom they had dealings.[1]

Even though physical control of an area through intimidation may be more important than the possibility of total political control, it would be mistaken to view the Camorra as a purely criminal organisation. The Camorra's governing drive remains economic and not political or social: physical control over a given territory and domination of local politicians, i.e. the exercising of power, are means employed towards the end of capital accumulation and enrichment.

In recent years Camorra gangs seem to have undergone a further mutation: once total physical control of a given territory has been achieved there appears to be a specialisation in particular activities. According to Judge Giuseppe Borrelli, there is now a fundamental difference in how gangs operate in the city of Naples and the surrounding Province:

The metropolitan gangs are made up of 50–70 people per area. The activities of criminal organisations in Naples are primarily aimed at drug trafficking ... This kind of activity is such that normally it becomes a mass Camorra, which recruits a very high number of people for preparation and distribution, etc ...

Numbers are smaller in the Provinces, on average 30–40 people: these organisations generally have a history, so they are very well-established and strong. They carry out activities in traditional sectors such as usury, public sector contracts, extortion on public sector contracts and consequently, they are linked with local councils ... There are entire areas in which drug dealing is banned. Given that these organisations have a very strong control over their territory, in reality they have always wanted to avoid bringing attention upon themselves. And wherever there is drug dealing, the police normally have a strong physical presence. They are also very worried about the possibility of police informers.[2]

It may be more accurate to describe activities such as racketeering, illegal gambling and the street selling of drugs and cigarettes as *Camorra-controlled* rather than as activities directly engaged in by leading members of major gangs. Drug dealing, for example, is sometimes carried out by drug addicts themselves, who because of their erratic lifestyle are not considered reliable enough to join a gang, or far more often by juveniles who are too young to be prosecuted.

However, once young people's delinquency brings them into direct contact with a gang, as with selling drugs, we are normally dealing with activities which involve the threat or use of violence.

For most ordinary people, the fear of violence is far more threatening than any specific criminal activity, and politicians tend to devote much of their time and ultimately public and police resources to this low-level crime, thus leaving higher Camorra levels untouched. Indeed it is arguably the 'foot-soldiers' who are the 'fall guys' for the real *camorristi*.

The thousands of young people who sell contraband cigarettes and small amounts of drugs, extort money through protection rackets and organise illegal gambling rings are individuals with no direct influence over a gang's policy; they simply have to accept their boss's word and decisions as law. These people are likely to die very young or spend long periods in jail, as they lack the money to either hire good lawyers or to gain influence within the judiciary, which would enable them to obtain acquittals or suspended sentences. They are also useful cannon fodder for politicians who need to silence any criticisms that they are 'soft on crime'.

Some youngsters do make the leap into a criminal gang, and at this point their personal situation can change with astonishing speed. As one observer has written of the Mafia:

> There is a kind of 'criminal career' that often begins with theft or hold-ups carried out individually or by small gangs, which then leads boys of 16 or 17 into contact with the Mafia and eventual membership. These are extremely upwardly mobile careers that sometimes end in death as a result of the frequent shootings which punctuate life in our country.[3]

Young men under the age of 18 are particularly encouraged by Camorra gangs to take part in armed robberies or murders as they cannot be tried as adults. The number of under-age boys and girls charged with crimes doubled during the 1980s, and increased by 28% between 1990 and 1992 alone, with the largest increase, 93%, relating to under 14 year olds, who cannot even appear in court. Although Campania only contains 10% of the Italian population, the national percentage of under-age Campanians held in borstals awaiting trial in 1992 (see Table 7) clearly illustrates the Camorra's ability to recruit young people and so to reproduce itself extremely effectively.

Whereas thirty years ago a 'criminal career' leading to the top of a major gang may have taken decades to complete, with the huge financial profits nowadays available mainly through drug trafficking, a young man can be a major gang leader and billionaire before he is thirty.[4]

This tendency towards rapid growth, plus the lack of a clear hierarchy and division of interests, differentiates the Camorra from the Mafia, as it has never managed to create a stable federal structure. This makes the Camorra more difficult to eradicate through crude repression: while the Mafia is like an octopus, (a single head with powerful tentacles), the Camorra is more akin to the Hydra, the monster of Greek myth which sprouted two heads for every one that was cut off. Indeed a rapid rise to immense wealth in just a few short years is an irresistible temptation for young people who otherwise face a lifetime of unemployment or at best underemployment. This prospect guarantees the social reproduction of criminal gangs regardless of new laws or investigative techniques.

It is important to stress again the distinction between working under Camorra control and membership of an organised gang, as it has been repeatedly shown that repression of criminal-controlled activities such as the sale of contraband cigarettes does nothing to stop the socio-economic conditions which push so many people to work illegally. The only effective strategy is to target the criminal bosses at the top, but even this would be pointless unless it is combined with a total change in the conditions that enable powerful criminals to provide employment and to gain some form of respect and social acceptance.

A young man generally becomes a member of a Camorra gang without any kind of ceremony; Cutolo's NCO appears to be an exception – an unrepresentative throwback to the rituals of the last century. However, one common feature of all Camorra groups is the fact that family links, while important, are not always essential. This is a fundamental difference from the family-based Mafia structure.

The people who eventually become gang leaders tend to be members of a family notorious for its criminal behaviour, and/or those who are clearly willing to engage in acts of violence. As Pasquale Galasso has explained:

Every Camorra group has a leader, around whom there are a number of trusted members who have distinguished themselves during gang wars and difficult periods either through their ferocity, their managerial skills, or their ability to communicate with the non-criminal world and other social classes. These figures emerge and surround the leader, who is at the centre of this leadership group. This group then decides everything.[5]

And in Alfieri's gang at least, these decisions also included murders, as Galasso again explains:

> The choice is made over who to kill and you wait for the right moment, in the sense that the victims might be in jail, not living locally, or well protected; when all the signs are good the boss and the leadership group decide how to carry it out and the killers are chosen and organised.[6]

Leaving aside the question of violence, the average kind of Camorra leader nowadays is extremely sophisticated and economically powerful, as a local trade unionist explains:

> What we are seeing is an entire generation of criminal businessmen who have made a qualitative leap. Every time a boss is arrested now, we discover that he's got a portfolio of hotels, supermarket chains and businesses. The 'poor' Camorra is a rare sight these days: generally they are small fry, who are given 'minor' tasks such as managing protection rackets.[7]

Intimidation and extortion

This is the oldest form of Camorra activity, which is still important today. Compared with other activities such as usury, drug dealing and public sector contracts, it is labour intensive, risky, and brings in relatively meagre profits. These two activities are generally *Camorra-controlled* activities, in that a gang's control of a given territory gives it the right to expect a cut from any protection racket taking place.

Often the first rung on the ladder of a criminal career, it is also one of the most 'invisible' activities since it is one of the least reported crimes. In 1992 the shopowners' association ASCOM estimated that 46% of shops paid protection money in Naples, compared to a national average of 12%.[8] Yet for obvious reasons the number of cases actually reported is very low: just 542 in the whole of Campania in 1993, 563 in 1996 and 480 in 1999.[9]

The relationship between shopowners and criminals may not always involve cash payments – shopowners may be required to assist with money laundering by cashing cheques or, as is often the case with usury, they may find their businesses slowly bought up and taken out of their hands. Alternatively, a shop can become a drug distribution centre like an electrical goods shop in Secondigliano, for example, where a day's supply of heroin for the area, 120 doses at the time, was deposited and collected from a microwave oven on display.[10]

The relationship may not be solely based on the threat of violence. Indeed on some occasions the laws of capitalism tempt some shopowners to 'invest' in a protection racket: the close relationship one shopowner develops with a local gang may give him the competitive edge over another economic rival.

The establishment of public links with shopowners, a generally respected group in society, is also a means by which Camorra gangs gain public recognition. But there is another equally important reason for developing a relationship with shopowners – they are economic agents who regularly order a whole range of goods and services. Not only can gangs then think about providing these goods and services in exchange for reducing the protection payment, they can also make offers to buy into the business.

The money extracted is in the region of several billions of dollars a year, and thousands of people are involved. Perhaps the chief importance of this activity is the legitimacy that gangs gain from what can often be small payments: the very fact that prominent members of the community feel obliged to pay extortion money is a clear sign that organised crime has come to dominate a particular area.

The other main economic activity subject to extortion demands is the construction industry – and the following case is an excellent example of the grey area between legality and illegality. In the area of Pianura a construction company, engaged in the building of unauthorised housing, kept having cash flow problems both in terms of their general activities and their need to pay for protection. The local gang then arranged a kind of 'postdated extortion': it would receive 10% of the houses' sale price.[11]

Illegal gambling

Illegal gambling, like extortion, is another activity which has existed in an organised form in Naples since at least the start of the last century. It takes two forms: placing bets in an illegal system, and illegal gaming houses.

The latter have always been a feature in many urban areas of Campania, and in Naples small printing shops were particularly favoured as premises for many years, although now all manner of places are used.

An illegal betting system, in contrast, requires quite a high level of organisation, and the extent of this activity should not be underestimated. For example, in Naples in October 1982 police discovered an illegal bookmaker's office containing 500,000 receipts, and in 1986 another office was found with receipts worth $8 million.[12] In 1989 it was estimated that the annual turnover throughout Italy for illegal betting reached the incredible figure of $4 billion, with clear profits of around $16 million.[13] In 1991 the finance police estimated the annual turnover to be $3.2–$4 billion, or over $80 million a week.[14] (These national figures include systems run under Camorra control in Florence, Milan, Rome and Sicily.)

In Naples itself it is estimated that more people bet illegally than in the state-run lotteries, as payouts are almost immediate and winnings are not taxed. Like the trade in contraband cigarettes, it is commonly seen as harmless and as providing both jobs – up to 5,000 people are employed, mainly women – and winnings. For the Camorra it represents not only profits, but also a means to relaunder drug money when payouts are made. Furthermore, the prompt and full payment of large winnings massively increases a local gang's popularity and prestige. In Naples, the main area of illegal gambling in Campania, it has been estimated that the turnover per week reaches several million dollars.[15]

One example which illustrates the potential scope of this activity allegedly took place in the late 1980s. In 1987 the Naples football team led by Diego Maradona, arguably the world's best player at that time, won the Italian league title for the first time in the club's history. The celebrations went on for days, yet many Neapolitans also had something else to celebrate – their winnings on the illegal betting system run by the Camorra, in which they had bet on Naples winning the championship.

The following season, Naples played equally well, until just a few games before the end of the season, when their form suffered an inexplicable collapse. The rumour which circulated then, and which has repeatedly resurfaced, was that Maradona and other players accepted bribes from the Camorra to lose matches: paying large sums of money to players would have cost the Camorra less than paying out half the city had Naples won the league again.[16]

Usury

The widespread practice of usury (specifically, private money-lending), is closely linked to the historical development of employment in Naples and the major towns of Campania. Because so many people have no permanent full-time job, they normally have no access to credit, so in cases of emergency they have to turn to private moneylenders.

Usury increased widely in Italy during the economic recession of the early 1990s. Compared to other European countries, Italy had been relatively untouched by the recession of the early 1980s, and so the impact of the new economic world order caught many people unprepared. Small businesses desperate for a loan because banks are unwilling to grant credit are the main users of this system, as they need to pay for supplies, or pay rent or taxes.

The Association of Italian Bank and Finance customers (ADUSBEF) estimates that usury accounts nationally for a total of $10 billion,[17] while the main shopkeepers' association, CONFESERCENTI, estimates that one in five shops, bars and restaurants is caught in a private debt trap. But as with extortion, the number of people who actually report this crime is very low: in the whole of Campania just 431 accusations were made in 1993, 606 in 1996 and 360 in 1999.[18]

Because of their dire economic situation, many individuals and small businesses may default at the original rate of repayment, often around 10% per month; their debt then quickly escalates as interest rates spiral to 30% or more per month, with annual interest rates often over 100%. It can also be a very opportunist crime: when a landslip blocked the main road to Sorrento, local hoteliers, shop and restaurant owners became desperate for cash, and ended up with annual repayment rates of between 120–180%.[19]

When repayment is impossible, debt collection then falls into the hands of organised crime, if it was not under their control in the first place. And Camorra bosses can propose various 'solutions': gaining control of the enterprise concerned, demanding that the debtor carries out some illegal action such as transporting drugs, or simply force the debtor to provide employment to certain individuals.

It is particularly difficult to prove the existence of this crime, and if so-called 'financial consultants' fail to provide tax inspectors with documentary evidence of the source of their earnings, the fines for not obeying regulations are very minor. Similarly, senior bank clerks who deny customers credit are sometimes in contact with moneylenders, and earn a commission for bringing the two together.

The whole system, therefore, provides an excellent opportunity for money laundering, as well as for investment in legal enterprises.

Public sector contracts

As the scandal of earthquake reconstruction shows, public sector contracts are of vital importance to the Camorra. In fact one can say without fear of contradiction that the Camorra has only achieved its present position of strength thanks to the help it has received from politicians in gaining contracts.

The relationship can be so close that criminals and politicians appear indistinguishable, as was the case with Carmine Alfieri's economic empire:

> In many cases business relations with public administration appear to have taken on the character of true symbiosis. Indeed, this was demonstrated by the fact that the continual awarding of contracts, sub-contracts and authorisations to the business segments of the criminal organisation had its accompanying counterpoint in violent and intimidatory actions aimed at eliminating even marginal competition.[20]

And as a leading member of the Alfieri gang, Pasquale Galasso, has outlined:

> The relationship between politicians and bureaucrats, businessmen, and then *camorristi*, is ultimately realised and achieves total fusion in the mechanism of public sector contracts. On the

basis of all that I have noticed personally in my legitimate business activities and my work with Carmine Alfieri and other *camorristi* and businessmen, it is clear to me that the politician who manages the financing of a contract, and therefore the awarding of a contract, is a mediator between the Camorra and a large company, which is nearly always from northern or central Italy. Such mediation takes the form of demanding a bribe from the company for himself or his representatives, and the awarding of sub-contracts to companies directly controlled by Camorra groups.[21]

Yet the relationship between a 'clean' firm and the Camorra does not remain a distant one for long:

Even if it did not exist at the start, what happens is that all the firms holding contracts slowly become subject to Camorra influence, and end up being entirely at the disposal of the leadership of a criminal gang. This occurs in various ways: from outright intimidation to joint financial and economic operations. Once the Camorra has taken total control over a single firm, you will notice that the individual businessman is always available for the Camorra; this obviously includes [the Camorra's] general business capacity and its whole public relations structure.[22]

And there are simply so many contracts to be awarded. One fairly representative example which illustrates the amount of money involved, and the environment in which contracts are awarded, occurred in September 1990, when rubbish collection contracts for Naples city estimated at $280 million were awarded to five private companies. When the new companies took over, their workers were repeatedly intimidated through warning shots and physical attacks. They eventually went out with a police escort of over a hundred – many rubbish bins had also been deliberately destroyed. It was presumed that rival gangs whose tenders had failed were demanding a 'piece of the action'.[23] Just over a year later further threats made by armed men wearing balaclavas necessitated further police escorts – Naples must be the only city in the world where rubbish has a police escort.[24]

The awarding of public sector contracts has been a national scandal for many years, for example an investigation of local councils by the National Audit Office found that in 67% of cases the rules governing contract tendering had been breached, to the tune of $3.2 billion.[25] The Consumers' Union has estimated that the cost of public sector contracts increases by an average of 7% due to the need to pay bribes.[26]

Although new laws have been introduced, they have been by-passed in various ways: costs can be inflated during the course of the contract due to the 'discovery of unforeseen problems'; after a contract has been awarded many tasks can be sub-contracted for 'technical reasons' to the only companies apparently able to perform these tasks. Alternatively, the company which has won the contract can simply cut corners, as a trade unionist recounts:

In the area of hospital services, such as the canteen, they initially win the contract by excluding competitors even before the contract is tendered. Then, with the complicity of someone from the accounting department, they regularly provide a quarter, at times just a fifth, of the amount written on the contract. All the rest is profit.[27]

Another technique is the creation of a cartel of interested companies (often linked to the same Camorra group) in order to inflate the average price of tenders. A good example of this was revealed by investigations carried out by the finance police in late 1991 into contracts for waste removal and disposal awarded by 104 councils in the Province of Caserta. In depressingly familiar tones the Anti-Mafia Commission commented:

> In the councils disbanded for Mafia infiltration in line with the anti-Mafia laws, a generalised presence of Camorra companies was noted. Firms with all kinds of names submitted tenders, but in effect it was always the same Camorra group through its local networks and company managers. Tenders were submitted at levels two or three times higher than the market average, and there was no space for competitors.[28]

The increasing deregulation and privatisation of council services, as a result of EU and 'globalisation' pressures,[29] will probably only make matters worse.

The trade in cigarettes and drugs

Contraband cigarettes normally cost 40% less than the official government price in the state monopoly sector.

In Naples legal sales of cigarettes have fallen every year since 1985, with a 27% drop being recorded in 1993 alone – although this may have been partly due to a state tobacconists' strike early in the year.[30] On the other hand, when supplies from Montenegro were cut off during the Kosovan war in 1999, sales of state cigarettes rose by 30%.[31]

The contraband market was restructured in the mid 1980s, when prices were lowered primarily with the aim of creating more jobs, although the chain of distribution was also modified. Instead of fast motor boats racing across the Bay of Naples, articulated lorries now picked up deliveries along the coast of Apulia and drove overland in convoy.

Profits are probably in the region of several billion dollars a year, although the market's importance for the Camorra lies not solely in the profits created but in the number of people who directly earn their living through this trade, estimated to be at least 30,000. Of all the activities outlined in this chapter, the sale of contraband cigarettes creates the greatest popular support for Camorra organisations, even though the actual street selling is again a Camorra-controlled activity rather than something in which gang members play a direct role.

As the major Camorra cigarette smuggler of the 1970s and 1980s, Michele Zaza once said (in terms that go some way towards explaining his nickname of 'mad Mike'):

At least 700,000 people live off contraband, which is for Naples what FIAT is to Turin. They have called me the Agnelli of Naples ... Yes – it could all be stopped in thirty minutes. And then those who work would be finished. They'd all

become thieves, robbers, muggers. Naples would
become the worst city in the world. Instead, this
city should thank the twenty, thirty men who
arrange for ships laden with cigarettes to be
unloaded and thus stop crime![32]

Indeed Zaza consistently denied that trading in
contraband cigarettes was a criminal activity, once
declaring 'I'm not a Mafioso, I'm not a *camorrista*, I'm
a simple cigarette trader.'[33] His wider criticisms are
not without foundation:

Isn't it a crime to demand 20% of public sector
contracts too? Who punishes politicians for that?
And the mysteries of Italy – the Lockheed affair,
the petrol scandal – who remembers them any
more? A cigarette smuggler doesn't hurt anyone,
he pays for the cigarettes and creates work for
loads of people.[34]

What is remarkable about this attitude is not the fact
that it is taken by a particular Camorra leader, but that
it is probably shared by tens if not hundreds of thousands of people in Campania. As one cigarette
smuggler said, echoing Zaza's sentiments entirely:
'It's tax evasion; don't industrialists avoid paying
taxes? Only we do it risking our lives.'[35] The frequent
and numerous deaths of cigarette smugglers along the
Apulian coast during the 1990s is evidence of the
accuracy of this statement.

For gang leaders the profit margin is enormous.
Despite the fact they are only one element in a three-
link chain, made up of the Camorra boss who imports
from overseas suppliers, the local gang leader who
controls distribution, and the street seller – overall the

profit in terms of street price compared to factory gate price has been calculated at 342%.[36] Current statistics estimate that an average of $80 profit is made per crate, so with approximately 48,000 crates being illegally imported per month the Camorra is enjoying an operating profit of nearly $4 million.[37]

Given the scale of contraband sales it is not surprising to learn that, according to Italian police, US tobacco multinationals such as Philip Morris and RJ Reynolds (manufacturers of Marlboro, Camel and Winston) have run a parallel system – 'export 2' – in which they sell their products to smugglers. A police report from the mid-1980s identified concessionary agents in Switzerland 'who directly supply Italian smugglers, who identify themselves as the representatives of specific criminal groups'.[38] Supergrass Salvatore Migliorino has also made the same accusation: 'We went and bought cigarettes in Switzerland and paid the multinationals ... We negotiated with people who represented Philip Morris, with whom we signed contracts for a thousand, two thousand or ten thousand crates of cigarettes.'[39]

The scale of tax evasion is huge, given that approximately 13% of tobacco sales throughout Italy are made by contraband sellers.[40] Government exasperation emerged in late 1991 when the Finance Minister rushed through a decree temporarily banning the sale in state-controlled tobacconists of Marlboro, Merit and Muratti, directly accusing Philip Morris of dealing with cigarette smugglers.[41] The European Union has recently lodged an action in New York against Philip Morris and RJ Reynolds, 'for their presumed involvement in cigarette smuggling within the European Union' under the terms of the Racketeering Influenced and Corrupt Organisation Act.[42] According to the Anti-Mafia Commission, such is the scale of Camorra operations that 'Campania has become the distribution centre for direct supplies to other countries in the European Union, such as Great Britain.'[43]

Profits in the drug trade are even larger. The Financial Action Task Force, a group set up at the Paris G7 summit in 1989, once estimated world turnover of drug trafficking at $320 billion a year, yielding profits of $90 billion.[44]

In Campania, according to Neapolitan sociologist Amato Lamberti, the local drug market was worth $3.2 billion a year in 1990, and employed a total workforce of 25,000.[45] More recent studies have estimated that there are 30,000 regular heroin users in Naples, who spend at least $80 a day on their habit, producing a daily turnover of $2.4 million, a monthly turnover of $72 million and an annual turnover of $860 million.[46] The amount of money generated by cocaine consumption is estimated to be much larger than heroin; and one should also add on large amounts for marijuana, amphetamines and synthetic drugs.

One of the Camorra's specific methods of dealing in drugs, as opposed to most other major criminal gangs who predominantly use addicts, is to use whole families in their distribution network. Adults normally negotiate the price and receive the money while their under-age children deliver the drugs. In such a system it is almost impossible to obtain convictions, as for obvious reasons the adults are extremely unwilling to confess.

Although serious Camorra involvement in drugs only began in the mid-1970s under the control of the Mafia, trade mushroomed to such an extent that by the early 1980s the Neapolitans' gang warfare had spread even as far as Peru, where they would fight over control of exports and where a large laboratory for refining coca leaves was also discovered.

It seems that during the mid 1980s Michele Zaza had a contract for cocaine from Peru and Bolivia worth $800 million a year, making it the third largest commercial operation in Campania – after the Alfa Romeo car factory in Pomigliano d'Arco and the steel-works at Bagnoli on the western edge of Naples. Around 70 kg a month were imported, almost a tonne a year, with the operation being run jointly by South Americans and Neapolitans, until a series of arrest warrants were issued in 1987. The drug was sent from Bogota by air couriers passing through Frankfurt and Madrid, and was then distributed throughout Italy.[47]

The drug trade is international by definition, and one of the best examples of the 1990s was the 'Green Ice' operation, launched in September 1992 by Italian and US authorities. This saw the arrest of 34 people in Italy, 167 in the US and 2 in Costa Rica. A total of 682 kg of cocaine was seized, along with goods and currency worth $58 million, including a 22 m^3 store-room in London stuffed full of dollars waiting to be laundered. Carmine Alfieri's gang were the Camorra representatives in this huge operation, relaundering money through the current account of an 80 year old ex-primary school teacher. The Italian laundering quota was $400,000 per week.[48]

Organising something on this scale means that some of the most powerful or influential people in society are involved. But there is no iron law which stops these individuals from 'doubling up' and becoming drug traffickers themselves. This was the case of Pasquale Centore in the town of San Nicola la Strada, which borders on the city of Caserta: a

Christian Democrat mayor in the day, by night he was a major drug smuggler, bringing in tonnes of cocaine from the shores of Venezuela to various European cities. Consequently, he owned various companies and tourist resorts, had close relations with *camorristi* for distribution, with local businessmen for money laundering, and so on. The price he paid for most cocaine consignments was about $1 million each.[49]

As indicated by Judge Giuseppe Borrelli earlier in this chapter, the massive profits available in the drug trade may well be leading to profound changes in terms of what activities Camorra gangs tend to specialise in. One factor is the speed of capital accumulation: 'The very availability of large amounts of money which arrive continuously, favours the faster and faster conversion of a *camorrista* into a businessman.'[50] The financial and social stability brought about by such rapid enrichment has led many major gangs to move away from the high-risk area of hard drugs. The advantages of moving away from drugs are numerous, most notably increased social consensus. As the Anti-Mafia Commission explains, once a Camorra gang decides to ban drug dealing: 'the criminal organisation becomes the real "guarantor" of "tranquillity" within a given area, thus creating consensus among a sizeable proportion of the local community'.[51]

In Campania drug dealing takes place mainly within the city of Naples, and often in just a small number of peripheral enclaves such as Secondigliano, Caivano and the Resina area of Herculaneum. Elsewhere: 'Low level drug dealing has become the prerogative of non-EU citizens, who often sell bad quality drugs at very low prices.'[52] The official statistics bear this out: nearly a third of people arrested for drug offences in Italy in both 1998 and 1999 were not Italian citizens. More importantly, deaths from drug overdoses have not changed much over time: 974 in 1989, 867 in 1994 and 1,002 in 1999.[53]

Money laundering and going 'legit'

The term 'dirty' money is a misnomer, as the only major cases in which it is necessary to launder specific banknotes are kidnap ransoms and bank robberies, both fairly rare activities for organised crime in general and for the Camorra in particular. The problem for most criminals is not so much 'dirty' money as 'funny' money – the possession of large amounts of money which cannot be accounted for. For major criminals the problem is finding the means to render legitimate, anonymous or untraceable huge amounts of money that have been earned illegally, and not the fact that possession of individual banknotes might somehow constitute proof of illegal activities.

In general laundering involves three stages: the first is the *placement stage* – the depositing of cash. This has traditionally been done by opening a variety of accounts using the names of people without a criminal record, both at one individual bank and at several different banks, who then frequently deposit small amounts of money. The second stage, *layering*, involves the movement of money, and even its reconversion back into cash, in order to lose all trace of its origin. Only then is the *integration stage* reached – the full absorption of previously 'dirty' money into the 'legal' system.[54]

A friendly relationship with a bank or credit institution, or even outright ownership, is the simplest way of recycling 'hot' money. In recent years banking activity and deposits have grown rapidly in the Naples area: in the 1989–92 period the number of banking outlets grew by 21% in Campania, almost double the national average of 11%, while deposits increased by 19%, as opposed to a national average of 13.6%. The province of Caserta, where more local councils have been disbanded due to the infiltration of organised crime than anywhere else in Italy, enjoyed an increase of 29% in banking outlets and 24% in new deposits.[55]

Investigators also face obstacles placed in their path by the banks themselves. A bank manager may well be aware that behind the *testa di legno* (the straw man opening an account, who does not have a criminal record), there is in reality a wealthy *camorrista*; any refusal to open an account and to grant credit will mean the loss of an account often involving millions. And even if the police later begin making enquiries, the bank is unlikely to divulge all that it knows about the real account holder, as it would then be implicated and possibly prosecuted for facilitating money laundering.

The use of off-shore financial operations is also widespread. Although the actual financial operation may take place in the country of origin, in legal and accounting terms the transaction takes place in the Bahamas, Bermuda, the Cayman or Channel Islands, Gibraltar, Hong Kong, Liechtenstein, Switzerland, and so on. One of the reasons why the lax controls are never significantly tightened up is that many 'legal' businesses and financiers – such as Robert Maxwell – make use of the same facilities, often for the same reason – the need to lose all trace of origin.

Large commercial operations also provide a common method of laundering: the value of goods delivered or ordered is simply exaggerated, or non-existent goods are apparently sent or received. An investigating magistrate recounts one recent example:

> In Pompeii money laundering effectively took place in the following manner: they pretended to send consignments of flowers abroad, using accomplices overseas. Money should then have come back from overseas, but these payments were false: yet this system allowed certain individuals to justify their possession of the amounts which had apparently arrived from outside Italy.[56]

Alternatively, once the Camorra gains control of a smaller commercial enterprise its financial inflows and outflows can be used to launder 'funny money'. Property speculation is a classic instance of this particular method: buying land and building on it involves large sums of money in rapid circulation – a good example of this is the land bought by the Alfieri gang just outside Nola.[57]

The ownership and use of gambling casinos is yet another traditional means of money laundering for any large organisation dealing in drugs. This is why, from the early 1980s, New Family gangs began to invest heavily in casinos near the borders between France, Italy and Switzerland, and also on the Franco-Spanish border.

Apart from this rather exotic kind of investment, one of the most common and economically important areas of money laundering and legal investment is the service sector, where illegal earnings can be recycled in a range of retailing, tourist and cleaning services. For example in late 1991 the Camorra boss Ciro Mariano almost gained control of the city's major theatre, the Politeama.[58] In the late 1990s the Polverino gang in Marano bought several large super-markets in order to facilitate money laundering.

This may also be why there are still so many retail outlets in southern Italy: rapid inflows and outflows of cash are completely normal, and are difficult to trace. The resources needed to even begin monitoring these activities are clearly massive, and then the crimes committed are often fairly minor. A restaurant owner, for example, faced with the accusation that his huge operating profit is in reality due to laundering drug money, could easily reply that he under-declared his real turnover in order to avoid tax payments. The owner might still have to pay a fine for tax evasion, but would nevertheless be able to carry on his opera-tions and take more precautions in the future.

It is important to remember that laundering 'dirty money' is not always essential for the Camorra if, as is the case with Carmine Alfieri's gang, the bulk of profits comes from public sector contracts. In histor-ical terms however money laundering is an important development: in the space of three decades many Camorra leaders have moved from crude protection rackets and control over agricultural markets to become sophisticated financial operators.

Nowadays investigators are just as likely to find share certificates as shotguns when they raid a gang leader's house. The confiscation of $1,900 worth of shares in Berlusconi's Mediaset company belonging to Giovanni Citarella in the summer of 1998 may have created a political echo, but it was a very small amount. At the same time, pieces of Francesco

'Sandokan' Schiavone's financial empire were also being dismantled, with the confiscation of about 40 companies worth $380 million.[59]

The ultimate investment move is into government bonds, particularly US Treasury securities, and speculation on the stock exchange. Furthermore, countries such as Italy, with its chronic public sector debt, are frequently obliged to hurriedly issue government bonds as a means of obtaining finance.

International links

Hollywood films and newspaper articles often like to present an image of huge criminal alliances which span the globe, usually dealing in hard drugs. The reason why this is actually very rare is common sense, as one investigator explains: 'When they need to go and buy cocaine they just go and buy the stuff – they know where to go. They don't have any organic links because, strategically, it would be a mistake. The creation of organic links between criminal organisations is something which weakens organisations.'[60]

Furthermore, the extent of the Camorra's international links is severely restricted by the need to maintain power and influence through territorial control at home – moving overseas is therefore nearly always a step backwards in a *camorrista*'s criminal career. Once they move abroad major criminals do not wield the same influence they previously did at home, in particular they lack the political protection which often enables them to avoid arrest. Their anonymity overseas also makes it difficult for them to become involved in criminal activities at a similar level to which they did at home; and in major industrialised countries Italians are normally just one amongst a number of competing ethnic groups outside the majority population. Then there is often a fundamental language barrier which can be an even greater obstacle in the creation of a criminal reputation.[61]

A long stay abroad inevitably means that their power base at home starts to crumble. Not only will a strong rival be more likely to launch some kind of attack, rising stars within the gang can be tempted to make a bid for power, a move that can easily start with giving police overseas a tip-off to the address where their boss is now living.

All these reasons make it very unlikely that top criminals will go and live permanently in other countries, although it is highly probable that they regularly visit a whole range of nations. In all likelihood Italian criminal gangs are investing in a range of activities throughout Europe, and apart from drug deals these will usually be activities that either are 'legitimate' or do not involve the use or threat of violence. The main attraction of a country such as the UK for Italian organised crime appears to be twofold: the opportunity to launder money within the City of London, and the ease with which fugitives can merge into the population and, even if questioned, avoid returning to Italy as charges of conspiracy and Mafia association are not grounds for extradition.

The racist debate in the UK concerning organised crime and the relaxation of EU border controls, or the supposed criminal records of asylum seekers, avoids one very simple point concerning criminal infiltration: a major criminal who has a string of convictions will simply obtain forgeries enabling him to pass through a normal passport check. A senior British detective, specialising in Italian organised crime, played down any effect of a relaxation in border controls on Italian criminal groups:

> They've been moving drugs and illicit articles, in huge amounts, over a very long period of time. And to be honest, I don't see that the dropping of frontier barriers, so far as goods or people are concerned, is going to make any difference. They've moved enough in anyway – and they've not had a problem in the past.[62]

The only reported case of a presumed Camorra presence in the UK concerns the La Torre gang. According to one supergrass, the La Torres were given control of the town of Mondragone in 1982 by Antonio Bardellino, who in turn dominated the entire area around Caserta. Yet at that time, 'the La Torres were still an old-fashioned Camorra clan, in the sense that it was still patriarchal'.[63] However in subsequent years they extended their control over Mondragone and surrounding towns, spreading out as far as southern Lazio and specialising in heroin, cocaine and arms deals –[64] so much so that in July 1992 police impounded villas, import-export companies, supermarkets and luxury cars, worth a grand total of $400 million, all linked to the clan.[65]

Another supergrass, Carmine Schiavone, then recounts that during this period the brother of the gang leader 'had married a woman from Britain and was spending more and more time in Scotland, where he reinvested money from drug trafficking and extortion into restaurants, property and land'.[66] An investigating magistrate concurs as regards their investments, such as Antonio La Torre's ownership of a restaurant in Aberdeen, but suggests their presence has more to do with self-preservation: 'The La Torres have got very important investments in Scotland. But we don't believe they are behaving as criminals there: it represents an enclave in terms of security.'[67]

The fall of the Berlin Wall in 1991 and the unification of Germany provided significant opportunities for investment, and Camorra gangs quickly bought restaurants across the country. For example Lorenzo Nuvoletta was once almost arrested in a restaurant in Baden Baden but managed to escape. Gennaro Licciardi established his base of operations in Rostock, in eastern Germany, with his brother setting up a whole range of shops. Edoardo Contini's clan is reported to have sent ten men to Leipzig, where they have opened restaurants, boutiques and food shops.[68] Furthermore, two Camorra money laundering companies were discovered in Munich in early 1992.

The south of France has been important for its casinos, many of which – in Nice, Cannes, Mentone and Boulier-sur-mer – have suffered Camorra infiltration and have been closed down by authorities for long periods. One of the first indications of Camorra infiltration was the arrest of long-term Camorra leaders Nunzio Barbarossa and Nunzio Guida in Nice in February 1989. Another important area of investment in France for money laundering is private clinics, which account for 37% of French hospital beds. In these institutions money can be recycled quite simply, as a fake kidney transplant can easily 'cost' $160,000.[69] The murder of the deputy Mayor of Marseilles in January 1990 was viewed by police as being linked to this laundering system; their suspicion was heightened by the fact that he was also a private doctor.

Finally, the break-up of the old Soviet Union, which saw rapid and uncontrolled privatisation and financial deregulation, allowed organised crime to make investments from abroad. The Camorra also understood that the whole Eastern bloc was desperate for hard currency, and that many people were curious to try drugs for the first time, and so often they were offered at very low 'promotional' prices.

Arms dealing and drug trafficking quickly mushroomed, as did trade in antiques, so much so that in the first half of 1993 it was estimated that 531 criminal gangs were operating within the Commonwealth of Independent States, and by the second half of the year this rose to 3,000 gangs with a membership of 15,000. Apart from selling drugs, arms and stolen cars, many criminal gangs are able to recycle their money through buying into privatised companies and illegal trading of the rouble, as well as setting up prostitution rings, protection rackets and robbing banks.

Elsewhere, production of opium has reached significant levels in Uzbekistan and Tajikistan, with the overland heroin route from the Middle East and South-East Asia often passing through Russia. Alternatively, heroin is brought into Italy by central African couriers who work as illegal labourers around Caserta.[70]

Frauds concerning the European Community could virtually fill a separate book given their sheer scale – in recent years it has been estimated that fraud amounts to at least 10% of the EC's Common Agricultural Policy expenditure. Yet these frauds are more the result of the general climate of illegality rather than operations being run under the control of Camorra gangs.

Nevertheless, EC fraud can involve: false receipts for activities never carried out, non-existent companies making orders, false declarations concerning the quality of a particular product; or adding water to goods to increase their weight.

One example in the 1991–93 period concerned false receipts amounting to $37 million in the Apulia-Campania area, which led to the release of $4 million of EC subsidies for the apparent sale of olive oil. Companies issued receipts for non-existent activities, while bottling plants declared they had produced non-existent goods, hence the EC easily fell into the trap.[71]

Yet the most significant international development for the Camorra in recent years has been the series of wars in ex-Yugoslavia, which has created the greatest opportunities in the Republic of Montenegro.[72] One of the main attractions of the small states born from a series of civil wars during the 1990s is that they are very near Italy, but most of them do not have an extradition treaty with Rome. Although there is some evidence of arms smuggling and human trafficking from this area, the main activity has been contraband cigarettes, and the largest trade so far emerged with the arrest of Gerardo Cuomo in Zurich in May 2000.

Cuomo owned 38 companies in Switzerland, specialised in buying and selling goods liable to duty. Both to protect this economic investment, and to maintain his residence permit for Switzerland – in view of extradition warrants requested by Italy – Cuomo needed legal protection. He found this in Judge Franco Verda of the Lucerne Courts, who would drive around in one of Cuomo's chauffeur-driven limousines, as well as taking a trip to the US at Cuomo's expense.[73] Verda is now on trial for aiding and abetting Cuomo in his dispute over his residence permit, and other legal matters. This was Cuomo's protection at the level of the judiciary: Cuomo was helped to prepare for his trial hearings by his lawyer, a Mrs Rinaldi – Judge Verda's wife. His money laundering was presumably done by Alexander Hagsteiner, now ex director of the Lucerne branch of the Banque National de Paris, currently under arrest.[74]

Agreements would be signed with cigarette multinationals in Switzerland, mainly Philip Morris, and the crates would then be shipped from Rotterdam to Montenegro. Using a line of defence often employed by politicians such as the British Conservative Kenneth Clarke, Cuomo once said: 'I sell to registered companies, it's got nothing to do with me where the goods end up. I can't stop them from engaging in smuggling.'[75] Cuomo alone has been estimated to shift 250 tonnes of cigarettes a month from Montenegro to the nearby coasts of Apulia in southeast Italy.[76]

This particular business began in 1992, when a man called Branko Perovic worked for *Jet* airlines in Rome, and facilitated the transportation of cigarettes into Montenegro.[77] Cuomo's main partner in this affair, Francesco Prudentino, then paid $2.5 million in 'security' to the Montenegro authorities in 1993 for the exclusive right to sell Philip Morris products within the Republic for a single year. From then on, the authorities imposed a tax of $7 on each crate sold; but anyone who wanted to buy the cigarettes could only buy them from Prudentino or Cuomo.[78]

Prudentino also contributed $240,000 to the building of a hospital in Montenegro, and owned the only casino in Podgorica, situated in the centre of the capital right in front of the government buildings. Such is the poverty of a small country like

Montenegro, that the Italian finance police have esti-mated that bribes and 'taxes' paid to local authorities amount to 60% of Montenegro's gross national product.[79]

When this story emerged Italian politicians ignored two individuals, currently still under indictment for trial in Naples for 'aiding and abetting cigarette smug-gling' and 'external involvement in a Mafia-type association': Milo Djukanovic and Branko Perovic.[80] The period in which the charges became public explains the politicians' lack of interest: the Kosovan war against Slobodan Milosevic's Serbia in 1999. At that time NATO powers were wining and dining all manner of Balkan politicians, singing their praises and trying to get them to support the West's bombing campaign against Serbia. Two of these politicians were Djukanovic and Perovic, President and Foreign Minister of Montenegro.

The broad picture given in this chapter has not even discussed other highly relevant Camorra activities, such as arms trafficking, the production of counterfeit goods, earth moving and excavation, human traf-ficking, prostitution and the disposal of human and industrial waste.

In any event, the Camorra's economic and social power means it creates huge profits, recycling massive amounts of money into the legal economy and directly or indirectly providing work and a living for up to half a million people. Indeed as one of Naples' leading investigators once noted:

> The Camorra has probably become more dangerous than the Mafia because the presence of organised crime in Campania is so widespread

that it is definitely more difficult to eradicate. Given that it is not a monolithic group [i.e. it does not have the same structure as the Mafia, in which the following scenario could develop] – you get the boss and his deputy, and you decapitate the strongest gang, the others get disorientated. On the contrary here [in Campania] you decapitate one, and the others remain as they were.[81]

If the activities detailed in this chapter comprised the full extent of Camorra power then their defeat would be extremely difficult. But the creation of such power could never have been achieved without the support and connivance of local politicians, the very people entrusted with any solution to the problem of organised crime.

CHAPTER 7

Criminal politics

The old mayor, a Christian Democrat, was a thief – but he helped everyone. He stole but he gave us welfare cheques, cheese as well – he never made us pay for water or electricity. Now there's a new communist mayor and he has reported us to the police because we don't pay our bills.

Unemployed Castellammare man

There must be sincerity and justice in the activities of the council and of the state, and it is necessary that citizens have faith in them. In Naples, on the contrary, citizens have lost all faith in their rights and in the justice handed down by the council and the state.

This is not due to ancient traditions which should have disappeared by now, but to new forms of private despotism, clientelism and Camorra, that are different forms of private organisations which tend to administer justice in their own fashion, outside the law and the state and, where necessary, against the law and the state. Citizens only have faith in favours.[1]

The reality of recent political life in Campania makes the above report, written one hundred years ago,

extremely relevant today. The underlying theme of
this chapter is that if the problem of links between
politicians and professional criminals recurs so
frequently, then perhaps another solution needs to be
found, rather than simply repeating variations of solutions which have been found wanting over more than
a century.

The most worrying aspect of the links between politicians and professional criminals is that not only has
the relationship become closer and more intertwined
over the last two decades, the balance of power moved
in the criminals' favour throughout the 1980s. It
could easily be argued that at the time of their 'fall' in
1993, Antonio Gava and his Christian Democrat
machine in Campania needed the Camorra for their
political survival far more than individual Camorra
bosses needed leading politicians to survive.

The decade between the decline of Cutolo in the
early 1980s and the arrest and subsequent collaboration of first Pasquale Galasso and then Carmine Alfieri
in the early 1990s is the crucial period in this evolu-
tion. Cutolo's 'mass Camorra' remained largely
outside the political structure, in some sense the NCO
was a more modern and violent version of the
Camorra racketeering dominant in the first two or
three decades of the postwar period. On the contrary,
it was the rise of the Nuvoletta and other New Family
gangs which represented the development of a more
sophisticated Camorra, both economically and
politically.

In economic terms Camorra gangs became far
wealthier – and their turnover and subsequent rein-
vestment in legal activities became a vital element in
the survival of the precarious Campanian economy. The
mechanics of money laundering and diversification

into legal areas necessitated working relationships
with the local political ruling class, who became
increasingly aware of the Camorra's enormous financial wealth. These relationships often started thanks to
politicians' encouragement – although if this was not
forthcoming, connections would be nurtured by the
Camorra through intimidation, violence and alternative candidates.

These relationships have now existed for so long,
and have become so intertwined, as to appear both
normal and essential. The long-term interdependence
of senior criminals and local politicians has probably
allowed the Camorra to overcome the uncertainty
caused by the collapse of the Christian Democrats in
the early 1990s – which for nearly fifty years could
claim to be 'the natural party of government'.

The last few years have witnessed an alternation of
political parties in government, which may well have
contributed to what appears to be a far lower level of
corruption and illegality at a national level. But things
have not changed so much at a local level: in
Campania the post-Christian Democrat era has been
very much one of 'business as usual'.

Local councils

During the early 1980s the relationship between the
Camorra and local politicians was still rather unstable,
but over the next few years it became clear that many
local politicians were at least under the influence of
the Camorra and very often conniving with them.

The late 1970s and early 1980s saw a large number
of political murders. In April 1981, the Christian

Democrat Regional councillor and ex-mayor of Marigliano, Alfredo Mundo, was murdered; a Social Democrat councillor, Giuliano Pennacchio, was killed in Giugliano in July 1982; the following month a DC councillor, Giuseppe Caso, was killed in Poggiomarino, and in October the Socialist Party mayor of San Gennaro Vesuviano was gunned down. In December 1984 Crescenzo Casillo was killed – an especially important target as he was the mayor of a major town, Casoria.[2]

If one looks beyond murders to the level of intimidation the picture becomes even clearer: between April 1982 and March 1983 there were 17 bomb attacks against local administrators, 5 attacks against trade union offices, 16 assaults on trade unionists, 5 murders of council committee chairpersons and 14 attacks on councillors.[3] This sudden and systematic attack was the result of two factors: the internal growth of Camorra gangs in the second half of the 1970s, and the massive increase in council budgets following the earthquake.

By the mid-1980s the Camorra was engaged in a campaign for direct political involvement. Its economic strength had increased massively thanks to earthquake reconstruction, and in social terms association with the Camorra also provided both an economic and political niche for a class of young architects and engineers. A new professional middle class was emerging during reconstruction, unwilling to be dominated by the old Christian Democrat method of clientelism.

A new type of politician had also emerged, different from the old-style political liberals of the 1950s and 1960s who had used Camorra *guappi* for clientelistic mediation. These new men, often from relatively poor backgrounds and with a limited education, were ambitious and not afraid to take risks. In many cases they were 'a new low-quality political grouping, who have totally committed their professional future to politics, and whose relationship with the Camorra is not so much based on personal enrichment as on the means to begin and maintain their political career'.[4] The Camorra was thus being fully integrated into the political system.

These 'rampant' elements were often either members or close associates of the Socialist Party. For example, Ernesto Bardellino was Socialist Party mayor of San Cipriano d'Aversa in 1982–84, and it was widely known he was the brother of one of the Camorra's most notorious gang leaders, Antonio.

For those politicians who opposed the Camorra, or who were perhaps associated with a gang that was losing a war, the price continued to be high. In what can only be seen as a deliberate strategy, twelve councillors were assassinated in Campania between 1984 and 1985. Yet assassinations are generally the exception – as kneecappings, beatings, threats against individual politicians or their families normally suffice.

These physical attacks, threats, and the whole process of conditioning and direct criminal infiltration all helped to seriously damage basic democracy. However it should always be remembered that many politicians had a traditional disposition towards high levels of illegality. In Marano in the late 1980s electioneering often involved the following scenario: 'Whoever was involved in politics guaranteed their electorate cancellation from the list of ratepayers. So if you vote for me, and I get elected, you won't pay rates.' When a reforming left-wing council was elected in 1993: 'We discovered that 9,000 people had been taken off the lists for the payment of rubbish collection rates, and nobody knew why.'[5]

The general social climate of illegality is therefore reflected within politics, although sometimes it takes the shape of just bending the rules. For example in 1985 the Italian Communist Party sent out a questionnaire to thirty Campanian councils and found that on average they held full council meetings only once every two months, although even this was within the legal requirement of two per year.[6] The absurd situation could easily be reached when there were literally hundreds of items for approval or debate – indeed in one meeting the Naples provincial council had 1,300 items on the agenda! On one occasion in Nocera Superiore, the mayor demanded that 323 items be voted on as one block.[7] The point to be borne in mind is that most of these items concerned ratification of contracts awarded. Furthermore, many of these contracts had been awarded solely as a result of private negotiation rather than public tendering, as was the case of Campania's third largest town council, that of Torre del Greco, which awarded contracts almost exclusively as a result of private negotiations in the 1984–85 period.[8]

By the end of the 1980s the Camorra had established itself within many local councils – indeed, rather than *camorristi* facing charges of intimidating politicians, many politicians were now facing charges of involvement with the Camorra. A *carabinieri* report detailed that in the 1988–89 period police investigated 192 local administrators and brought official charges against 126, of which 21 were accused of membership of a Camorra gang; 5 of these people were then arrested.[9]

The May 1990 council elections are a useful barometer of the Camorra's direct move into municipal politics. In a declaration that gives a clear indication of its profound impotence, the Naples police head-quarters stated prior to the elections that fifty-two of the candidates were suspected of having close links with the Camorra. Despite this warning, or in some cases because of it, 31 of these candidates were elected: 17 Christian Democrats, 8 Socialists and 4 Social Democrats.

Not surprisingly, during the election campaign senior magistrates were sounding the alarm:

> Nowadays Camorra clans are able to determine majorities and to guarantee the electoral success of a candidate – above all in the Province of Naples ... the Camorra boss contacts the politician directly, he speaks to him personally and it ends up with their deciding together on construction projects or anything else.[10]

The mutually beneficial nature of the relationship had been understood too: 'It is an exchange of favours amongst equals: the godfather guarantees votes, public order, in other words total support. On the other hand the politician commits himself to dividing up the cake.'[11] Yet warnings like this fell on deaf ears, as the politicians responsible for fighting organised crime had often become partners in a whole range of illegal activities.

It should therefore come as no surprise that a judicial inquiry into the May elections published in December 1990, revealed voting irregularities in seven constituencies: Casoria, Naples (2), Pozzuoli, San Giuseppe Vesuviano, Saviano and Torre del Greco. In some cases the number of votes cast was higher than the number of people on the electoral register.[12]

During this period the problem of illegality and links with organised crime was brought into focus most dramatically in Naples, the capital of both Campania and the whole South. Events within the council, the city's largest employer, are particularly illuminating. In the late 1980s, the warning signs had been numerous. For example, during his period as the Socialist Party's mayor of Naples from 1987 to 1990, Pietro Lezzi had to be interviewed as a witness or make statements to magistrates in judicial enquiries on ten separate occasions.[13] And in December 1991 Socialist councillor Silvano Masciari, who had been groomed to succeed his party colleague Lezzi, was sentenced to fourteen months in jail for having provided council jobs to two known members of the Mariano gang.[14]

In September 1990 it emerged that out of the 80 city councillors, 38 were under police investigation for association with the Camorra. One of them was a communist, but the other 37 belonged to the five ruling government parties, with only 19 councillors from government parties not under investigation.[15]

It was hoped that things would improve as a result of the June 1992 Naples council elections, yet even before voting took place it became clear that any potential clean-up had little chance: of the 923 candidates, 189 already had criminal records.[16] And over the following year 18 councillors out of 80 ended up facing charges for various crimes: 7 Socialists, 5 Christian Democrats, 2 Republicans, one neo-fascist of National Alliance and a member of the centre-left DS. The symptom rather than the cause was then addressed, with fourteen of these councillors being substituted by the various parties – but some of these 'substitutes' were then arrested and accused of other crimes![17]

By early 1993 the collapse became total. A new ruling group was cobbled together, but politics had by now taken on a surreal tinge, as many of the difficulties in creating a new administration were due to councillors being under arrest, on the run, or continually helping police with their enquiries. During the spring several meetings were inquorate due to the fact that many councillors were either under arrest or undergoing questioning in the police station next door.[18]

In May the ruling group on the city council passed a motion declaring its bankruptcy, with debts amounting to approximately $800 million. Three months later, as councillors were again bickering over forming a new ruling alliance, black gunge instead of water started coming out of many taps in the city, a problem which was not new, but which had supposedly been solved. Fearing a repeat of the rioting that had ensued in Ponticelli in May 1990, which had led to the resignation of Mayor Lezzi, the President of the Republic signed a decree on 12 August disbanding the council and providing emergency funding. The most important reason given was that of maintaining public order.

Apart from this generalised illegality and inefficiency, it is difficult to monitor who may have links with the Camorra. The Mayor of Naples Francesco Tagliamonte admitted in mid-1993: 'In this great confusion of things that need to be done concerning 17,000 council employees, identifying who has connections with *camorristi* is a totally impossible task.'[19] Such an opinion appears to be perfectly rational, however. Official statistics show that in the period from 1984 to 1993, in the Province of Naples, 902 council administrators were the subject of legal proceedings, 60 of them for Camorra membership.[20]

If large numbers of politicians behave in this fashion, then it can only be expected that bureaucrats will do so as well. The main cases of bureaucratic corruption in Naples' council during 1992 were the following: in June two librarians were arrested and charged with usury, forgery of legal documents, embezzlement and criminal association; in July a maintenance worker at the council court was sacked when it emerged that his sons were members of a Camorra gang; in October the chief technical officer of the food supplies division was arrested for extortion; in February 1993 the head of the council police and another employee were arrested and charged with extorting money from a businessman who had applied for a trading licence. A water board official was also arrested and charged with defrauding the board.[21] This brief outline of bureaucratic corruption and criminality is to show that any 'clean' administration which is elected will find itself being serviced by a bureaucracy with these kinds of ingrained habits.

Nevertheless, the election of centre-left politician Antonio Bassolino as Mayor of Naples in November 1993 certainly was a breath of fresh air. Rather than being on friendly terms with *camorristi*, he often needed sizeable police protection just in order to make an orderly speech in Camorra-ridden towns.[22] Yet despite his many reforms, council employees continue to break the law and work with organised crime. One example was a scam involving the Polverinos from Marano: three council technicians brought temporary council workers to Marano to remove vegetation from an area which the Polverinos had a contract to develop. Although Naples council employees actually did the work, the scam concerned a false payment of

$19,130 to a private company, which was shown as having apparently carried out the work.[23]

In the post Christian Democrat era one of the main tendencies outside Naples has been that of local councillors politically 'relaundering' themselves, i.e. moving away from a clearly discredited party to a 'clean' one. A good example comes from Afragola, a town of over 60,000 just to the north of Naples. In March 1999 a government commission was brought in to investigate the council, and see whether it should be disbanded due to Camorra infiltration. One of the key figures was deputy mayor Franco Costato, who before being elected as a councillor for the 'post fascist' National Alliance in May 1997, had been a member of the Social Democratic party for many years.[24]

Police sources soon discovered that a notorious Camorra family 'were particularly active in Costato's election campaign' in May 1997.[25] Not only was Costato a local politician, he was also a lawyer whose specialisation was defending people accused of illegal construction work. The other politician under suspicion was the President of the council, Vincenzo Nespoli, another National Alliance member. Following a familiar pattern, Nespoli 'effectively' (but not officially) had a major share in a private security company, which subsequently won a contract from the council in highly irregular circumstances. In all probability, this company provides employment for people with long criminal records, and another major shareholder is a close associate of a notorious local *camorrista*, who again according to the police: 'was very prominent in the most recent municipal elections in pushing for the election of Nespoli'.[26]

Sadly, examples such as this are a paragon of virtue compared with some other local councils.

'Abandon hope all ye who enter' – political criminality in Sant'Antonio Abate

Political and criminal activities in Sant'Antonio Abate, to the south-east of Naples and Vesuvius, are probably no worse than in many other towns in Campania. The choice of presenting this town as an example of the intermeshing of criminal and political activities is dictated to a large extent by the details which have emerged in a number of trials; although the town also has a historical importance as it was one of the power bases of Antonio Gava, who was arguably the most important politician in Campania over a 25 year period which began in 1968 and ended in 1993 with his being charged with membership of a criminal organisation.

The town has a population of 17,000 and an electorate of 9,000, and for many years was the fiefdom of Giuseppe D'Antuono, described by supergrass Pasquale Galasso as 'simultaneously, a man of Antonio Gava and of Carmine Alfieri'.[27] D'Antuono was first elected mayor in 1973, and held the position for almost fifteen years until September 1988, although there was an interruption between December 1981 and March 1983 when he was in jail accused of membership of Cutolo's NCO.[28] Although the charge was dismissed in court due to lack of evidence, it probably furthered his political career rather than handicapping it.

In the early years of D'Antuono's rule, Sant'Antonio Abate seemed a normal small town politically dominated by the Christian Democrats. In a typically clientilist fashion he illegally took on twenty-eight people as council employees in 1978,[29] and the overall council workforce rose from 42 in 1973 to 292 in 1988, even though regulations stated that no more than 206 could be employed.[30]

As we have seen in earlier chapters, it was during the early 1980s that a huge gang war broke out across Campania over the contraband and drugs trade, as well as earthquake reconstruction contracts. Sant'Antonio Abate was by no means immune to these pressures, and D'Antuono's release from jail in March 1983, in time for the council elections, brought some of these tensions out into the open.

Two Catholic-inspired lists were presented at the elections, with the DC list proving victorious: gaining 5,913 votes out of a total of 8,886, and therefore winning 21 seats; the other Catholic list won 6 seats, whilst three went to other minor parties.[31] As a member of Gava's DC faction, D'Antuono was due to become mayor again, but then internal dissent broke out. The alternative Catholic list had been led by Mario Savarese and Giuseppe Abagnale – at that time the latter was a member of Carmine Alfieri's gang. After the election seven DC councillors led a break-away group which intended to stop D'Antuono becoming mayor. Negotiations were held between these seven and the Savarese/Abagnale grouping, but these soon stopped once a series of violent attacks began: DC councillor Orlando Cinque was shot at, whilst three others received phone threats.[32] Not surprisingly, a few days later they put an end to their factional activities, rejoined the DC group, and D'Antuono became mayor once again.

Behind the scenes an agreement was reached which allowed Abagnale to cross over from his original grouping to become in effect a DC councillor. However his nominal political affiliation meant very little when compared with his membership of Alfieri's gang: in the past Abagnale had been convicted of murder, attempted murder and membership of a Camorra gang.[33]

Despite the fact that he was a wholesale butcher by trade Abagnale became chairman of the public works committee, and soon after his appointment a decision was made to build a slaughterhouse worth $330,000. But as happened so often with earthquake reconstruction contracts, once approved the price quickly rose to $490,000 and later to $1,920,000.[34] It would appear that this was mainly a manoeuvre to gain access to money, as the actual building work was delayed for many years, probably to allow Abagnale to keep his monopoly position in meat production. As outlined previously, the Christian Democrats were always riven by internal faction fights over resources: it was the internal pecking order which dictated the amount of resources and privileges a political faction controlled.

During the mid-1980s the sheer scale of money available in earthquake reconstruction contracts caused increasing tension between competing political and criminal factions. As regards his criminal affiliation, Abagnale left the Alfieri gang in the mid-1980s and joined the more locally based Rosanova clan. One of the Rosanova brothers later recounted that during this period: 'Abagnale and us had enormous economic and business resources thanks to the contracts we obtained from Fantini.'[35] Antonio Fantini – a Christian Democrat politician at one point facing six separate charges linked to earthquake reconstruction – was president of the Campanian regional council from March 1983 to November 1988, a position which automatically made him one of two Special Commissioners appointed by the government

to supervise reconstruction. He was therefore a
linchpin in the distribution of major contracts and
favours, such as a $200 million contract for a water
treatment plant – and he seemed to be linked to the
Rosanova gang.

On a national level Fantini was part of Giulio
Andreotti's faction within the Christian Democrats, in
opposition to that of Antonio Gava, as Alfonso Ferrara
Rosanova explains:

> After Giuseppe Abagnale moved towards Fantini,
> a politician of Andreotti's faction, and obtained
> the contracts I've already mentioned, D'Antuono
> automatically moved towards Andreotti's faction
> … It was clear that Gava was losing power at S.
> Antonio Abate; and once the contract for the
> water treatment plant had been awarded Fantini,
> along with Giuseppe Abagnale, had created a
> very strong electoral base.[36]

The tension behind this jockeying for position to win
huge contracts, or rake-offs from contracts, resurfaced
the next time the cake was due to be divided: the
municipal elections of May 1988. D'Antuono and
Abagnale's official Christian Democrat list gained
4,987 votes and 15 seats, and as Abagnale had now
passed over into their 'sphere of influence', the
Rosanova gang supported the DC list.[37]

The 'opposition' to the Christian Democrats took
the form again of an alternative Catholic 'civic list',
and was led by one Antonio D'Auria. His participation
was highly significant, as he had been Antonio Gava's
personal secretary for many years. This was highly
unorthodox behaviour, and was evidence of intense
tension among all the interests that the party

represented. The former Christian Democrat MP Alfredo Vito has testified that:

> It was absolutely obvious that the list that was officially closest to Gava was the civic one and not D'Antuono's: and you could notice this from hundreds of signals which could not go unobserved – the Ministerial machine put itself at the civic list's disposal.[38]

Gava's own personal actions also illustrate his factional position; his refusal to come and speak in the town, given that he would have been duty-bound to support the official DC candidate, went against one of his long-standing traditions during election campaigns. Superficially there did not seem to be any real political differences between the two lists, apart from some rather vague local references in the 'civic list'; what was really at stake, of course, was control over the Christian Democrat spoils system.

Yet the election did not resolve the issue as the DC, with 15 councillors, failed to achieve an absolute majority given that the civic list had won 12 seats, with the socialists, communists and neo-fascists all gaining one seat each.[39] One of the reasons for the DC's failure was the fact that a few days before the election a Dr Calabrese suddenly withdrew his candidature, subsequently depriving them of a majority – apparently his withdrawal was due to pressure from four *camorristi*: Ciro D'Auria, Catello De Riso, Gaetano Mercurio and Bernardo Santonicola.[40]

The intimidation of a Christian Democrat candidate, who was supported in turn by Fantini at regional level, Andreotti at national level, and by the Rosanovas at a criminal level, obviously suggests that it was the politician Antonio Gava and the gang leader Carmine Alfieri who were applying pressure. The involvement of Gaetano Mercurio, suspected of the Alfieri-inspired Torre Annunziata massacre, lends weight to this hypothesis.

A clear division emerged five weeks after the election, when Pasquale Galasso ordered the killing of two Rosanova brothers, Aniello and Luigi, as well as Diodato D'Auria, a DC councillor who was also coincidentally a distant relative of Antonio D'Auria. The murders had the desired effect: three DC councillors immediately moved over to support the alternative Catholic list, thus giving it the majority. Giuseppe Abagnale, the ex Alfieri gang member who had crossed over to the Rosanovas and become a DC councillor, went into hiding in fear of his life.[41]

The balance of power was now clearly established in the town: the losers were the official Christian Democrat list and its councillors, and therefore Antonio Fantini at a regional level together with Giulio Andreotti at a national level and the Rosanovas at a criminal level. Given the circumstances it is not surprising that one of the Rosanova brothers has stated: 'I believe Antonio D'Auria and Antonio Gava to be morally responsible for my brothers' murder.'[42]

The motive behind these murders and acts of intimidation was clearly not morality but political power and the financial resources that came with it. One other point to bear in mind is that during this period (1988–90), Antonio Gava was Minister of the Interior and ultimately responsible for police activities.

The new council was agreed upon in December 1988 and excluded both D'Antuono and Abagnale, selecting Bonaventura Rispoli as mayor and quickly disclosing the illegality of D'Antuono's administration and its $8 million debt. The change in political power was also confirmed at a criminal level. Once Abagnale lost his position as councillor he clearly lost a degree of protection, and both Giuseppe Abagnale and his brother Carmine were murdered by the Alfieri clan in June 1990.

Yet D'Antuono was far from resigned to his fate, and what probably helped him were his connections with Minister of the Interior Antonio Gava. Otherwise, it is difficult to explain how D'Antuono managed to extricate himself from his legal problems in the early 1990s, when he was facing two separate trials concerning his past administrations, the possibility of being placed under preventative house arrest for five years and having property confiscated as a result of demands being made by the State Prosecutor's office in Naples.[43]

The fact of the matter is that he made a successful political comeback in 1993, and was elected Christian Democrat mayor once again in June. He won his election under a new electoral system, which had been strongly supported by Christian Democrat reformers such as Mario Segni and the ex-communist DS, as they believed that the elimination of preference voting and the institution of a direct ballot for the position of mayor would somehow magically end the links between criminal politicians and political criminals.

Soon after D'Antuono's election, the authorities began to receive complaints concerning threats he apparently made to rival candidates, and he was subsequently charged with criminal association and ballot rigging and suspended from his post in August 1993. In a forlorn attempt to salvage some shred of credibility, the authorities decided to disband the council the following month and appoint an unelected government commissioner for eighteen months. The motivation behind this presidential decree was 'the resumption of democratic principles and collective freedom'.[44]

Matters did not seem to have improved much when elections were held two years later. Individual houses were canvassed and people were promised jobs, as well as being given crates of tomatoes as 'gifts' – although in order to monitor their votes they were also asked to write their voters' registration number on a 'questionnaire' they were given. Thirteen left-wing MPs denounced these activities, accusing a right-wing candidate, who also owned a tomato canning factory.[45]

In a recent trial the seemingly insignificant election of Vincenzo De Rosa, first as a Christian Democrat councillor in 1990, has taken on far greater importance. A major trader in flowers in the Pompeii area, he has essentially been an integral part of the Cesarano clan, which took criminal control of the area following the demise of Alfieri and Galasso. De Rosa has been involved in usury and handling stolen cheques – his business activities made banking cheques particularly easy, as he admitted during an argument with Vincenzo Cesarano on 11 November 1999 which was bugged by the police: 'They gave me two stolen cheques, two, and I banked them, and then I had to answer to the judge.'[46] Earlier in the same conversation he complained about a frequent activity of the Cesarano gang, extortion, but only because on this particular occasion his interests had been damaged: 'He was sorting out all those clients and then he shot at one of mine. And if I've got small clients, it's because I've won them off the wholesaler, right? But now thanks to him I can't go near them.'[47]

In essence, over a 25 year period the names of the
parties have changed, the names of individual politicians and *camorristi* have changed, but what never
seems to change in towns such as Sant'Antonio Abate
are the social and economic conditions.

Regional councils and the health service

Barely thirty years after their creation in 1970, Italy's
twenty regional government authorities now account
for nearly 10% of the country's gross domestic
product. They are generally responsible for agriculture, economic development, housing, hospitals and
health services, public works and urban affairs.

Yet despite their demands for more power to raise
taxes independently, in 1989 they were financially tied
to national government for 98.2% of their expenditure.[48] Perhaps even more important than this is the
fact that regional government has no real history in
modern Italy – to a large extent these authorities are
hollow shells, devoid of any political tradition, colo-
nised by national parties and politicians, who have
also brought in their traditional practices. Furthermore, election as a regional councillor is very often a
stage in an upwardly mobile trajectory: while over the
1970–90 period 19.2% of Campanian regional councillors were elected from the ranks of the Naples city
council alone,[49] at a national level at least 20% of all
regional councillors left for seats in the national
parliament.[50]

Apart from this general picture, in relative terms it
is not surprising to learn that major research
conducted over this period has shown Campania to

come nineteenth out of Italy's twenty regions in terms of general administrative performance, and last as regards public satisfaction and bureaucratic responsiveness.[51] In other words, the local political culture of inefficiency and illegality has simply been reproduced on a grander scale.

However there is one very obvious difference compared with municipal administration: the lack of political murders. It is highly likely that regional politicians have been conditioned by the Camorra's move into local politics during the 1980s and, given their own political traditions, were quite willing to come to an arrangement with it. Indeed, we are often dealing with the same politicians who had previously been elected as municipal councillors.

The major area of regional government expenditure is the financing and management of local heath authorities, the *aziende sanitarie locali*, or ASLs. Although Campania comes only seventh nationally in terms of its total number of public hospital beds, in line with a familiar pattern it is second in terms of its public health budget, which in 1992 amounted to $6 billion.[52]

One of the most scandalous example of wastage and Camorra infiltration took place at the end of the Christian Democrat era, and concerned ASL 35 in Castellammare di Stabia, Antonio Gava's home town. One of the earliest signs of corruption was a contract signed in 1982 for in-patient catering, which cost $10 per meal, an improbably high figure for the period. Not surprisingly an investigation was begun and in 1986, when a new contract was signed, costs were reduced by more than half. In the long term, however, this was not a solution – in late 1991 patients refused to eat meals in protest at the poor-quality food they were being served.

The construction of a new hospital wing took more than 10 years to complete, while costs increased from $1.6 to $8 million; it also appears that up to 20% of the total cost may have been spent on bribes.

In 1988 the son of the local hospital's main cardiologist and the son of the Socialist vice-president of the ASL were both promoted to jobs they were not qualified to perform. In October 1989 an investigation began into the legitimacy of the decision to rent a flat for $650 per month to an employee of the ASL, Dr Adriana Ingenito, who also happened to be the wife of DC Senator Francesco Patriarca.[53]

The level of nepotism became even more bloated in the spring of 1991 when dozens of sons, daughters, grandchildren and other relations of the ASL 35 management committee and local councillors were all given jobs.

These are only a few specific examples which help explain why by 1992 ASL 35 had an operating deficit of over $80 million and over a thousand workers on its payroll. The scandal involved not only politicians, but also trade union officials within local hospitals, who also faced charges of membership of a criminal organisation and extortion.

It seems that the Camorra's murder of Sebastiano Corrado in March 1992, a PDS councillor and member of the ASL 35 management committee, was linked to his involvement in a bribe regarding the refurbishing of a nursing school – in this case 15% of a $200,000 contract.[54] Most of the companies involved in building work or cleaning services were controlled by *camorristi*, and it seems that Corrado, who worked in the finance office, had done something to anger a particular gang. But once again it is the patients who suffer the most: orders for new equipment mysteriously disappear, wards and kitchens are infested with cockroaches due to lack of cleaning and so on. As a doctor based in a cardiology department stated: 'We are operating without being able to offer guarantees to a patient who comes to us asking to be cured.'[55]

The links between DC and PDS politicians in this scandal were taking place at a highly significant period: the end of the DC's domination of local and national politics. And the events surrounding the election of the next regional council illustrated that the centre-left PDS was not prepared to make a 'clean sweep' either. The new Campanian regional council met in April 1994 to vote on who should hold the various administrative positions, with PDS politician Giuseppe Venditto being voted in as president by other councillors. This caused a storm of protest, as other left-wing parties had insisted that the ten councillors out of sixty then under investigation, for corruption and membership of the Camorra, should not vote in these elections. However Venditto's election, and control over regional council committees, was determined by these councillors who took an active part in voting.[56]

Five years later a subsequent president of the regional council, National Alliance politician Antonio Rastrelli, was under arrest accused of fraud, corruption and criminal association. The scandal revolved around the massive contracts for the TAV high-speed rail line between Rome and Naples, and Rastrelli's role was that of manoeuvring the council into awarding contracts to certain companies he was linked with, which in turn would often sub-contract work to Camorra-controlled firms. Rastrelli received various kinds of political support, wrote the investigating magistrate, including 'the presence of crowds at his public meetings'.[57]

National government

Until the fall of the Christian Democrats in mid-1993 there was little evidence of direct Camorra involvement at the national political level, although some circumstantial evidence had previously pointed in that direction.

For example, during a police raid on Lorenzo Nuvoletta's house in the 1980s, a letter from a lawyer named Palumbo was found, in which he urged the Nuvolettas to 'direct their votes towards Antonio Gava'.[58] During another *carabinieri* raid, Antonio Gava's business card was found in the pocket of Domenico Di Maro, a builder later convicted of a series of crimes, including membership of the Nuvoletta gang.

A raid on Carmine Alfieri's house as far back as March 1976 revealed that he had six different telephone numbers for the DC Senator Francesco Patriarca, known in Camorra circles as 'Frankie the promise' for the favours he would often try to do.[59] Further evidence of Patriarca's contacts emerged in 1983: between 1974 and 1976 he had written three letters to Ciro Iavarone, a NCO member in jail, in which he thanked him, among other things, 'for your help during the election campaign, which led to my election'. Even more disturbing is the fact that Patriarca was a member of the Parliamentary Justice Commission and then later the Anti-Mafia Commission.[60]

Although these examples (and many others one could give), do not constitute definite proof of illegality, the undisputed power of the Camorra makes it very likely that close links with politicians do exist. It would be very improbable, given the sheer size of the

Camorra's economic empire, that the most entrepreneurial and powerful gang leaders are not consulted regularly by politicians.

The examples quoted here are therefore in many ways the tip of the iceberg – they are just a few of the cases which have come to light. However, in both the economic and political spheres, the Camorra is naturally obliged to use personnel without criminal records, so their influence and actual penetration within political institutions is impossible to quantify.

Nevertheless, evidence has started to accumulate concerning Camorra infiltration of national politics. But its relationship with national politicians is less organic and direct than with local councillors; the main role of the national politician is one of delaying or deflecting government policies that might damage their criminal friends, while approving laws that facilitate criminal penetration of the public sector.

A brief review of the activities of a few MPs brings into focus a disturbing picture, such as the case of Socialist MP Raffaele Mastrantuono, former vice-president of the Parliamentary Justice Commission, which has the role of monitoring and amending laws relating to organised crime. The sensitive nature of this position is not, one would think, entirely in keeping with the fact that the town council of Villaricca, of which he was mayor from 1975 to 1984 and again in 1990–93, has been disbanded due to Camorra infiltration.[61]

Mastrantuono became the right-hand man of the Socialist Party's deputy National Secretary, Giulio Di Donato, and often had a strange relationship with the judiciary. As part of the Justice Commission he once repeatedly interrupted a trial and insisted on telling two judges details about a local Camorra gang operating in his home town. Not only was this completely inappropriate behaviour, it also created suspicion that Mastrantuono wanted to damage a rival gang.[62] As one author has written: 'He was open to all requests: house arrest, parole, compassionate leave.'[63]

The vice-president of the Justice Commission between 1992 and 1994 was the Liberal MP Alfonso Martucci, elected at Casal di Principe near Caserta. Before becoming an MP he had been a lawyer, special-ising first in defending NCO members, and later members of the Bardellino and Mariano gangs. When he decided to stand as a Liberal candidate, the party's vote in the town leapt from 1.2% to 26.7%, the Liberal Party's highest ever vote in any election, giving rise to strong suspicions of Camorra support.[64] Martucci was later convicted of electoral fraud through 'the use of Mafia methods', but like so many politicians convicted in this period, avoided jail through plea bargaining.[65]

In more general terms, however, the accusations made by Pasquale Galasso in 1992–93 have thrown a different light on the traditional view of the relation-ship between politics and organised crime. It is no longer simply a question of the Camorra manoeu-vring votes towards 'friendly' politicians in exchange for favours and protection. Many politicians of the Christian Democrat era have been accused, and some convicted, of being part of the Camorra. The question is no longer one of 'bad government' or clientelism but in some cases total commitment to a violent and illegal organisation. Once again, these issues also point to the fact that the Camorra is far more than an organisation that relies solely on acts of violence and its control of the drugs trade – in fact public sector contracts could even be its largest source of profits.

Although the precise nature of these links may never be proved satisfactorily, it is certain that close links existed, and in any event many, but unfortunately not all, of these politicians have been found guilty at least in a political sense. One telling example is Carmine Alfieri recalling for magistrates a meeting allegedly held at Lorenzo Nuvoletta's house in late 1980 or 1981: 'Antonio Gava was at that meeting. You can appreciate, your Honour, that with this kind of protection *you sort out* trials, you can do business, the police leave you alone.'[66] A more graphic example of this protection occurred several years later when Gava was Minister of the Interior: in a major report on organised crime presented to Parliament on 5 December 1989, Gava omitted to even mention the existence of Alfieri's gang, despite the fact that it had been common knowledge for several years that Alfieri had superseded Cutolo as the Camorra's strongest leader in 1981–82. This is how Alfieri describes his response:

> A few days after this piece of news came out in the newspapers, at one of the meetings at my farmhouse to which I summoned Senator Vincenzo Meo, I asked him to thank Antonio Gava for the 'interest' he had shown in not mentioning my name. Meo assured me that he would have conveyed my gratitude to Gava.[67]

Cases of clear collusion between politicians and *camorristi* have been far rarer since the demise of the Christian Democrats: in essence a system which had worked for decades has become far more unsafe and uncertain. Many recent cases involve 'recycled' politicians, such as the ex-Christian Democrat MP Carmine Mensorio, arrested for Camorra membership in July 1995, when he was a Senator for the CCD, a new Catholic party.[68] He was accused of having half of the shares in Camorra-controlled private security companies in the Nola area, but unfortunately the Senate refused to lift his parliamentary immunity. A year later magistrates requested another arrest warrant, this time for membership of a Camorra gang, writing in the indictment: 'The judicial developments of recent years have destroyed a series of political reference points which were clearly linked to organised crime, [Senator Mensorio] has sought to extend his own interests in the shape of Camorra co-management of private security firms.'[69]

In September 1996 a series of arrests were made over construction of the TAV high-speed rail link between Rome and Naples, initiated by the creation of a holding company in July 1991, comprising 40% of state capital and 60% of private investments. Many of the contracts were awarded to ICLA, one of the most notorious companies from the earthquake period, and according to the Anti-Mafia Commission: 'made up of individuals and groupings of organised crime, from both a Camorra and Mafia background, with the mediation of personalities from the political and business world who have been involved in serious cases of political corruption'.[70] In the government's 1994 budget alone, $1.2 billion was set aside for the work; some of the bureaucratic string-pulling emerged with the arrest of Vincenzo Chianese in June 1999, inspector-general of the Treasury Ministry. He advised his 'friends' exactly how to pitch their tender to the government in order to win contracts, and for investigating magistrates he was a key member of 'a perfect business-administrative-Camorra board of directors'.[71]

So far we have focused our attention on how criminals seek to exploit their relationship with politicians, but for criminals to gain these advantages, politicians must receive something in return. And as far as both local, regional and national politicians are concerned, the vital link with Camorra gangs is their ability to deliver votes, the very lifeblood of professional politicians.

Given the political history of Naples and Campania over the last century and a half, it is not surprising that politics has almost lost any pretence of honesty or genuine democratic debate. The following scenario, sketched out by a senior investigator, paints an accurate but at times almost incomprehensible picture of political criminality, beginning with a *camorrista*'s approach to a voter:

> They know who is going to vote in that individual ballot box, so the *camorrista* says to himself: from family X (who has been contacted) there have to be so many votes …
>
> Apart from voting for this candidate because I tell you to, if you vote for Fred Smith you get something in return: there are council jobs to be given out, contracts to be awarded, certification of disabilities in order to get a pension, and so on …
>
> They check up on and control the voting, but above all they control the successful candidate. The candidate has to then act so that the promises made beforehand are actually kept afterwards.
>
> If a politician says: 'Dear voter, if you vote for me, and after my election I'm sure you voted for

me, I'll get your daughter a job in this particular office' – then the person in question who has been promised this by the politician, and who knows that if he is elected he will probably keep his promise, will then go out and vote for him.

At the very least he signs a blank cheque, but what choice does he have? There is this politician who has promised a job for his daughter, and another who has promised nothing.

But the politician hasn't promised these things to individual voters but to a Camorra leader …

The *camorrista* never worries about whether somebody is going to keep his promises because he can solve the problem. If a businessman or politician gets elected he has to keep the agreement he made previously with the *camorrista*, when he told him – 'Don't worry, you get me elected and then I'll always act in your favour.' If he then becomes mayor or chairman of a committee, and doesn't keep to this agreement, the *camorrista* doesn't have many options, he's not going to wait for five years … as a matter of course they kill him. And there have been several local politicians eliminated in this fashion – and the background is always the same – the agreement had been broken and at a certain point they have been eliminated …

It is not unusual to see politicians who belong to different party factions, or even to different parties, being elected with votes controlled by one individual Camorra gang.[72]

In other words, one might argue that a politician elected with Camorra votes is more 'honest' than one elected without their help, in the sense that promises are generally kept, and expectations accurately reflect what is then achieved by the politician elected. This scenario also partly explains why right and centre-right parties such as the 'post fascist' National Alliance and Silvio Berlusconi's Forza Italia, have generally performed better than the left, which is far less likely to make deals with organised crime. The left is therefore deprived of a reservoir of votes which goes to those candidates who make deals with *camorristi*.

The best example of the uphill battle an honest left-wing council faces comes from Marano, long-term stronghold of the Nuvolettas, but interestingly, the only council in the whole of southern Italy controlled by the far left Communist Refoundation party. One local councillor describes the problems they often face on polling day:

> They stand outside and make sure they're seen by the people they've giving voting indications to, and they accompany them inside the building. They only leave them on their own when they walk up to the ballot box, and then they walk outside with them again. They're not intimidating them directly, but they make sure they understand: 'Here I am. I've asked for your vote throughout the election campaign. I came round to your house and left you a leaflet, I came back again and left another one.' Every election we're on the phone to the police all day, asking them to move these people on, to keep the entrances clear, and so on.[73]

What is important to note here is the scale of resources employed by Camorra gangs during election campaigns, often at dozens of polling stations in medium-sized towns. The only reason such an effort is made is that local gangs understand the very high level of potential profits that can accrue from controlling 'friendly' councillors who will place expensive council tenders with certain companies.

The crucial element at work here is the *camorrista*'s influence within a given community. Not only does he enjoy obedience as a result of his violent reputation, he also enjoys a certain level of support as it is known that many semi-legal jobs, such as selling contraband cigarettes, have been created thanks to his illegal activities. The most important factor however is the common knowledge that he is the mediator with the political system in terms of public sector jobs, contracts, pensions, various services and so on. As Pasquale Galasso puts it, a relationship previously based on fear, respect, or semi-friendship is transformed:

> When a person comes to ask us for favours, such as a low-class job, and it is given to them – at that moment this person swears allegiance towards whoever has done him the favour. There are other favours as well: whoever has problems with VAT, a builder's licence, the tax office, the bureaucracy, permits, and so many other problems which are part of our society.[74]

Long-term unemployment and poverty are the essential factors in explaining the strength of this system: there are simply so many people desperate for a job or some kind of financial help that they are prepared to accept arrangements of this kind. One of the classic scenarios is a *camorrista* employing construction workers illegally, who then wants his employees to vote for a certain politician. The following

sequence of events can often take place, with the
camorrista:

> managing to link their voting intentions with the
> permanence of their job. The following exchange
> takes place: 'If you want to carry on working
> here, this is who you vote for. You, your relatives
> and your friends.' And afterwards they even
> manage to make an overall check in the various
> polling stations where these people vote, and see
> whether these voting instructions have been
> followed.
>
> You can find out from the electoral register
> who is enrolled to vote in which polling stations.
> So let's say as a *camorrista* I've got lots of building
> workers who live in one particular area, so I do
> my sums: if I've got 100 workers, my candidate
> should get 100 votes, and at least 50% of the
> votes of their relatives and 50% from their
> friends. Then I go and check how many votes my
> candidate got from that polling station ...
>
> There isn't any individual monitoring going on
> here, but verification of whether, according to the
> *camorrista*, the right-sized package of votes which
> that area should deliver has materialised or not.[75]

Gang leaders often recognise that providing electoral
support is a vital component in their own self-preservation, as a *camorrista* once explained:

> This [electoral] support may not even cost a
> candidate anything. If he is a capable politician
> and the organisation sees that they can exploit
> his election in the future they won't ask him for a
> penny, on the contrary they will spend money on

posters, leaflets, meetings … It is an investment, because once he is elected the candidate will make himself available.

But if he just wants a bit of help, then he has to pay. A thousand guaranteed first-preference votes from a given area in Naples council elections cost $240–$320,000. The person who wants this help normally has a strong electoral base of around 10,000 votes, and those extra preference votes are intended to gain him chairmanship of a council committee …

The Camorra isn't interested in parties but in people. A local Camorra leader needs just a single afternoon to get a thousand votes: seven youths on mopeds who give people written or verbal 'messages'.[76]

Nowadays there are many factors that link politicians to the Camorra, the major one obviously being the need for election. Yet there is also the persuasive power of intimidation, or blackmail as a result of previous links with *camorristi*, the need to finance party organisations or factions, or simply personal greed. Given the nature of the Camorra, it is impossible to quantify its general political influence and the extent to which it can dictate voting patterns, but it seems beyond doubt that its influence is highly significant, in that Camorra votes can often make the difference between electoral defeat or victory.[77]

According to Galasso, by the early 1990s Carmine Alfieri's gang virtually held the upper hand in its relationship with politicians:

In the six-month period preceding elections there is a coming and going of all those politicians who have had links with our Camorra group, who push themselves forward in order to get votes – they therefore demonstrate their continuing availability – and at that point things turn into a market place.

In the end Alfieri and the rest of us measure up what a politician can offer us in exchange: if he is useful as a politician or if we can use him for his friendships within institutions, particularly the judiciary. In the end politician X is 'weighed' to see whether he really has that power.

It's a bit like in our own Camorra group: what Pasquale Galasso says has a certain power, but if someone else says the same thing it's hot air. Basically it's the same thing.[78]

Galasso also tells a revealing story about his first meeting in September 1991 with Alfredo Vito, who was then preparing his campaign for election as a DC MP in the April 1992 elections, in which he was elected with the highest personal vote of all Campanian candidates. Galasso was on the run at the time from a 10-year sentence for Camorra membership and extortion:

What made me almost laugh was to hear the ideas put forward by this future MP; I heard Vito talking about fighting the Camorra, and even though I was on the run I was due to meet him in a few minutes … He told me that he knew all about my situation and promised to take an interest in it particularly as regards my trial at the Court of Appeal in Naples, as he had lots of friends within the judiciary …

After the March 1992 sentence, in which all my

family was acquitted of the charge of constituting a Camorra gang ... I honoured our agreement, which [here a name has been censored in the original document] reminded me of, I think that Vito drew heavily on the Camorra's vote.[79]

Vito later confirmed that he met Galasso at a DC election meeting, telling magistrates: 'It's true, I have met Pasquale Galasso. But it was a trap, your Honour, believe me – I was naively caught in a snare without being guilty of anything.'[80]

Magistrates are currently investigating accusations of electoral fraud in Naples during the May 2001 general election, a suspicion that was immediately voiced widely given the chaotic and inexplicable scenes many people witnessed at polling stations. One student recounted that after he had voted:

I went out and realised there was a group of suspicious looking people who were waiting for voters outside the building. They checked the official stamp on the polling card, thanked them, and then paid them: $5, $25 or $50 notes were being sprayed about ... The Camorra isn't stupid, it got paid loads of money for these elections and doesn't want to let down those who gave it to them.[81]

Over the last ten years it has become clear to most voters that nearly all major parties, including the left of centre DS, are corrupt. Sadly, most of the left in Campania has adapted to the right's political outlook, absorbed many of its general policies, values and methods of operation, and has discarded any thought of a different world being possible. The *inevitability* of corruption – the predominance of political favours over rights – has become pervasive.

This lack of hope in the future, and the common knowledge of cross-party corruption, creates great difficulties in terms of effecting real changes:

> In the South elections no longer represent consensus or dissent towards whoever is administering the political system, as they do in other democracies. In the South votes represent economic hardship and are directed towards whoever controls resources; it is not consensus but necessity, you vote for them but you hate them.[82]

And it is to this area – the social, political and judicial forces outside of the centre-right parties, which are normally seen as an alternative to the criminal politics of these parties – to which we now turn.

CHAPTER EIGHT

Who will stop the Camorra?

Why don't all those people do something?
Don't they get angry about anything?
Aren't they angry about the police on every street corner?
Aren't they angry about the homeless without even a
cigarette?
Aren't they angry about the pissed-off unemployed
hanging around?

If you're not really angry
Don't do a thing, don't bother
Do something really useful and make everyone happy
Go and sit down quietly in Parliament.

99 Posse

Any political party committed to maintaining the institutions of the political system within which it operates cannot but share and apply the values of that system in practice.

Such a simple statement takes on a specific meaning in modern Italy: because the whole postwar system has functioned on institutional corruption, patronage and nepotism, none of the minor or potentially progressive forces, either within or outside of government, can be immune to the system's values.

Destroying this ethos, and its toleration not only of illegality but also of organised crime, means over-throwing this system and replacing it with something really democratic. Yet the political debate between various parties revolves around how to manage the system and maintain its intrinsic values (including its links with organised crime), not how to dismantle it.

The level of corruption and illegality which has historically been tolerated within state institutions makes any notion of piecemeal reform a pipedream. It should come as no surprise, therefore, that the tolera-tion of illegality and organised crime emerges most sharply within the legal system, the very institution entrusted with preserving legality.

Watching the detectives (1): *criminal investigations*

What concerns most ordinary people is whether the police and judiciary are actually managing to solve crime, and the statistics clearly demonstrate that they are not. A close analysis unmistakably shows their inefficiency; recent statistics show that overall 83% of crimes are never solved. Only 36% of murders are solved, compared to a shocking 2.5% of all burglaries.[1] (Tables 8 and 9 illustrate in greater detail the inability of the Campanian police to make any impact on lawbreaking.)

The main underlying reasons for the failure of the police to apprehend lawbreakers and obtain convic-tions is the alienation of most ordinary people from institutions of the state, as the Head of the Naples Flying Squad once admitted:

We receive some anonymous phone calls, but nothing more ... it is impossible to find a witness, even one, who will point his finger and say: it was he who came into my shop and demanded protection money. In Naples investigations hardly ever end in the capture of a criminal, given that nobody helps us to find the evidence which would justify an arrest.[2]

But, as he goes on to acknowledge, the police's failure to complete investigations successfully is the result of long-term popular scepticism:

A section of the population does not love us, they do not see the police as the incarnation of the state and the defenders of freedom and people's rights. In those desolate areas it is Camorra bosses and not policemen in uniform who are figures of authority. In Forcella, whoever suffers a wrong or an act of violence doesn't turn to the police but to the Giuliano family.[3]

Magistrates too have sometimes recognised that it is mass distrust of institutions which makes investigative work almost impossible:

There is a lack of confidence in the judicial system and in the state in general. There is a belief that the ordinary police and the finance police do not function very well, that in the field of casual employment safety regulations are ignored, that Health and Safety inspectors do not exist, that public offices in general – and the financial ones in particular – are insufficient and inadequate.[4]

In short, it is the very inefficiency and corruption of the institutions that make people hostile towards them. However hostility towards authority and the legal system also has an economic basis, as Table 10 illustrates.

While the unemployed accused of relatively minor crimes are sent to jail on remand, they see leading politicians accused of serious crimes frequently avoiding both arrest and trial, and even if they are finally convicted, the courts either agree to a plea bargain or a suspended sentence, so none of them ever gets a prison term. Throughout the 1990s the Italian parliament has repeatedly denounced corruption and the infiltration of organised crime into politics, but only to then repeatedly refuse to lift an MP's parliamentary immunity from prosecution.

In June 1994 Silvio Berlusconi's first government immediately tried to pass a decree which facilitated the release from jail of politicians facing trial, but it was hastily withdrawn following widespread public outrage and protest. Seven years later one of the first announcements of Berlusconi's second government, in June 2001, made it clear that the crime of false accounting would be struck off. As a media tycoon, rather than as Prime Minister, Berlusconi was facing three separate trials in which his companies were accused of false accounting.

All this should be compared to the situation of Italy's 'ordinary' prison population: at a national level 50% of all inmates are people held on remand awaiting trial, whilst in Campania the number of prisoners on remand in September 1993 was 67% of the total prison population.[5] The basic reason behind this scandal is the snail's pace of the legal system. It is so bad that in 1999 Italy had more judgements passed against it by the European Court of Human Rights than any other country – 44; whereas Turkey received 18, France 16 and the UK 12.[6]

Once incarcerated, inmates then suffer over-crowding: Italy's jails currently detain 55,000 people in institutions meant to hold no more than 42,700. Naples' Poggioreale jail currently holds 2,500 prisoners although its official capacity is 900: 17 inmates often spend 22 hours a day locked up in a room five metres by four.[7] Nationally, the Prison Service only has 608 staff employed to re-educate inmates, a ratio of just 1:90.[8] In this context it is therefore understandable why wives and partners of presumed or convicted *camorristi* once demonstrated outside Naples' Law Courts carrying placards with slogans such as: 'The real "*camorristi*" are the politicians. Their problems get solved, what about ours?'[9]

The problem the police face in terms of law enforcement is not a lack of resources, as the President of the Province of Naples and major sociologist of the Camorra pointed out: 'In Campania there is one law enforcement officer for every 100 inhabitants, compared to a European average of 500.'[10] What is lacking is public support for the police and the judiciary; in other words, many people see the police and the judiciary as part of a system which encourages organised crime.

And it is not surprising that people should have these views: examples of members of the police force with Camorra connections emerge practically every week in Campania, and the links encompass all levels of police activity. Here is the first example:

In 1997 it emerged that anti-Camorra efforts in Naples had been seriously compromised by several police officers whose 'salaries' from the leading crime families ranged from $1,300 to $2,800 per month. Nineteen officers were arrested in January. In February the former head of the Naples Flying Squad was arrested, followed by three more officers from the city's drugs squad in May. It was alleged that the men regularly faked investigations into the criminal activities of the Camorra factions who were paying them, while arresting members of rival clans.[11]

A statement by Camorra supergrass Ciro Vollaro led to the arrest of a senior policeman in December 1998, accused of throwing investigations concerning the Vollaro clan off-track for a monthly 'salary' of $715.[12] In June 2000 two policemen and two *carabinieri* were arrested for Camorra membership, specifically for warning gangs of impending police raids in the Aversa area.[13] In March 2001 two *carabinieri* were arrested for aiding a fraud by a Camorra gang, which supplied sub-standard products to the cosmetics industry.[14] In June 2001 an investigating magistrate's secretary was given an 18 month sentence for revealing information about the nature of investigations being made against the powerful Fabbrocino clan.[15]

Many more similar examples could be given, but as the Anti-Mafia Commission recently pointed out, the important thing to understand is not the quantity of scandals, but the environment from which they emerge: 'The exceptional seriousness of this phenomenon has not been mentioned simply because of the sheer frequency of verified cases of corruption, which is relevant in itself, but also for the number of deep-rooted cases of institutional deviation recorded, which in some cases has involved entire departments.'[16]

Essentially the very people entrusted with stamping out illegality are often breaking the law themselves, even at the highest level.

Watching the detectives (2): *judging the judges*

There is a fundamental difference between the legal systems of Anglo-Saxon and Continental European countries in the way they investigate crimes and obtain prosecutions. In Italy, although the police deal directly with issues of public order and the documenting and assessment of all reported crimes, for major investigations they work largely under the direction of the judiciary.

Historically there have been many examples of low level police corruption and collusion with criminals, but it was only in the 1990s that the same pattern was revealed at the level of the judiciary. By late 1993 there were twenty magistrates in Campania facing either criminal charges or internal disciplinary procedures, and an examination of the alleged activities of just two magistrates gives an indication of the level of collusion which appears to have taken place.

The most serious charges were made against Alfonso Lamberti: criminal association, corruption, extortion and possession of explosives. It is thought that his systematic involvement with the Camorra came about as a result of personal tragedy: the murder of his twelve year old daughter Simonetta in 1989. After that he earned the nickname 'handcuffs' at the Salerno court where he was based for the frequency with which he issued arrest warrants, although it is widely thought that these measures were almost exclusively directed against the gang he believed was responsible for his daughter's death. Later, he apparently asked Alfieri's gang to murder the presumed killer of his daughter, and celebrated his death with a champagne meal with Alfieri.[17]

However, it is his period as president of the inspection branch of the court of Naples (which deals with the supervision of convicted and remand prisoners), that has given rise to greater concern. It is presumed that he granted favours to Camorra prisoners – the inspection branch also has powers to revoke 'internal exile' in towns far away from Naples and Campania – and that he ordered the return of goods seized by police as illicit gains.[18] Lamberti was also accused of making deals with Giorgio Nocaro's gang in Ponticelli, some of whose members allegedly came to see him offering him $40,000 to release goods which had been seized. Lamberti is said to have replied, 'Either $120,000 or nothing; here things are split three ways.' Whatever the truth of such accusations, what is beyond doubt is that Lamberti signed an order in November 1988 for the release of the Nocaro gang's assets.[19]

Another allegation concerns his intervention on behalf of two men whose assets had been seized as a result of various investigations. It appears that this manoeuvre, started at Alfieri's instigation, was rewarded with $120,000 and two gold Rolex watches.[20] During his deposition to the Anti-Mafia Commission Pasquale Galasso defined him in the following terms: 'Lamberti was another magistrate in our hands. We had a direct link to Lamberti, we could meet him whenever we wanted and I remember that more than once he, Alfieri, Lamberti's cousin and I all had meetings.'[21]

Armando Cono Lancuba faced similar charges, particularly concerning his role as an appeal court judge who passed a series of 'light sentences'. One notable case was the appeal trial over the August 1984 Torre Annunziata massacre, the worst ever gangland murder in Italy.

At the first trial Carmine Alfieri and others had been convicted of having organised the murders, and were consequently given life sentences.[22] Yet on appeal the very same people were acquitted, and without going into detailed arguments concerning evidence, this was viewed at the time as a particularly surprising decision, given Alfieri's criminal record.[23] This is how Pasquale Galasso describes the help both he and Carmine Alfieri received from Cono Lancuba: 'On appeal [Alfieri] was acquitted thanks to the intervention, once again, of some politicians, whose interests were taken care of by Lancuba. He advised us on how to bring our influence to bear and how to present our written evidence.'[24]

This pattern of first conviction and then acquittal on appeal is perhaps the most worrying aspect of such 'light' sentences or acquittals. Harsh sentences at the main trial create the perception in the public's mind that criminals are being convicted and put behind bars. Once public interest wanes and a few years pass, the sentences are then either drastically reduced or simply overturned on appeal. Even though the release of a notorious criminal may cause disquiet in some quarters, the fact that criminals have been in jail for a few years leads most people to believe they are no longer dangerous.

Cono Lancuba was also the appeal court judge who decided to return to Pasquale Galasso $24 million worth of assets that had previously been impounded with the intention of permanent confiscation. Apart from these cases and several charges of corruption, Cono Lancuba was also accused of being Alfieri's 'judicial counsellor' as well as of Camorra membership. As reward for his services, it has been established that at the very least he could stay rent-free in a luxury flat in Positano every summer and was also given fur coats as gifts for his wife.[25] In addition, Alfieri bought him a legal office in central Naples.[26]

Prior to these events he had been criticised for many of his activities, such as the fact that he was one of the magistrates employed as inspectors of building sites following the 1980 earthquake. And for many years he was in charge of perhaps the most vital and delicate office in the Naples law courts: the declarations office.[27] It is here that accusations and tip-offs are made, and where police, *carabinieri* and finance police reports are sent. All information is then filtered and assessed, and passed on to the Federal Prosecutor for a decision.

Cono Lancuba was also Deputy Federal Prosecutor during the investigations concerning the Cirillo affair, and is now thought to have tried to cover up the fact that the Christian Democrats negotiated with Raffaele Cutolo. Amongst his alleged manoeuvres in this context were: privately advising witnesses not to mention certain facts, rewriting certain passages of an indictment written by another magistrate, and forging a letter supposedly written by Judge Carlo Alemi.[28]

Supergrass Salvatore Migliorino has stated that when he was facing trial for extortion at the Torre

Annunziata fish market, once he had paid $55,000 to a go-between who took the money to Cono Lancuba, 'The trial went really well – it was never spoken about again', i.e. all charges were dropped.[29]

However, this is not to say that all judges are corrupt and linked to the Camorra, far from it. Investigating magistrates are probably the people most at risk from assassination, they work in inadequate conditions, and in the majority of cases are really dedicated to their job. The point is that, while a majority might well be honest, a powerful minority are not, and these dishonest ones have powerful political friends.

Furthermore, senior judges are also senior members of the Italian state. As a group, for decades they turned a blind eye to the rampant corruption and bribery among politicians and the business community, as well as to politicians' links with organised crime. In the final analysis they are an integral part of that system, and it is in their own interests to defend it. In other words, magistrates are part of a ruling class, and even Pasquale Galasso, who was outside this grouping, was able to identify the common ground they shared:

> At the bottom of it all there is a strong sense of friendship between Gava and Lancuba, or Gava, Scotti and Lancuba, or Gava, Scotti, Lancuba and Bargi and others, it was a bit of a magic circle. Over time, between 1986 and 1987, I then found out that other people were part of this group: journalists, and representatives of various institutions.[30]

Maybe this magic circle came into play again when Cono Lancuba was recently convicted of these crimes, including membership of a Camorra gang, or perhaps it was the sheer familiarity of these events which led the Anti-Mafia Commission to complain: 'It was greeted with very little interest by the local press.'[31]

As to the judiciary's relations with politicians, it is the widespread toleration and practice of illegality by politicians themselves that lead the judiciary to be selective in the application of the law, as any campaign for consistent judicial values would entail a head-on collision with the judiciary's political over-seers. Consequently the administration of justice, too, is far from equal: an unemployed seller of contraband cigarettes is far more likely to spend time in jail than a gang leader accused of murder or drug trafficking.

But as has been the case with politicians defending their interests as a group when faced with requests to remove parliamentary immunity, so too will the judiciary defend its own power and privilege. During his period as Naples' federal prosecutor, Alfredo Sant'Elia once explained why he asked a deputy prosecutor to reduce the seven-year sentence demanded for a regional councillor facing charges of extortion. Sant'Elia began by telling his subordinate that the accused was:

a person of higher social extraction, so I gave him the same explanation I normally gave when I was at the bench myself. The physical and moral suffering which is inflicted on a prisoner of a higher social extraction is far greater than that of a common prisoner or a common criminal, because I believe that if any of us were to be so unlucky as to end up in Regina Coeli or Poggio-reale, our suffering would be totally different from that endured by somebody born in the backstreets of Trastevere or Via Toledo.[32]

Not surprisingly, even the most senior members of the judiciary have now been forced to admit the real extent of the problem. Soon after his appointment, the current federal prosecutor Agostino Cordova was very pessimistic about the possibility of cleaning things up. If, as the government's senior legal representative in Naples, Cordova could publicly outline the area under his jurisdiction in the following terms, then the idea of the system reforming itself appears naive in the extreme:

> a territory totally penetrated by the Camorra and political-administrative poisoning which implies above all – and this is an aspect which has been completely ignored – the poisoning of the bureaucracy. The various individuals under investigation, who have managed senior government responsibilities, have placed their followers throughout all structures of the state and public bodies; these people have stayed at their posts because nobody has identified them. If these polluted structures survive it is an illusion to believe that the situation will change, as the old perverted system will remain along with the same secret power groups, but with different faces.[33]

Cordova was discussing the Christian Democrats without naming them, and wondering, pessimistically, whether their system could be overcome. Several years later, after the experience of Italy's first centre-left government in the postwar epoch, he was probably even more downbeat: 'Criminality has never been as powerful as it is today. In Naples the state is a vague, virtual and random entity. I'm only talking about the official state, not the real one. The only one that people in Naples really fear and recognise is the Camorra.'[34]

Such an opinion calls for a discussion of the main left party, the Left Democrats (DS), and their recent role in positions of power.

The failure of the DS in Campania

For decades the Italian Communist Party (PCI) was the main political opposition to the Christian Democrats. In 1991 the PCI became the openly social-democratic PDS, and in 1998 changed its name again to the DS, moving even closer to the political centre. Not only is its history of opposition to the dominant system important, the real nature of some of the local councils it has controlled also needs to be discussed.

When the PCI gained control of Naples city council in 1975 there was dancing in the streets, such was the enthusiasm of its members and supporters. Yet the very years of Maurizio Valenzi's administration, 1975 to 1983, were the crucial years of Camorra expansion, due to contraband cigarettes, drugs and earthquake reconstruction contracts. Sadly, the history of Valenzi's council is a useful illustration of the futility of trying to effect lasting change through the existing system because there was a fatal flaw at the administration's heart: a keen willingness to govern with elements who view corruption, clientelism and links with *camorristi* as being the most normal thing in the world.

The power of the forces that Valenzi now recognises he had to contend with during the earthquake reconstruction period provides sobering thought:

After the earthquake, organised crime began finding political friends in the opposition, in the construction business, in the city's infrastructure. With their political friends, they held up the money for the reconstruction until after the election of 1983, so we were seen to fail, and they to succeed.

Contracts would disappear up north and come back as sub-contracts to *camorristi*. We realised that we had no real control.

Now, they simply pick candidates off the lists; they offer to get them votes in return for contracts and favours. And it's not just the politicians – it works right across the system. There is a trial, so they need lawyers. You go in a lawyer, you come out a *camorrista*.[35]

Most of the period of the Valenzi council coincided with the PCI's 'historic compromise' with the Christian Democrats, a policy that led to profound demoralisation within the party, and eventually, to significant levels of corruption.[36] Although the PCI never governed directly with the DC in Naples, the whole party was nevertheless orientated towards the maximum accommodation possible.

One of the immediate consequences of the historic compromise was a haemorrhage in party membership: in the period from 1976 to 1981 the PCI lost 33,825 party members in the South, or in other words a 10% fall in five years.[37]

Consequently, at their February 1982 southern conference, party leader Enrico Berlinguer called for the PCI to become a 'party of struggle' and to forget about becoming a 'party of government'. But despite the authority of his leadership:

Berlinguer's strategy, and the strategy of most of the party's national leadership, was not at all popular among some sectors of the PCI; this was particularly so with party members active in local administration in the South. Berlinguer and Occhetto were reproached for proposing 'a far too rigid political orientation, exclusively based upon struggle and not upon proposals for government'.[38]

After so long in opposition, communists who had finally tasted power were unwilling to break comfortable working alliances and risk their position by launching a radical political campaign against the Christian Democrats. And Neapolitan communists, whose vote had held up better than the communist vote in most other areas of the South, were amongst the strongest critics of Berlinguer's new strategy.

In other words, communist militants had begun to be seduced by the temptation of power and privilege. And as the years progressed, some senior communists were sucked deeper and deeper into the shady and corrupt world inhabited by Christian Democrats and Socialists, and significant numbers ended their political careers sharing their values.

Antonio Pastore, the PCI's administrative secretary in Naples from 1975 to 1991, was arrested in April 1993 and charged with soliciting and obtaining bimonthly bribes for the party from companies building the new Naples underground line. The agreement, to finance all major parties, appears to have been made prior to 1980, even before the Camorra's systematic rise to power – and at the very time when 'the party of clean hands', the PCI, was controlling the city council. Apparently $720,000 per year was paid to the main parties: the DC and PSI sharing 40% between them, while the PCI took 40% on its own.[39] For the PCI this meant $288,000 per year.

Both Pastore and Berardo Impegno – a senior councillor for most of the 1980s within the communist opposition group on the city council and provincial party secretary – who acted in tandem, took kickbacks of $200,000 for building work related to the 1990 World Cup. Part of the agreement between the PCI and companies hoping to gain building contracts was that communist councillors guaranteed their appearance in council meetings in order to make them quorate. In other words, they were being paid appearance money, both in the sense of their physical presence and their apparent opposition to certain decisions.[40]

Impegno also seems to have been the leader of a group of PCI councillors and party bureaucrats who took $400,000 for themselves during 1988 and 1992, as a result of a council plan to privatise rubbish collection. The money was given in order to guarantee a 'soft' opposition to privatisation when it was debated in the council and in the appropriate committee.[41]

Impegno went to jail for these crimes, but also faced charges of taking a $80,000 bribe in 1991 from a major builder, who needed the full approval of Naples city council for the building of 140 houses at Soccavo worth $18.4 million. The Christian Democrat deputy mayor allegedly told the builder: 'My dear fellow, you either give them something or they will hold up construction until you die.' The investigating magistrate eloquently wrote in his indictment:

This matter testifies to the enslavement of public administration to corrupt politicians, and shows how both differences and battles between political parties, and the disputes between the ruling group and the opposition, are merely a facade which hypocritically masks premeditated decisions and precise agreements over the division of illegal gains.[42]

This particular payment was only one in a series which were made to four other major parties.

This is not to tar all of the DS with the same brush. After all, had the entire party had been as corrupt as the Christian Democrats it would have suffered the same fate and imploded under mass arrests.

Instead, the DS regained control of Naples city council in November 1993, electing Antonio Bassolino as mayor. Although people did not dance in the streets this time as they did back in 1975, Bassolino's administration was certainly very popular in its early years. The city centre became cleaner, safer, and tourists were visiting the city once more. This popularity was proved again in 1997, when Bassolino was re-elected mayor with a huge vote of 73%.

Yet over time the council's intrinsic economic weakness began to tell. Although it is the largest employer in the region, the council employs just under 20,000 people in an urban area of three million; thus it cannot change unemployment levels by direct recruitment. In financial terms it is not independent, it relies on state contributions, and therefore state politics, for 60% of its income.[43] So although Bassolino may have cleaned up and reopened historical buildings in the city centre, life in the suburbs and nearby towns changed very little. A survey published by the Italian equivalent of the *Financial Times* in 1999 put the Province of Naples in 101st place out of the 103 Provinces in Italy as regards the general quality of life. It was 98th out of 103 for unemployment, and bottom in terms of the city's services and environmental quality.[44]

This growing dissatisfaction explains Bassolino's decision to retire early as mayor in May 2000. However, despite his personal honesty and commitment, his behaviour has often not been replicated by other DS politicians in Campania.

DS politicians were already linked to the Camorra in the early 1990s: when the town council of Pagani was disbanded for presumed Camorra infiltration it had a DS mayor, similarly DS councillors were part of the ruling group in the disbanded councils of Herculaneum, Nocera and Sessa Aurunca.[45] Even Pasquale Galasso, in his small home town of Poggiomarino, could notice a certain social ambivalence in supposed 'communist' councillors: 'They are good professional people who I have always admired. I used to go to University with some of them.' [46]

Another worrying sign was the agreement by the DS to run joint tickets with the Popular Party, essentially the remnants of the Christian Democrats, during the local council elections held in many Campanian towns in November 1994.

A Camorra supergrass named Ciro Vollaro made serious allegations against the DS mayor of Portici, Leopoldo Spedaliere, in December 1998. Although it is possible that Spedaliere may have been unaware of the gang's electoral support, Vollaro has also stated that in addition he gave the mayor a weekly supply of cocaine. In return, according to Vollaro, the mayor facilitated the gang winning several important construction contracts, from which the DS later got a kickback of up to 20% of the tender price. Vollaro also says the gang refurbished DS party offices in Portici.[47]

Giovan Giuseppe Palumbo, the DS mayor of Pigna-
taro Maggiore near Caserta, was first accused of being
the front man of a local gang by the *carabinieri* in 1994,
soon after being elected. In the summer of 2000 it
emerged that he had kept a judicial order to seize land
and property from a local gang secret from the rest of
his administration for up to three years; when this
was discovered most councillors resigned, thus
forcing his resignation as well.[48]

But the most serious recent case involving the
Camorra and the DS occurred in the town of Pompeii,
next door to the World Heritage archaeological site. In
April 2001 police arrested 57 people, also impounding
39 companies, 124 properties, 54 cars and 107 bank
accounts – all linked to the Cesarano clan. A press
release spoke of their 'absolute and complete control'
of the local area, including 'direct intervention in both
the contracts awarded by the local council, and more
in general, in all the sensitive decisions made by the
administration'.[49]

It soon emerged that the DS mayor, Giovanni Zito,
was under investigation for association with the
Camorra, while another DS councillor and president
of the council, Giuseppe La Marca, was immediately
taken to jail accused of being a member of the Cesarano gang.[50] Supergrass Domenico Cuomo recounted
La Marca's long-term links with the Cesarano clan:
'He was a building surveyor who told us about jobs
he had heard about; this carried on from 1988–89
until my arrest … Apart from him telling us, we also
used him to 'close' the extortions … The money was
given to Giuseppe La Marca, who then brought it to
us.' [51]

Another *camorrista* had a lesser view of La Marca's
role:

In reality I didn't need La Marca because the situation was so tight that it was the builders of Scalati themselves who contacted me when they were about to start work ... I closed the extortion on my own, I don't remember the precise amount now, but it was between 4% and 5% of the total value of the contract.[52]

In a bugged telephone call Camorra businessman Luigi D'Apice showed that the gang effectively controlled council contracts. In the middle of a conversation with La Marca present, he criticises the head of the council's technical services division, who was obviously not part of the gang: 'There's no reason for him to know whether Giuseppe La Marca, Luigi D'Apice or Donnarumma are behind that contract: "The councillor has said that this is what has to be done, full stop." He shouldn't know who is behind it – this is what it means to have a strong council!'[53] Of course there was never any real 'politics' associated with La Marca's membership of the DS. Similarly, the Cesarano clan deliberately supported both opposing lists in the June 1999 elections, in order to influence both groupings and make them aware of the gang's ability to mobilise votes.

The primary purpose behind listing these specific cases is not to attack individual politicians but to illustrate the atmosphere that exists within the DS. None of these individuals could have made these decisions without many other senior party members being aware of their actions. Ultimately one has to make a collective judgement on the nature of the party, putting to one side the latest individual scandal.

Despite its origins in Italian communism, the DS leadership remains thoroughly committed to defending existing institutions and power blocs, or in other words, a ruling class which has always had close links with the Camorra: from ordinary police officers to senior officials, from court ushers to senior judges, from council clerks to government ministers, and from small businesses to international conglomerates, the DS essentially wants to maintain the current system of power.

But DS members, as well as their many working class supporters, have interests diametrically opposed to a system dominated by the ruling class and the Camorra: it is in their interests to destroy the present system and create a new one based on political and economic equality.

Some people may say this is a dream, yet it is both a necessary and feasible dream, and infinitely preferable to the very real nightmare which most people have experienced in Naples and Campania throughout the last century.

The inhabitants of Campania and Naples have a long history of fighting from below to get rid of the Camorra. The case for the importance of mass resistance to the Camorra relies on two main arguments: the first is that it is the most efficient way to counter Camorra intimidation. While it is easy to threaten individuals, the continued mass harassment or general social isolation of even low-level Camorra activities is a method over which Camorra gangs cannot bring direct pressure to bear. Strike action against Camorra infiltration of a workplace, or local harassment of drug pushers, or even contraband cigarette sellers, would be concrete steps not only towards combating the Camorra, but crucially towards socially isolating Camorra activity.

The second argument is broader but strategically linked to the first: it is ordinary people who suffer most from the dominance of the Camorra, and who therefore have the greatest interest in establishing a new political system in which organised crime is not supported by state institutions. Indeed, ordinary people have been systematically deceived by those institutions, which have historically perpetuated a socioeconomic environment of mass unemployment, illegality and violence. In more than a hundred years, no attempts at 'reform' have substantially solved the problems which have afflicted Naples and Campania. None of the major political parties has been prepared to overthrow the existing system of capitalism, the only way in which the dominance of illegality and criminality can be brought to an end.

Yet, despite frequent racist stereotyping, Campania also has a long and impressive history of mass movements against both the existing political system and organised crime in particular.[54]

The first modern movement developed in the early 1980s, when it became clear that the Camorra was attempting to gain control of reconstruction contracts and obtain influence over many local councils. In late 1982 groups of students began to organise systematic protests against the Camorra: in early November several dozen held a demonstration during a funeral at Acerra, and two weeks later 5,000 marched in Ottaviano – the home town of Raffaele Cutolo – then at the height of his power.

On 24 November another 5,000 students took to the streets in Torre del Greco, this time supported by trade unionists and a delegation of students from Palermo; shops also closed as a sign of solidarity. A few miles to the north, at Afragola, hundreds of students crowded into a library to debate how to fight the Camorra.[55]

Three days later another demonstration of 5,000, mainly made up of students but also including workers, was organised by women's committees in Castellammare.[56] And two weeks later students, teachers and other workers marched from Nocera to Pagani, while on the other side of Vesuvius two simultaneous marches were organised: one from Afragola and one from a factory threatened with closure at Casavatore, which met up at Casoria in a rally of 10,000. In a particularly important development, building unions organised a simultaneous half day strike in the same area against Camorra infiltration of sites engaged in earthquake reconstruction work.[57]

The following week Cutolo's home town of Ottaviano witnessed a second, larger demonstration of students and workers, whose main demand was 'jobs to beat the Camorra'.[58]

After Christmas, activity moved to Naples, where shopowners organised a two-day strike against Camorra protection rackets, an action which turned the city into a ghost town.[59] The high point of this whole campaign occurred two weeks later, with a massive national demonstration of at least 100,000 in Naples, backed up by a two hour general strike. The march was a mile and a half long, took 90 minutes to pass, and included significant delegations from all the Italian regions, and numerous contingents of blue and white collar workers, the unemployed, and women's organisations.[60]

The demands raised by this movement revealed an incisive political understanding, for example one of the banners read: 'The Cirillo affair taught us that the Mafia and the Camorra are inside the state.' This slogan summed up a contradiction which existed – and still remains – at the heart of any strategy aimed at defeating the Camorra: the very institutions called upon to defeat organised crime both tolerate and encourage it. This is why such an impressive movement eventually went down to defeat. The politicians called upon to take action, indeed some of the very politicians who received a delegation from the February 1983 demonstration, were discovered ten years later to have been in league with the Camorra even then.

Some priests too have taken a courageous stand against the Camorra. The most famous recent example was Don Peppino Diana, notable due to his murder in March 1994. His town, Casal di Principe, was infested with the Camorra: two years before his death the council was disbanded for Camorra infiltration, and the local MP was Alfonso Martucci, mentioned in chapter seven. Despite this atmosphere, he organised marches, wrote articles, mobilised young people, refused donations to the parish from certain individuals, and was murdered three days after a long meeting with investigating magistrates.[61]

The unemployed too have frequently made the link between the growth of the Camorra and high unemployment, and have periodically demanded jobs – something absolutely essential as the long-term unemployed are the people most likely to join a gang. Not only has there been an organised movement of the unemployed in Naples for nearly three decades, the unemployed in towns such as Acerra periodically protest and demand work: in the mid-1990s the town experienced 100 demonstrations in a single year.[62] The problem they face, as ever, is an economic system dominated primarily by considerations of private sector profit.

The previous year the nearby town of Aversa had seen a national 'march for legality' of over 10,000 people: made up mainly of young people, but also trade unionists, temporary workers, pensioners and Mayor Bassolino from Naples.[63] One wonders, given past history, whether all the 100 MPs and 60 Senators who took part were genuine in their anti-Camorra commitment?

One positive development in recent years has been the creation of a tradition of strong public protest immediately after a specific Camorra outrage. For example, following the murder of an innocent passer-by, 5,000 students took to the streets in September 1997.[64] Similarly, a week after a car bomb exploded in the Sanità area of Naples, 3,000 people marched demanding the Camorra leave the area.[65] And in Caserta, 4,500 marched against another outrage in January 1999.[66]

One of the best responses in recent years was the decision of the trade unions to hold their traditional May Day march in 1997 not in the city centre but in Secondigliano, following yet another Camorra murder.[67] Similarly, there was a general strike of all unions in Campania in March 1998, with one of the main demands being that the institutions launch a serious offensive against the Camorra.

These examples show that Neapolitans want to be active in getting rid of the Camorra from their lives. Although most demonstrations have now become a bit ritualistic this is far from saying these activities are useless. Neither is it being suggested that demands should not be made of the institutions and leading politicians. What is essential in any long-term strategy is clarity over the fact that the institutions will frequently lie and stubbornly resist any substantial change. A radically different approach is needed to combat the Camorra, one which is outlined in greater detail in the concluding chapter.

Ha dda passà 'a nuttata[1]

Words are easy words are cheap.

Yothu Yindi

As we have seen, over its recent history the modern Camorra has taken on three distinct forms: Raffaele Cutolo's 'mass Camorra', Lorenzo Nuvoletta's 'business Camorra' and Carmine Alfieri's 'political Camorra'.

The most recent form of Camorra is 'political' in the sense that for many gangs based outside Naples the main source of profits is probably public sector contracts awarded by politicians, rather than the drug trafficking or contraband cigarette activities favoured by many Neapolitan clans.

This 'political' form of Camorra has also been innovatory in its attempt to create a federation between gangs to overcome the mutual suspicion and blood letting which has normally prevailed.

The attempt to reach a wider agreement between gangs began in the mid-1980s, when the 'maxi-blitzes' of 1983–84 were in the past, and when Cutolo's NCO had clearly been destroyed. The fact that by then most reconstruction contracts had been assigned also led to a decrease in friction.

The end of the Bardellino-Nuvoletta war, which had culminated in the Torre Annunziata massacre of August 1984, ushered in a few years of relative peace. But following the slaughter of Gionta's gang in Torre Annunziata, and the murder of Ciro Nuvoletta two months earlier, the balance of power was shifting increasingly in favour of Carmine Alfieri.

Alfieri wanted to set up a unitary vertical structure within Campania to replace the traditional unregulated 'horizontal' system in which no one gang ever attempted to give orders to the others. However, he had learnt from Cutolo not to try to impose an oppressive monolithic structure, and one of his key allies in this project was Gennaro Licciardi, who had built up a lot of respect and notoriety in Naples over the years thanks to his ability to act as a mediator between various gangs.[2]

While Alfieri's gang dominated the area around Nola, within Naples at this time the major gangs were led by Gennaro Licciardi, Edoardo Contini in the Arenaccia, the Giulianos in Forcella and the Lo Russos in Secondigliano. However, the dividing lines between territories were sometimes quite mobile, and control of some spheres of operation extended far beyond a particular gang's area; furthermore gangs would often cooperate on operations that required large amounts of capital or human resources. Nevertheless, the plan was that Licciardi would control Naples and Alfieri the Provinces.[3]

Alfieri's grouping was the dominant element in this tentative alliance. It is clear that between 1984 and 1989 he managed – through a toleration of local, lower-level autonomy – to gain control of a huge area surrounding Vesuvius. This ran from his home town of Nola in the north-east, to San Sebastiano in the

north-west, down to Castellammare di Stabia in the
south-west and Pagani in the south-east.[4] The various
local gangs in this alliance included Michele
D'Alessandro in Castellammare, Mario Fabbrocino's
gang based in San Giuseppe Vesuviano and the
surrounding towns and the Galassos in Poggiomarino.

The relative calm of the late 1980s suggests that a
higher degree of agreement between gangs had been
achieved. A key element in this coordinated strategy
was to keep Camorra activity out of the public eye. For
example, instead of bombing building sites as an
intimidatory warning, two people would be sent on a
scooter to fire warning shots at workers; while this
was perhaps even more frightening than an overnight
bombing, it did not normally lead to media attention.
One reason for the decrease in the murder rate was
that the number of kneecappings rose to over 200 in
the Province of Naples alone during 1988,[5] indicating
a deliberate policy of not drawing attention to
Camorra activity and rivalry.

Pasquale Galasso has confirmed this strategy, but
has also revealed the existence of different levels of
'Camorra':

Things were getting out of hand so people
thought it would be useful to create a coalition of
the most violent groups, the ones which were
more rooted in local areas, so that all those little
vendettas and wars could be brought to an end
and peace could be established. This is convenient for the more powerful Camorra groups
given their links and agreements with other institutional and political circles ...

When there's no war, when nothing's
happening, you can work in peace. Certain

relationships can be made stronger, and all our
movements take place smoothly, the police have
no need to harass us and we aren't distracted by
worries.[6]

The success of this strategy was such that by 1990
investigators had reached the conclusion that Alfieri
had created:

a kind of anti-state, with its own laws and regulations, such as to guarantee for the organisation
uncontested engagement in typical criminal
activities and other activities associated with
Mafia methods. Furthermore, all of this took
place mainly through the conditioning of, and
often the open complicity of, public administrators and officials.[7]

However the plan soon began to unravel for a variety
of reasons, the most immediate being the revelations
of a number of supergrasses, beginning with the
professional killer Pasquale Frajese in March 1990. It
was these supergrasses who initially destroyed
Alfieri's grand design, in that between 1991 and 1992
most major Camorra gang leaders were captured by
the police: Carmine Alfieri, Michele D'Alessandro,
Valentino Gionta, Gennaro Licciardi, Ciro Mariano
and Lorenzo Nuvoletta. It would appear that they
were caught largely as a result of tip-offs, although
there was also an element of investigative skill in
some cases.

The instability caused by these arrests led to a
number of notable massacres during 1992: five
people were killed in Acerra on May Day, another five
in Secondigliano seventeen days later, with another

four murders in Mugnano, near Marano, in September.

Another key reason for the collapse of this more federal structure was widespread political instability within Italy. The fall of the Berlin Wall in 1989 had removed the main justification for keeping the Communist Party out of government, which in turn led to a loss of credibility for the Christian Democrats. Once the stability and permanence of the old political system were cast into doubt, relations between politicians and *camorristi* entered a state of flux, which still seems to prevail today. This instability deepened in 1992 with the beginning of the *Tangentopoli* scandal in Milan, with the old Christian Democrat order finally being overturned in the March 1994 elections.

In assessing why Carmine Alfieri was unable to create a stable federation of Camorra gangs before his arrest in 1992, one must not underestimate the underlying general importance of the social and political structure of Campania. As the American academic James Walston has argued, while in the provincial towns 'gangsters might control the local council ... in the city and region as a whole there is too great a heterogeneity for one social group to gain control'.[8] And he adds: 'Neapolitan society is too fragmented, as indeed one would expect of a city of two million people to be, to allow a single figure (or group) to control the whole or even a fractional part of the whole.'[9]

However there are also subjective reasons for the lack of a unified structure and a single leader, as a senior investigator has argued:

The reality of the Camorra is that there has never been one, and probably there could never be one

... for a certain period this was the dream of Raffaele Cutolo, i.e. becoming the undisputed leader of the entire Camorra, but his evil dream was shattered by the New Family alliance ...

If we were to define criminal organisations as being made up of logical, rational and sensible people – people who are building for the future – and who are therefore able to give something up in order to create this future, then we would never have had outrageous actions which have led either to the defeat or weakening of criminal organisations.

For example we wouldn't have seen Judge Falcone killed, or Borsellino, because they were very negative moments for the Mafia. We wouldn't have had the massacre of Torre Annunziata or many of the other massacres perpetrated in Naples, which have definitely been negative moments for them.[10]

In the final analysis, it is the attacks on 'internal' targets rather than 'external' ones which prevent the creation of a unified structure. As another senior investigator has commented recently:

Neapolitan criminality is different from Sicilian criminality because it is characterised by a series of vendettas which are never-ending. Therefore it is difficult to bring about reconciliation among people who have suffered mutual deaths ... And then the Province of Naples is characterised by a very high number of organisations in comparison to Sicily.[11]

None of these limits on greater Camorra unity makes the sum total of Camorra gangs any less dangerous.

Compared with the Mafia, the Camorra has more of a 'horizontal' than a 'vertical' structure, so individual gangs act by and large independently of one another. On the whole, this makes the Camorra more resilient when top leaders are arrested, or when a gang war erupts. In Pasquale Galasso's words, 'Campania can get even worse because you could cut into a Camorra group, but another ten could emerge from it.'[12]

This tendency is described in greater detail by the Anti-Mafia Commission:

> The Mafia is separated from society; its hierarchical structure makes it an organisation which immerses itself in social life without being part of it.
>
> On the contrary the Camorra, with over a hundred gangs, its speedy substitution of leaders and rapid processes of disintegration and reconstitution, its use of social desperation, is capable of reproducing itself wherever an illegal avenue gives a young person the impression of being able to build a future.
>
> For the great number of the young and very young who can be manoeuvred by Camorra bosses, legality has never represented either dignity or a future. They have never managed to identify with legality; on the contrary, all they have seen is the crisis of institutions which should have preserved, defended and administered legality.[13]

There was considerable optimism in the mid-1990s that the Camorra was facing a massive defeat. Not only had Alfieri and others been arrested, other bosses such as Gennaro Licciardi, Lorenzo Nuvoletta and

Michele Zaza all died in mid-1994. Another reason for hope was the rapid rise in the number of super-grasses: Pasquale Galasso decided to collaborate with investigators in mid-1992, Umberto Ammaturo in 1993 and Carmine Alfieri in early 1994.

The optimism over supergrasses displayed an igno-rance even of recent Camorra history, in the sense that previous waves of supergrasses did not stop the overall growth of the Camorra over time.[14] This opti-mism was even more misplaced because it ignored the social and economic reality which leads to the growth of the Camorra. The 1990s saw, essentially for the first time in modern Italian history, an alternation of right and left-wing parties in government; an event that may have blinded some observers as regards one crucial factor which has remained unchanged. Despite this political variation, unemployment in the South has continued to rise: in 1993 the rate in Campania was 18.9%; in 2001 it was 23.3%.[15]

The consequences in terms of criminal behaviour can be predicted quite easily. As an ex-*camorrista* has simply observed: 'If you've got a job and I haven't, if you've got a house and I haven't, it's obvious I'm going to come and steal from you.'[16]

This underlying reality explains why, despite some partially favourable circumstances in the mid-1990s, the Camorra has maintained its strength, and even made another attempt at creating a more organised structure – what became known as the 'Secondigliano alliance'. Gennaro Licciardi built up his gang in the early 1990s in Secondigliano, a northern suburb of Naples. One investigating magistrate characterised their strength thus: 'It was based on the number of members they had. They recruited by the hundred, even giving people guns in their hands.'[17]

Gennaro Licciardi's death in 1994 produced some uncertainty and some bloody bids for power, but over the years his role was slowly taken on by his sister, Maria. Despite being able to build alliances throughout the city and to its north, the characteristic nature of Camorra gangs eventually made itself felt once again. The Lo Russo family eventually split from the alliance, in a dispute over a $400,000 drug payment,[18] causing a general destabilisation and a massive gang war, including the use of car bombs and bazooka attacks. Despite spending much of her time in the Czech Republic, Maria Licciardi was finally arrested in June 2001,[19] an event which probably signals the end of the Secondigliano alliance.

The names of current gang leaders who may prosper, die or be arrested, are: Edoardo Contini, Giuseppe Misso, Pasquale and Salvatore Russo and Michele Zagaria. Given the nature of the Camorra, it is pointless to try and make any accurate predictions over its future; what is more useful is to examine why so many strategies have failed to prevent its resurgence in the past.

Failed economic attempts to curb the Camorra

As we have seen in chapter one, during a period of significant industrialisation in the early part of the last century, and the subsequent growth of a working class, the Camorra went into decline. In other words, real economic development can make a difference in reducing the appeal of criminal activities.

However, following the hiatus of the inter-war Fascist period, the major postwar innovation throughout the

South was the setting up of the Southern Development Fund in the early 1950s. In the short term this was aimed at alleviating the immediate economic hardships which the southern population endured, and in the long term, at closing the huge economic gap between the North and the South.

By the 1960s it had become clear that its original targets were not being reached, so it was hoped that a law passed in 1971 – which restructured the financing of the Fund through a new policy of 'intervention through projects' – would overcome many of the problems. Some of the new proposals involved plans to end pollution in the Bay of Naples, intensive meat production and better communications within Campania. But with hindsight it can be seen that the improved communications and better meat production achieved also led to the strengthening of political clientelism and the growth of the Camorra, and the Bay of Naples is still severely polluted.

By the 1980s the whole Fund had become a public scandal as it was clear that it had achieved very few of its objectives, and was therefore wound up. It is estimated that the almost inconceivable figure of $320 billion had been spent on fixed capital investment in the South over a forty-year period, with the money mainly going to public works programmes, infrastructure and industry.[20] Yet more than anything else this expenditure aggravated regional differences and bolstered a corrupt political system, the exact opposite of what its original supporters had intended.

The same tendency can be seen again in two further specific events: following an outbreak of cholera in Naples in 1973, millions were spent on water and sewage plants, yet once again the sea remained as polluted as ever. More recently there has been the scandal of the billions disappeared from earthquake reconstruction funds during the 1980s. Of the $40 billion spent on earthquake reconstruction, it has been estimated that $20 billion went to 'create an entirely new social class of millionaires in the region', $6.4 billion went 'straight into the pockets of the Camorra' and $4 billion went to politicians in bribes. Only the remaining $9.6 billion, i.e. just 24% of the total amount, was actually spent on people's needs.[21]

The Anti-Mafia Commission recently stated what has been the norm in Campania for at least the last two decades:

> The conclusion to be drawn is certainly a bitter one: public sector contracts continue to be a major area of interest for the Camorra, and this carries the grave risk that the more the state invests in the South (a necessary and urgent activity in order to intervene upon the socio-economic fabric which lies at the roots of the expansion of Mafia-type phenomena), the more the Camorra will build up its business affairs.[22]

However it would be a mistake to respond to all this by accepting one of the key economic mantras of the witch-doctors of privatisation currently applying their 'medicine' in many advanced countries, i.e. 'You can't solve problems by throwing public money at them.' The real problem in Campania and the rest of the South has never been that money was simply thrown into the wind; more often than not it has been pocketed by corrupt politicians and businessmen, or alternatively passed on to the Camorra or the Mafia. The crucial issue as regards economic development – whether in Italy, Britain or the US for that matter – is the political control of public finances, not that money well spent is unable to make a positive difference.

The fundamental purpose of public expenditure should be, in the long term, to create the conditions for independent economic development. Yet Campanian politicians have used finances in such a way as to delay development and make people even more dependent on state handouts. Organised crime also holds back development, as it is largely parasitical on public sector contracts and generally invests in either non-productive or labour-intensive industries.

The problem therefore has never been a lack of money, but a political system unwilling or unable to generate economic growth. In 1997 just 16.6% of EU regional development funds set aside to alleviate unemployment in Campania were actually spent.[23] Two years later Prime Minister D'Alema admitted that Italy was only using 7% of the EU funds available in 1997, but stated that by 1999 the figure had risen to 58–59%.[24] The explanation for such behaviour, as we shall see below, is that real economic and social development of the area would jeopardise the control of the local ruling class.

Having analysed the difficulties associated with economic development, we now turn to the issue of crime repression, another area commonly held to be fundamental to any strategy for defeating organised crime.

The failure of repression

In 1963 Italy was outraged by the massacre of seven policemen in the Sicilian town of Ciaculli. One knee-jerk reaction was to send 10,000 troops to Sicily, who quickly arrested 1,200 people, mainly at roadblocks. On a political level, all parties united in condemning the attack, and after many years of resistance the Christian Democrats finally agreed to create a permanent parliamentary committee, the Anti-Mafia Commission. Over nearly forty years it has published dozens of hefty volumes of testimony and evidence. However, as one Mafia expert has commented, 'One has the impression that this institution has been used as a gym in which government forces allowed the left-wing opposition to land anti-Mafia punches on them, as long as they were thrown in a vacuum.'[25]

The Commission's first report took fifteen years to produce, and even then there was one majority report, and two minority reports written by left and right-wing MPs respectively. During its first decade the Commission largely analysed the Mafia as a mainly Sicilian phenomenon. Although the president of the Commission Francesco Cattanei produced a very perceptive report in 1972, as one historian has argued, 'One cannot avoid asking why twenty (or close to thirty) years have passed in vain since the Cattanei report; allowing the Mafia to penetrate further into state institutions, local administrations and the social fabric of Italy throughout the 1990s.'[26]

It was only in the 1970s that organised crime became a serious problem in other regions of the South, as well as branching out overseas and within the ranks of government in Rome. The growth of organised crime in the 1970s forced politicians to move beyond the mere analysis presented by the Anti-Mafia Commission and take more concrete measures. The Mafia had by now not only managed to dominate and increase the international heroin trade but had also left behind a series of 'illustrious corpses', primarily policemen, politicians and journalists. The most prominent corpse of this period was General Carlo Dalla Chiesa, who had played a major role in defeating the Red Brigades in the 1970s.

Despite the fact that he was given unprecedented powers and enjoyed considerable public support, he was murdered in a car bomb attack in September 1982, just three months after arriving in Sicily. Public outrage exploded at a similar level to that which followed the death of Judges Falcone and Borsellino ten years later, and a new investigative judicial structure was immediately created, the High Commission against the Mafia.

However it soon became clear that the High Commission was being used by the government as a means to deflect public criticism, as a kind of shock absorber for the Christian Democrats. Indeed Giovanni Falcone wrote shortly before his death: 'Ministers of the Interior and the government as a whole have been able to place the blame on the institution for anything which hasn't worked, and attribute to it responsibility for every failure.'[27] Even when the High Commission was given greater powers in November 1988 there was no improvement in its activities, as a minority parliamentary Anti-Mafia Commission report noted: 'After more than a year since the passing of these reforms, compared with the considerable extension in the High Commission's powers, there has not been a corresponding increase in anti-Mafia action.'[28]

Nine days after the murder of Dalla Chiesa, i.e. at the same time as the High Commission began its work, the 'La Torre' law (named after an MP murdered shortly before Dalla Chiesa), was also passed. For the first time this introduced the specific crime of Mafia membership, as well as the right to seize illegal assets.

A further spate of laws were passed in 1991: in March Parliament introduced measures giving greater protection to supergrasses, in May it passed a law that required greater openness in the tendering of public contracts, and in December an anti-extortion law was approved. In the same month the DIA (the National Anti-Mafia Coordination) was created; it largely superseded the High Commission and, like an Italian version of the FBI, was designed to coordinate all three police forces.

In July 1991 the Minister of the Interior was given powers to disband councils believed to be infiltrated by criminal organisations and to call fresh elections 18 months after their dissolution. Yet the fact that *all* councillors are thrown out of office simply produces greater cynicism and does not help people to distinguish between politicians presumed to be honest and those suspected of criminal activities.

But, as with so many of these laws, it is a case of window dressing, in the sense that they only deal with the symptoms of a problem rather than the cause. The arrival of one honest Extraordinary Commissioner cannot drastically change the way medium-sized towns have been run for several years, so it is not surprising to learn that: 'The Extraordinary Commissioners have in many cases taken on absolute power without, however, radically changing things, as was requested.'[29]

In February 1994 a new law came into force against the buying and selling of contraband cigarettes. Anyone who bought illegal cigarettes would now have to pay a $65 fine; while street sellers risked up to four years in jail. As was predicted by some, the law was not really enforced due to the social tension it would have created. As the Anti-Mafia Commission recently admitted, 'It did not lead to a significant change in behaviour,'[30] either by street sellers, or by local policemen. But even if it had been enforced, the people who earn their living in this way would simply have been forced to move on to other activities, with predictably negative consequences.

Once again, tackling the symptoms of crime will have no long-term benefit if the causes of crime are not eradicated – and the causes are quite obvious. As an ex-*camorrista* once remarked about his own area where, he estimates, 90% of the population earn their living illegally: 'It's enough that these 90% are put into a different situation – and this is what they really want – they want legality, they want to lead a normal life, to go off to work in the morning and not have anything to do with guns, violence or prison.'[31]

The main effect of most of these laws is to fill up jails with people on remand – almost half of those in Campanian jails are there on remand, and although the jails were only built to hold 4,822, there are in reality 6,597 inmates.[32] And those closer to the ground have an accurate picture of what such imprisonment may mean, as the Naples police chief once said: 'The majority of crimes which happen outside are organised from inside jails.'[33] Even in free market capitalist terms, this is all proving to be a huge waste of money. Under the law of 'unjust detention', in 1992 the Italian state was forced to pay out $2.2 billion in 197 cases; in 1999 this had trebled to $6.4 billion and 738 cases. The Naples Appeal Court dealt with 449 cases, the highest of any courthouse.[34]

Meanwhile, law-makers are incessantly trying to legislate away problems: for example the law on preventative custody was changed thirteen times in the period from 1986 to 1996.[35] And between 1975 and 1994 Parliament passed thirty-five laws relating to organised crime.[36]

The other response is a knee-jerk military reaction following some particular outrage. In 1994 'Operation Partenope' was launched – over 500 soldiers were stationed to guard courthouses for eighteen months.[37] In September 2000 'Operation Gulf' was announced; another 500 soldiers at a cost of $2.7 billion per month.[38]

But as the jails fill to bursting, the MPs debate and pass laws late into the night, and the army patrols city streets, organised crime continues to grow to unprecedented levels. One recent report has estimated organised crime's economic activities to be worth the equivalent of 15% of the nation's GNP: moneylending and extortion rackets alone are estimated to bring in $20,000 billion, the equivalent of the government's entire public sector debt.[39]

There is a strange irony to the fact that it is ex-*camorristi* who are able to recognise, albeit in a distorted fashion, the brutal truth of 'law and order' campaigns: 'Through this instrument – the struggle against the Camorra and the Mafia – they create Camorra and Mafia. They create and use it for anti-democratic goals.'[40]

If attempts at economic improvement have failed due to the vested interests of the local ruling class, and repression has failed for the same reason – but also because masses of desperate people are forced to risk death and imprisonment just to survive – then there clearly needs to be a fresh and broader approach.

The solution to the deep-rooted nature of organised crime in Campania needs a far more radical solution than the user-friendly packaging and right wing revivalism which characterises Silvio Berlusconi and his Forza Italia organisation.

What is urgently needed is real grass-roots campaigning. Two positive developments in this area during the 1990s have been a growth in demonstrations against the Camorra, and a widespread 'education in legality' programme within schools. But these initiatives by and large do not involve those people who are close to the Camorra out of economic necessity – i.e. poor working-class people. The dangers of middle-class campaigning have to be learned from Sicily, where the extraordinary mobilisation following the murders of Judges Falcone and Borsellino in 1992 led to the growth of many anti-Mafia associations. Yet a survey later revealed that 63% of the leaders of these associations were over 40, and 60% had university degrees.[41] To put things bluntly, because this movement was unable to mobilise working-class people with ideas and proposals which appealed to them, many of these people quickly reverted back to being influenced by the Mafia.

The creation of a climate of legality, or to be more precise the freedom to engage in democratic debate and activity without arbitrary intimidation, has rightly always been a basic demand of any grass-roots campaigning. But it should be borne in mind that the whole tradition of the state structure in the South, as a leading DS politician from near Naples, Isaia Sales, has pointed out, has always relied on a rather flexible notion of legality:

> Variations in the level of legality have served as an instrument of social control in the South. This

unusual political adaptation of the concept of
legality has meant that for long periods the South
did not socially explode but instead imploded
along criminal lines.[42]

Any left-wing government intending to initiate
radical reforms would find itself immersed in this
tradition of ambiguous and shifting legalities. It
would rely on the existing judiciary, police forces and
state bureaucracy to carry out its plans for fighting
organised crime. In other words, it would not be in a
position to solve a contradiction which has been
repeatedly highlighted: 'Even though there are laws of
the land, the men who manage these democratic laws
are anti-democratic.'[43]

Examples of the futility of relying on the state
machinery have been seen first with the Communist
Party Naples council from 1975 to 1983, and in a
different fashion with the DS-led Bassolino administration from 1993 to 2000. It has of course been seen
on a national scale during 1998–99, i.e. during the DS-
led government of Massimo D'Alema.

Even if a local or national government far more
radical than those above were ever elected, powerful
economic forces have a variety of tactics to bring politicians back in line: companies could go on
investment strike nationally and invest overseas; they
could destabilise the currency through speculation
and pressure on interest rates; they could refuse to
provide credit to government organisations or to place
orders with them. The problem for radical politicians
in all these circumstances is that Parliament has no
power to control such manoeuvres.

The same can be said for the machinery of state. If
certain reforms were perceived as damaging to the

interests of the state bureaucracy or the judiciary, they could either be circumvented or delayed for long periods by provoking administrative chaos or simply refusing to obey instructions. If, for example, senior investigators were to refuse to investigate the foreign bank accounts of senior politicians or business people on the pretext that the request had a political rather than a judicial basis, then there would be no other body capable of taking on this task.

Why the institutions cannot beat the Camorra

What is striking about the Camorra is that, in the space of twenty years, an organisation which was believed to be on the verge of extinction grew to rival the Mafia in terms of power and influence.

Over these two decades the more powerful gangs became semi-autonomous from local politicians and were no longer purely parasitical in the way they accumulated wealth. Their control over significant economic resources has meant that the traditional patron-client relationship with politicians has in some cases been turned upside down. Many politicians, judges, businesses and even parties have sponsored the Camorra within their own field of influence, thus becoming lobbyists for Camorra interests.

Although the Mafia may still have more international power, the Camorra can draw on far stronger social and economic roots than its Sicilian counterpart. It commands a higher level of mass social legitimacy due to its capacity to provide employment for tens of thousands of people. As one magistrate put it: 'In many areas of this region the Camorra is not viewed as a negative phenomenon to be fought, but as the expression of a justified revolt against a corrupt, distant and inefficient state.'[44]

The Camorra probably has an even closer relationship with the local ruling class than the Mafia, a hypothesis supported by the lack of 'illustrious corpses' left behind by Camorra gangs. The local political traditions of extreme centralisation, bureaucracy and clientelism, have always nurtured a network of local mediators and brokers. These, in turn, have favoured the involvement of organised criminals, first as a group of subaltern brokers hired to provide votes, and later as semi-independent power-brokers in their own right.

However the advantages which politicians receive have always gone beyond the creation of an electoral base. It can easily be argued that organised crime performs a vital, and perhaps even more efficient role of social control than the official representatives of law and order, as the fear it instils in the population, and the precarious or oppressive nature of employment in criminal enterprises, serve as useful shock absorbers for ruling politicians and powerful business interests.[45]

One only needs to imagine what a huge difference it would make if organised crime lost its dominance in the urban areas of the South: firstly, there would no longer be such widespread fear of speaking out against a whole series of injustices, and secondly – and perhaps more importantly – it would change people's expectations concerning employment.

Once violent intimidation and a climate of illegality are removed from the workplace, workers would begin to organise and come to expect a whole series of changes as their automatic right: permanent employment contracts, the application of health and safety legislation, payment of overtime and shift work rates, trade union representation, regular pay increases and so on.[46]

But in an atmosphere of widespread illegality, things are often distorted and are not what they seem. For example building workers have fought long and hard to get rid of Camorra intimidation within their workplaces, and now they sometimes find themselves in the opposite situation, i.e. with a suspiciously high level of wages and decent conditions. One trade union leader in Naples recounts:

Where the Camorra does exist, things are often done legally. This is because the Camorra's profits don't come from that particular workplace. A Camorra company, or a company linked to the Camorra, doesn't want to 'waste time' keeping its workers off the books. It would be like a bank robber escaping down the motorway at 100 mph only to get stopped by the police for speeding. The earnings of the Camorra, especially when it becomes a business, come from money laundering, through false accounting.[47]

Another official from the same trade union concurs: 'We often find that they pay all their taxes and social security contributions. And the salaries can even be generous. They recognise trade unions; we're allowed to hold meetings, we've never been threatened.'[48]

This is a perfect illustration of how deep-set problems are, and how it is not enough just to mobilise working-class people for rights which are taken for granted in many other countries. The Camorra is so deeply embedded in society, that to defeat it society needs to be rebuilt from the bottom up.

Therefore the changes which the extinction of organised crime would bring to the South would be
extremely threatening to the ruling class: most businesses would face higher wage bills as workers began
to organise themselves, and politicians would be
selected or deselected on the basis of their
programmes rather than the favours they are
presumed to be in a position to make.

In short, for the southern ruling class organised
crime has become a vital mechanism in maintaining
its power and privilege. During his deposition to the
Anti-Mafia Commission, Pasquale Galasso spoke for
many of his fellow Neapolitans when he challenged
the MPs listening to him to undermine their own
position by dealing with the social causes of organised
crime. His statement also perhaps revealed some of
the reasons which led him to cooperate with the
police:

At the end of the 1970s I used to socialise and
take part in political meetings. Everybody liked
us; I met Gava and all those politicians.

Then at a certain point in my life I became a
criminal and met them again, this time in meetings on the other side of a table – even a young
bobby on the beat knows about this!

This is something that you don't want to deal
with or perhaps you don't want to believe, also
because you're split into so many corporations.
Forgive me, these are my ideas, I want to
unburden myself and bring them to your attention.

This is too much! Can't you see the state
Naples is in? My contemporaries, people who
studied with me and who now have degrees,

after thirty years of studying have to turn to their fathers every Friday and Saturday for a fiver because they're unemployed ...

If you don't change this social reality, if you don't get at its roots, how do you think you're going to beat the Camorra? My own personal belief is that criminals will spontaneously disappear if each one of you plays your part.[49]

But the southern ruling class does not want to deal with the root problems within society, which lead people towards criminal activity, because this would place its own rule in jeopardy. It will therefore resist fundamental change and have no scruples about encouraging illegality and the growth of organised crime if this helps to defend its power and privileges. This is why any strategy for defeating organised crime has to involve the overthrowing of the ruling class and their capitalist system through the creation of a completely different system.

A different system of economic and social equality, in other words a socialist system, would vastly reduce the temptation for masses of people to embark on a life of crime. The widespread material desperation and long-term insecurity in southern Italy makes a criminal choice inevitable for large numbers of people; the possibility of huge wealth compared to a normal miserable existence is a temptation difficult to resist.

Although they are a small minority in society, it is encouraging that notorious ex-*camorristi* or super-grasses have begun to understand how the existing capitalist system destroys the lives of so many ordinary people in the South. As Pasquale Galasso again has observed:

Over the years I have understood that the whole
sequence of murders which destroyed me and my
family, and many others throughout Campania, is
in the final analysis a part of these politicians'
manoeuvres. They are prepared to run away and
wait for the winner, with whom they will then
make an alliance to manage elections and business affairs.[50]

And elsewhere he comments: 'My town, Poggiomarino, is a backwater, it is a town mistreated by these
politicians and the government. There's nothing
there, no industry, not even a tiny little factory of ten
workers.'[51]

In terms of creating a political alternative to the
present system, the fundamental problem with
choosing a criminal career is not that current laws are
not respected, but rather that poor people look for an
individual solution to their common situation of
poverty. Any political strategy aimed at ending organised crime and the political system it is part of, and
which involves masses of people, clearly needs to
resolve this weakness.

Even the realisation of the need to become politically active implies a monumental improvement in
traditional political awareness; in the words of Nunzio
Giuliano: 'Those who have ruled the South have never
had the intention of creating mass awareness; they
have wanted to perpetuate, at all costs, a low level of
culture or even ignorance.'[52]

In order for these political, economic and ideological changes to take place, the southern masses,
together with their counterparts in the North, need to
organise themselves collectively into a party which is
prepared to lead the way towards these changes.

What is beyond doubt is that the main political parties are unwilling to take on this role. Just as the Christian Democrats started to work with organised crime from 1945 onwards, so did the Socialist Party several years after joining government in 1963, and so has the DS at a local level. The track record and traditions of Italian political life illustrate that any solution to the problems posed by the Camorra cannot come from government and its state machinery – they are very much part of the problem rather than part of the solution.

The wealth of evidence of the links between organised crime and the political and economic elite can only lead to one conclusion: any political strategy that leaves the foundations of the existing system intact is a proposal which accommodates to and favours organised crime.

In recent years a new set of ideas which reject the capitalist system have been growing around the world, including Naples and Campania. One of the main slogans of this movement is very adapt in describing the qualitative leap which needs to be taken to rid Naples of the Camorra: *another world is possible.*

Tables

Table 1: Comparative statistics of Camorra and Mafia activity

	Camorra/ Campania	Mafia/ Sicily
Councillors debarred for illegal acts (1990–93)	64	26
MPs/Senators indicted for criminal association (1993)	8	3
Magistrates indicted for favouring crimin. assoc's (1993)	16	3
Value of assets impounded in $million (1993)	210	105
Murders linked to organised crime (1991–97)	874	816
Councils disbanded for criminal infiltration (1991–97)	44	27
Estimated no. of members of organisations (1997)	6,700	5,500
Total no. of extortions reported (1993–99)	3,480	3,375
Total no. accused of usury/money-lending (1993–99)	2,924	2,594
Total no. of arrest warrants (1992–2000)	1,739	1,579
Value of assets confiscated in $million (1992–2000)	375	3

Source: Anti-Mafia Commission, DIA, EURISPES, Ministry of the Interior.

Table 2: Sectoral employment in Campania, 1911

Province	Agriculture and fishing	Industry
Avellino	161,209	8,466
Benevento	108,270	6,363
Caserta	260,073	26,674
Naples	109,277	91,389
Salerno	178,154	25,227
Total	816,983	158,119

Source: F. Barbagallo, 'Sviluppo e sottosviluppo agli inizi del Novecento', pp 395 & 397, in F. Barbagallo (ed.), Storia della Campania, vol. 2. (Guida Editori, Naples 1978)

Table 3: Unemployment among 14–24 year-olds in 1979

Region	Unemployment (%)
Calabria	40.5
Campania	38.2
Lombardy	15.6
Piedmont	20.7
Sicily	33.6
Veneto	17.2

Source: D. Sassoon, Contemporary Italy. Politics, Economy & Society since 1945, p 112. (Longman, Harlow 1986)

Table 4: Murders in Naples and the Province of Naples, 1975–92

Year	Deaths	Year	Deaths
1975	49	1984	160
1976	56	1985	150
1977	51	1986	106
1978	62	1987	134
1979	85	1988	171
1980	148	1989	231
1981	235	1990	230
1982	265	1991	233
1983	197	1992	174

Source: I. Sales, La camorra, le camorre, p 252. (Editori Riuniti, Rome 1993)

Table 5: Southern politicians charged with 'neglect of public duty' (as a percentage of charges nationwide)

Year	%
1976	56
1977	48
1979	51
1980	52
1982	63
1983	61
1984	60

Source: M. Cammelli, 'Governo locale e sistema amministrativo nel Mezzogiorno', p 433, in Il Mulino no. 329, no. 3 May/June 1990.

Table 6: Councils classified as damaged before and after
May 1981

| Province | No. of local councils | Number of councils classified as damaged: | |
		before May 1981	after May 1981
Avellino	119	104	119
Naples	91	67	86
Potenza	98	46	98
Salerno	157	66	157
Benevento	78	–	78
Caserta	104	–	102
Matera	31	–	31
Foggia	64	–	14

Source: A. Becchi Collidà, 'L'evoluzione della legislazione post-
terremoto', p 24, in L'affare terremoto. (Comitato Regionale del
PCI campano, Naples 1989)

Table 7: Number of inmates in Campania's youth
detention centres as a percentage of detention centre
inmates nationwide

Charge	Percentage of national total
Murder	8.0
Attempted murder	22.6
Attempted robbery	10.6
Robbery	8.9
Violent robbery	36.5
Extortion	21.3
Drug-related crimes	23.8

Source: Anti-Mafia Commission report, 21 December 1993.
Published as Rapporto sulla Camorra; p 77. (L'Unità, Rome 1994)

Table 8: Crimes and indictments in Campania, 1989

	No. of crimes	No. of indictments	No. of unprosecuted crimes
Theft	102,436	4,427	99,315
Armed robbery	8,856	935	8,274

Source: ISTAT, statistiche giudiziarie.

Table 9: Crimes in Campania and number of cases in which legal proceedings had begun, 1989

	No. of crimes reported	Legal actions begun	No. of unsolved crimes
Theft	119,073	2,373	116,700
Armed robbery	15,889	347	15,542
Extortion	814	145	669

Source: ISTAT, statistiche giudiziarie.

Table 10: Economic status of those convicted in Campania, 1989

	Employed	Unemployed*
Contraband	106	278
Possession of arms	178	360
Extortion	45	111
Murder	124	234
Producing, selling and buying drugs	189	493

Source: ISTAT, statistiche giudiziarie.
*These figures include students, housewives and pensioners.

Notes

Introduction

1. *The Observer*, 3 February 2001.
2. *The Guardian*, 1 May 2001.
3. *Corriere della Sera*, 21 August 1993.
4. *The Economist*, 5 February 1994.
5. See D. Gambetta's review of L. Ricolfi, *L'ultimo parlamento: Sulla fine della prima repubblica* (Nuova Italia Scientifica, Rome, 1993) in *L'Indice,* July 1994.
6. Professor Claudio Lodici, in *The Observer*, 22 April 2001.
7. See *Il Manifesto*, 11 March 2001.
8. *The Observer*, 22 April 2001.
9. *The Economist*, 28 April 2001.
10. See A. Jamieson, *The Antimafia*, pp62–7. (Macmillan, Basingstoke 2000).
11. *L'Unità*, 24 August 2001.
12. *Il Manifesto*, 10 May 1994.
13. *The Sun*, 18 June 1983.
14. *Daily Mail*, 11 June 1991.
15. *The Guardian*, 29 March 1993.
16. Anti-Mafia Commission report on the Camorra approved on 21 December 1993, published in book form by *L'Unità* in February 1994 and entitled *Rapporto sulla camorra,* p166.
17. Commissione Parlamentare di inchiesta sul fenomeno della mafia e sulle associazioni criminali similari, *Relazione sulla criminalità organizzata in Campania,* 24 October 2000, p85. (Camera dei Deputati, Rome 2000).
18. *Il Mattino*, 7 June 2001. This is the main daily newspaper in Naples.

19. *Il Manifesto*, 13 February 1994.
20. *Il Mattino*, 24 September 1999. Many other examples are given in *Il Mattino*, 19 January 1999.
21. *Il Mattino*, 14 September 1999.
22. *Liberazione*, 24 February 2002.
23. *Il Mattino*, 16 February 1997.

Chapter 1: The origins of the Camorra and the Mafia

1. See M. Short, *Murder Inc.: The Story of Organised Crime*, p19. (Thames/Methuen, London 1984)
2. See I. Sales, *La camorra, le camorre*, p26. (Editori Riuniti, Rome 1993)
3. Ibid, p65. For a discussion on the origin of the word itself, see G. L. Messina, *L'etimologia di mafia, camorra e 'ndrangheta.* (Bonanno Editore, Arcireale 1990)
4. See G. D'Agostino, *Per una storia di Napoli capitale,* p131. (Liguori, Naples 1988)
5. Sales, *La camorra*, p32.
6. See J. A. Davis, 'Oligarchia capitalistica e immobilismo economico a Napoli 1815–60' in *Studi Storici*, 1975.
7. Sales, *La camorra*, pp35–6.
8. M. Monnier, *La Camorra: Notizie storiche raccolte e documentate,* p121. (Argo, Lecce 1994) This is a reprint of a book first published in 1863; written by a Swiss academic who lived in Naples from 1855–64, it is one of the best contemporary accounts of the Camorra's early growth.
9. Sales, *La camorra*, p72.
10. D'Agostino, *Storia di Napoli*, p146.
11. Monnier, *La camorra*, p47.
12. Ibid, p127.
13. Ibid, p128.
14. Ibid, pp112–3.
15. Ibid, p115.
16. Ibid, p118.
17. See D. Demarco, 'L'economia degli stati Italiani prima dell'unità' in *Rassegna storica del Risorgimento*, 44, 1957.
18. Monnier, *La camorra*, p84.
19. Ibid, pp129–30.

20. 'A curse upon this liberty.' This is a phrase from a song of one of the bandit groups which roamed the southern countryside after Unification, and refers to the lack of freedom experienced under the new Italian government.

21. L. Romano, *Memorie Politiche*, p50. (Naples, 1873)

22. See H. Acton, *The last Bourbons of Naples*, pp485–90. (Methuen, London 1961)

23. Monnier, *La camorra*, p138.

24. Ibid, p140.

25. M. Marmo, 'La camorra e lo Stato liberale', p19, in F. Barbagallo (ed.), *Camorra e criminalità organizzata in Campania*. (Liguori, Naples 1988)

26. See Demarco, 'Economia degli stati italiani.'

27. M. Marmo, 'Ordine e disordine: la camorra napoletana dell'Ottocento' in *Meridiana*, no. 7–8, 1989–90, p161.

28. Quoted in N. Dell'Erba, *Le origini del socialismo a Napoli (1870–92)*, p22. (Franco Angeli, Milan 1979)

29. Quoted in P. Ricci, *Le origini della camorra*, pp94–5. (Edizioni Sintesi, Naples 1989)

30. See Dell'Erba, *Origini del socialismo*, pp7 and 9.

31. Quoted in Sales, *La camorra*, pp100–1.

32. E. Ciccotti, *Come divenni e come cessai di essere deputato di Vicaria*, p63. (Naples, 1909)

33. See Sales, *La camorra*, p107.

34. Figures quoted in G. Aragno, *Socialismo e sindacalismo rivoluzionario a Napoli in età giolittiana*, p93. (Bulzoni Editore, Rome 1980)

35. *Guappo* is a Neapolitan word generally used to denote a senior member of a criminal gang, often prepared to use violence. Like *guapparia*, it can also refer to an individual's attitude.

36. See R. Minna, *Breve storia della Mafia*, pp17 and 25. (Editori Riuniti, Rome 1984)

37. See A. Blok, *The Mafia of a Sicilian Village, 1860–1960*, pp89–102. (Waveland Press, Illinois 1978)

38. Minna, *Breve storia della Mafia*, p30.

39. Ibid, p32.

40. Quoted in R. Catanzaro, *Il delitto come impresa: Storia sociale della mafia*, p99. (Liviana Editrice, Padua 1988)

41. See U. Santino's *Storia del movimento antimafia* (Editori Riuniti, Rome 2000) for an excellent rebuttal of the

stereotype that Sicilians have never opposed the Mafia over the last century.

42. Sales, *La camorra*, p37.

Chapter 2: The postwar development of the Camorra

1. See P. Ginsborg, *A History of Contemporary Italy. Society and Politics 1943–88*, p37. (Penguin, Harmondsworth 1990)

2. G. D'Agostino, *Per una storia di Napoli capitale,* p184. (Liguori, Naples 1988)

3. The *Risorgimento* was the movement which led to the unification of Italy in the last century; one irony of this today is that it appears that the main supporters of unification, chiefly Count Cavour and the ruling House of Savoy in Piedmont, only intended to unite northern and central Italy. It was an expeditionary force led by Giuseppe Garibaldi which eventually forced their hand into uniting the whole peninsula.

   Trasformismo is a political term, normally used to describe a process that characterised the Parliament between 1860 and Mussolini's seizure of power in 1922, which involved the absorption of radical opposition into a non-threatening parliamentary force.

4. See the tables in G. D'Agostino, 'La politica in Campania nel quarantennio repubblicano', pp1075–84, in P. Macry and P. Villani (eds), *Storia d'Italia. Le regioni dall'Unità ad oggi: La Campania*. (Einaudi, Turin 1990)

5. See R. Minna, *Breve storia della Mafia*, pp49–50. (Editori Riuniti, Rome 1984)

6. Ibid, p50. See also the relevant sections of R. Campbell, *The Luciano Project: The Secret Wartime Collaboration of the Mafia and the U.S. Navy* (McGraw-Hill, New York 1977). Many ex American agents also admitted as much in a BBC2 *Timewatch* documentary broadcast in 1993, entitled 'Allied to the Mafia'.

7. M. Pantaleone, *The Mafia and Politics,* pp60–61. (Chatto and Windus, London 1966)

8. Minna, *Breve storia della Mafia*, p50.

9. This included two Ministers and dozens of MPs, generals, admirals, and so on; it was a kind of state within a state, pledged to help fellow members above everything else.

10. Quoted in T. Cliff and D. Gluckstein, *The Labour Party: A Marxist History*, pp196–7. (Bookmarks, London 1988)

11. J. Follain, *A Dishonoured Society*, pp220 and 225. (Little, Brown & Co, London 1995). When Vizzini died in 1954 his role at the top of the Mafia was taken up by Don Giuseppe Genco Russo, whose criminal history was similar: in 1928 he was acquitted of five murders, in 1929 of four, in 1930 of three plus three attempted murders, in 1931 of being a member of a criminal organisation, in 1932 of three murders. However he was convicted of conspiracy to commit a crime in 1932, and served three years of a six year sentence. The Allies appointed him mayor of Mussomeli in 1943.

12. See for example the letter written by the American Consul General in Palermo to the Secretary of State on 21 November 1944, in A. Jamieson, *The Antimafia*, p75. (Macmillan, London 2000)

13. R. Catanzaro, *Men of Respect: A Social History of the Sicilian Mafia*, p115. (The Free Press, New York 1992)

14. G. Di Fiore, *Potere camorrista: Quattro secoli di malanapoli*, p134. (Guida Editore, Naples 1993)

15. P. Maas, *The Valachi Papers*, p139. (Panther, St Albans 1970)

16. Pantaleone, *The Mafia and Politics*, p64.

17. Ginsborg, *A History of Contemporary Italy*, p37.

18. A leading postwar *mafioso*, quoted in C. Sterling, *The Mafia: The Long Reach of the International Sicilian Mafia*, p68. (Grafton, London 1991)

19. Pantaleone, *The Mafia and Politics*, p64.

20. Ibid, pp64–5.

21. Ibid, p65. The original Italian edition, *Mafia e politica (1943–62)*, was published by Einaudi in 1962.

22. Minna, *Breve storia della Mafia*, p51.

23. Quoted in Sterling, *The Mafia*, p95.

24. Ibid, p97.

25. This is a legal measure, in which people considered to be potentially dangerous within their normal area of residence can be sent to another part of the country, where they are required to periodically report to the police.

26. 'La malavita organizzata in Campania,' in *Nord e Sud* no.18, April–June 1982, p15.

27. G. Fabiani and S. Vellante, 'L'evoluzione delle strutture agricole 1921–71,' p464, in F. Barbagallo (ed.), *Storia della*

Campania, vol. 2. (Guida Editori, Naples 1978)

28. Ibid, p456.
29. Ibid, p406.
30. Contemporary newspaper statistics, quoted in P. Allum, *Politics and Society in Post-war Naples,* p106. (Cambridge University Press, London 1973)
31. Ibid, p82.
32. N. Ajello, 'La camorra vestita di grigio' in *L'Espresso*, 15 November 1964. A *guappo* is a Neapolitan word generally used to denote a senior member of a criminal gang, often prepared to use violence.
33. C. Cederna, *Giovanni Leone: La carriera di un presidente*, p130. (Feltrinelli, Milan 1978)
34. G. Tutino, 'Camorra 1957', in *Nord e Sud* no.35, December 1957, p88.
35. C. Guarino, 'La Camorra', p553, in *Napoli dopo un secolo*. (Edizioni Scientifiche Italiane, Naples 1961)

These complaints raise the issue of developing a successful strategy for defeating organised crime, a debate which was to become far more important during the 1980s. The problem with calls for 'letting the police do their job' is that it ignores the political control which normally exists over the police in any parliamentary democracy. Although the secret services are often beyond parliamentary control, and senior policemen enjoy considerable operational autonomy at times of serious social unrest, such as riots and major strikes, this cannot be the case for a long-term campaign against a well-entrenched criminal organisation. In this case, any increase in police staffing, operations or powers, will almost invariably be initiated and supervised by politicians, the very politicians often suspected of being in league with organised crime. Furthermore, these calls for increased police powers also assume that the police are immune from criminal infiltration or blackmail.

The problem of the Camorra has not become so deep-seated in Naples because of a lack of police power; indeed police forces in the rest of northern and central Italy have managed to largely control organised crime using exactly the same powers which have failed in the South. The specific problem of the Naples area has been that long-term poverty has made criminal association an attractive prospect for large numbers of people.

36. See Sterling, *The Mafia*, p93.
37. *Nord e Sud* no.18, 1982, p12.
38. Ibid.
39. E. Mazzetti, 'Il "caso Campania" nell'evoluzione territoriale del Mezzogiorno', p105, in *Nord e Sud* nos.19–20, July–Dec. 1982.
40. Ibid, p113.
41. Ibid, p111.
42. Ibid.
43. Ibid, p113.
44. G. Montroni, 'Popolazione e insediamenti in Campania (1861–1981)', p250, in Macry and Villani, *Storia d'Italia*.
45. Allum, *Politics and Society in Post-war Naples*, p154.
46. Ibid, p160.
47. Mazzetti, 'Il "caso Campania" nell'evoluzione territoriale del Mezzogiorno', p109.
48. P. Villani, 'L'eredità storica e la società rurale,' pp88–89, in Macry and Villani, *Storia d'Italia*.
49. P. Cotugno, E. Pugliese and E. Rebeggiani, 'Mercato del lavoro e occupazione nel secondo dopoguerra,' p1173, in Macry and Villani, *Storia d'Italia*.
50. A communique released by the PCI branch nearest the docks on 22 March 1960, quoted by C. Guarino, 'La Camorra', p547.
51. See Sterling, *The Mafia*, pp190–1.
52. *Nord e Sud* no.18, 1982, p15.
53. Di Fiore, *Potere camorrista*, p150.
54. N. Chieppa, 'Dal contrabbando alla camorra e dal colera al terremoto' in *Osservatorio sulla Camorra* no.4, May 1985, pp59–60.
55. F. Barbagallo, *Il potere della camorra*, p6. (Einaudi, Turin 1999)
56. Quoted in I. Sales, *La camorra, le camorre*, p152. (Editori Riuniti, Rome 1993)
57. See Chieppa, 'Dal contrabbando alla camorra e dal colera al terremoto,' p59.
58. *Nord e Sud* no.18, 1982, p16.
59. Quoted in Sterling, *The Mafia*, p201.
60. Di Fiore, *Potere camorrista*, p165.
61. *Nord e Sud* no.18, 1982, pp16–17.
62. For further details, see 'Sentenza-Ordinanza n.1140/81 contro Sabato Saviani e 261 altri,' Tribunale Penale di Napoli, 21 January 1983, pp87–91. (Hereafter 'Sentenza contro Saviani'.)
63. P. Monzini, *Gruppi criminali a Napoli e a Marsiglia*, pp139–40. (Donzelli, Rome 1999)

64. R. Cutolo, *Poesie e pensieri*, p56. (Berisio, Naples 1980)

65. *Nord e Sud* no.18, 1982, p17.

66. See M. Massari, *La Sacra Corona Unita*, pp10–14. (Laterza, Rome-Bari 1998)

67. See 'Sentenza contro Saviani,' pp82–4.

68. Cutolo, *Poesie e pensieri*, p89.

69. 'Sentenza n.80/88 contro Cutolo Raffaele e 17 altri,' Corte di Assise di Napoli, 4 November 1988, pp364–5.

70. Statistics taken from ISTAT, the government's statistical office, quoted in D. Sassoon, *Contemporary Italy. Politics, Economy & Society since 1945*, p214. (Longman, Harlow 1986)

71. Statistics quoted in Sales, *La camorra*, p166.

72. L. Rossi, *Camorra: un mese ad Ottaviano*, pp32–33. (Mondadori, Milan 1983)

73. Statistics quoted in Sales, *La camorra*, p164.

74. 'Sentenza-ordinanza n.1935/84 contro Amendola Giuseppe e altri,' Tribunale Penale di Napoli, 28 March 1985, p15. (Hereafter 'Sentenza contro Amendola'.)

75. Ibid, p14.

76. Ibid, p16.

77. Sales, *La camorra*, p192. These figures can be compared to the 'roaring twenties' (1922–32) in Chicago, when 'only' 680 were murdered.

78. *Nord e Sud* no.18, 1982, p17.

79. S. De Gregorio, *I nemici di Cutolo*, p12. (Pironti, Naples 1983)

80. 'Sentenza contro Saviani,' p109.

81. De Gregorio, *I nemici di Cutolo*, p16.

82. Di Fiore, *Potere camorrista*, p176.

83. Commissione Parlamentare di inchiesta sul fenomeno della mafia e sulle associazioni criminali similari, *Audizione di Salvatore Migliorino, 12 novembre 1993*, p3090. (Camera dei Deputati, Rome 1993)

84. 'Sentenza contro Amendola,' p25.

85. F. Feo, *Uomini e affari della camorra*, p55. (Edizioni Sintesi, Naples 1989)

Chapter 3: The 'administrative economy' and the 1980 earthquake

1. The recollection of the communist Mayor of Naples from

1975–83, Maurizio Valenzi, in A. Wanderlingh, *Maurizio Valenzi, un romanzo civile*, pp21–2. (Edizioni Sintesi, Naples 1988)

2. I. Sales, *La camorra le camorre*, p151. (Editori Riuniti, Rome 1993)

3. See P. Allum, *Politics and Society in Post-war Naples*, pp297–307, (Cambridge University Press, London 1973), for a description of the Gavas' rise to power.

4. P. Monzini, *Gruppi criminali a Napoli e a Marsiglia*, p61. (Donzelli, Rome 1999)

5. F. Barbagallo, *Mezzogiorno e Questione Meridionale 1860–1980*, p84. (Guida, Naples 1980)

6. Allum, *Politics and Society in Post-war Naples*, p322.

7. Interview with Maurizio Valenzi, 8 December 1992.

8. I. Talia, 'Il decentramento urbano ed industriale in Campania' in *Nord e Sud*, July–Dec. 1982, no.19–20, p122.

9. G. D'Agostino, 'La politica in Campania nel quarantennio repubblicano,' p1059, in P. Macry and P. Villani (eds), *Storia d'Italia. Le regioni dall'Unità ad oggi: La Campania*. (Einaudi, Turin 1990)

10. See M. Clark, *Modern Italy 1871–1982*, pp391–2. (Longman, London 1984)

11. Barbagallo, *Mezzogiorno e Questione Meridionale*, pp90–1.

12. Sales, *La camorra*, p205.

13. Ibid, p209.

14. G. Falcone, *Men of Honour*, pp134–5. (Warner Books, London 1993)

15. M. Cammelli, 'Governo locale e sistema amministrativo nel Mezzogiorno' in *Il Mulino* no.329, no.3 May/June 1990, p436. Apart from the expense of maintaining public parks, Naples has very little green space compared to other cities: 1.2 m² per inhabitant. This can be compared to 10.9 m² per inhabitant in Rome, 24.0 m² in London and 50.0 m² in Hamburg. See *Il Manifesto*, 1 May 1994.

16. Interview with Franco Malvano, 3 December 1992. Malvano was head of the Naples Flying Squad from 1982–6, and then became the city's Deputy Police Chief. Following the disbanding of Marano council for presumed Camorra infiltration, he was also appointed Special Police Commissioner with government responsibilities for Marano in October 1991, after three civilian Commissioners had resigned in fear.

17. Sales, *La camorra*, p150.

18. D'Agostino, 'La politica in Campania nel quarantennio repubblicano,' pp1059–60.

19. F. De Rosa, *Un'altra vita: Le verità di Raffaele Cutolo*, p24. (Marco Tropea, Milan 2001)

20. G. Di Fiore, *Potere Camorrista: Quattro secoli di malanapoli,* p191. (Guida, Naples 1993)

21. *La Voce della Campania*, November 2000.

22. A. Becchi Collidà, 'L'evoluzione della legislazione post-terremoto,' p29, in *L'affare terremoto*. (Comitato Regionale del PCI campano, Naples 1989)

23. I. Sales, A. Lamberti, A. Dottorini, A. Leone, 'Il Commissariato Regionale alla Ricostruzione,' in ibid, p76.

24. See EURISPES, *Rapporto Italia '94*, p638. (Koinè, Rome 1994)

25. Sales, Lamberti, Dottorini and Leone, 'Il Commissariato Regionale alla Ricostruzione,' p77.

26. Ibid, pp78–9.

27. *Il Manifesto,* 9 October 1984.

28. *L'Unità,* 11 October 1982.

29. *Il Manifesto,* 9 October 1984.

30. 'Lo Stato "collaudatore"' in *L'affare terremoto*, p119.

31. Ibid, p118.

32. Ibid, p126.

33. Ibid, p123.

34. A letter dated 27 October 1980, sent by the Prefect of Avellino to the Scalfaro Parliamentary Commission of inquiry, copy in author's possession.

35. *La Voce della Campania*, January 1999.

36. Historian Francesco Barbagallo, writing in *La Voce della Campania,* April 1989.

37. *La Voce della Campania,* January 1991.

38. Vito Di Virgilio, owner of a small construction company in Potenza, quoted in *Panorama,* 14 February 1993. Yet many of these very businesses had not complained when *they initially offered* bribes to politicians, which was generally how the system started, in order that competing firms could be shut out of the market.

39. *Panorama*, 4 February 1994.

40. *Il Mattino*, 12 September 1995.

41. *Il Mattino*, 23 November 2000.

42. F. Barbagallo, *Napoli fine Novecento. Politici camorristi imprenditori*, pp79–80. (Einaudi, Turin 1997)

Chapter 4: The 'business Camorra' of the Nuvoletta gang

1. The documentation in question is Judge Paolo Mancuso's 'Sentenza-ordinanza n.1873/84 contro Nuvoletta Lorenzo e 29 altri,' Tribunale di Napoli, 29 July 1989. (Hereafter 'Sentenza contro Nuvoletta')
2. 'Decreto n.64/91 contro Lorenzo Nuvoletta e 10 altri,' Corte di Appello di Napoli, 4 July 1991, pp21–2.
3. 'Sentenza n.286/63 contro Angelo Nuvoletta,' Pretura di Marano di Napoli, 28 October 1963.
4. C. Sterling, *The Mafia. The Long Reach of the International Sicilian Mafia*, pp141–2. (Grafton, London 1991)
5. S. De Gregorio, *I nemici di Cutolo*, p89. (Tullio Pironti, Naples 1983)
6. 'La malavita organizzata in Campania,' in *Nord e Sud* 18, April/June 1982, p23.
7. Cited in De Gregorio, *I nemici*, p88.
8. Ibid, p73.
9. 'La malavita organizzata,' p14.
10. See *carabinieri* report no.455/1 of 22 July 1981, quoted in 'La malavita organizzata', p24. See also De Gregorio, *I nemici*, p86.
11. 'La malavita organizzata,' p14.
12. P. Monzini, *Gruppi criminali a Napoli e a Marsiglia*, p129. (Meridiana, Rome 1999)
13. See C. Stajano (ed.), *Mafia: L'atto di accusa dei giudici di Palermo,* p28 and p93. (Editori Riuniti, Rome 1986)
14. 'Sentenza di appello n.15554/R/G93 contro Baccante Luigi e altri,' Corte di Assise di Appello di Napoli, 7 July 1999, pp16–21.
15. As recounted to P. Arlacchi in *Gli uomini del disonore*, p134. (Mondadori, Milan 1992)
16. Commissione Parlamentare di inchiesta sul fenomeno della mafia e sulle associazioni criminali similari, *Audizione di Pasquale Galasso 13 luglio 1993*, pp2241–2. (Camera dei Deputati, Rome 1993)

    Galasso goes on to claim that Nuvoletta's protection was provided by Christian Democrat politician Antonio Gava. Riina, Provenzano and Bagarella were all senior members of the Sicilian Mafia.
17. 'Sentenza contro Nuvoletta,' p115.

18. *La Voce della Campania*, March 1987.
19. These statistics are taken from a finance police report dated 18 December 1985, quoted in 'Sentenza contro Nuvoletta', p115.
20. Ibid, p181.
21. Ibid, p119.
22. Ibid, p273.
23. Ibid, p279.
24. Ibid, p276.
25. Ibid, p279.
26. *La Voce della Campania*, January 1991, and 'Sentenza contro Nuvoletta', p138.
27. *La Voce della Campania*, April 1988.
28. See *Il Mattino*, 25 August 1983. Relatively little has been written about the role of organised labour in opposing the Camorra. This is unfortunate, as it is potentially the most effective method of opposition.
29. Quoted in *Il Manifesto,* 28 November 1984.
30. Statement quoted in 'Sentenza contro Nuvoletta', p127.
31. Ibid, p122.
32. Ibid.
33. Quoted in V. Faenza, 'La camorra nelle amministrazioni comuali,' p133, in F. Barbagallo and I. Sales (eds), *Rapporto 1990 sulla camorra.* (L'Unità, Rome 1990)
34. Ibid.
35. *L'Attesa* (Marano), December 1999.
36. *La Repubblica,* 31 May 1991.
37. Statistics quoted in Faenza, 'La camorra,' p133.
38. Interview with Franco Malvano, 3 December 1992. Malvano was Head of the Naples' Flying Squad from 1982–86, and then became the city's Deputy Police Chief. Following the disbanding of Marano council for presumed Camorra infiltration, he was also appointed Special Police Commissioner with government responsibilities for Marano in October 1991 because three civilian Commissioners had resigned in fear.

    While allowing for a certain amount of exaggeration, the frequent irrelevance of official political affiliation is also confirmed from the opposite end of the spectrum, by supergrass Salvatore Migliorino. When asked about the political affiliation of the mayor of Torre Annunziata, with whom Migliorino had dealings for many years, he answered, 'He appears to be a socialist'; he then described two councillors as 'Between Christian Democracy and the Socialist Party' and another politician thus – 'I don't know whether he was a Republican or Social Democrat, I can't really remember.' See Commissione Parlamentare di inchiesta sul fenomeno della mafia e sulle associazioni criminali similari, *Audizione di Salvatore Migliorino 12 novembre 1993*, pp3102 and 3137. (Camera dei Deputati, Rome 1993)

39. *La Voce della Campania*, September 1989.
40. *L'Unità*, 3 May 1990.
41. *La Voce della Campania*, October 1992.
42. *Il Manifesto*, 26 January 1993.
43. *Il Manifesto*, 9 October 1984.
44. 'Sentenza contro Nuvoletta,' p32.
45. Quoted in ibid, p21.
46. Stajano, *Mafia*, p87.
47. See 'Sentenza-ordinanza n.1935/84 contro Amendola Giuseppe e altri', Tribunale Penale di Napoli, 28 March 1985, pp148–152.
48. *L'Unità*, 31 May 1990.
49. *Il Manifesto*, 9 October 1984.
50. *La Voce della Campania*, March 1987.
51. *L'Unità*, 31 May 1990.
52. 'Sentenza contro Nuvoletta,' p182.
53. 'Mandato di cattura n.104/86 contro Di Somma Raffaele e 5 altri,' Tribunale Civile e Penale di Napoli, 9 April 1986, p25. See also Barbagallo and Sales, *Rapporto 1990*, pp162–3.
54. 'Mandato di cattura n.104/86,' p5.
55. Ibid, p6.
56. Ibid, p15.
57. F. Feo, *Uomini e affari della camorra*, p68. (Edizioni Sintesi, Naples 1989)
58. Ibid, p71.
59. Ibid, p72.
60. *Il Manifesto*, 11 October 1992.
61. 'Sentenza contro Simonelli Vincenzo e 8 altri,' Tribunale di Napoli, 19 July 2000, p79.
62. Ibid, p80.
63. Ibid, p239. The invoicing, for which payment was received, was either for non-existent goods or services, or for larger quantities than those actually used.

64. Ibid, p200.

65. Interview with Judge Giuseppe Borrelli, 21 November 2000. The word 'decina' means 'a group of ten', whilst a 'capo-decina' is the boss of such a group. See the diagram on p172 of G. Falcone, *Men of Honour* (Warner Books, London 1993) for a more detailed explanation of the structure of the Mafia.

66. See T. Behan, 'Communism and Camorra in Naples,' in *Crime, Law and Social Change*, vol. 35, no.4, June 2001.

67. *La Repubblica*, 18 May 2001.

68. Interview with Francesco Cirillo, 2 February 1994. Cirillo is head of the Naples office of the *Direzione Investigativa Anti-mafia*, or Anti-Mafia Investigative Commission, a kind of Italian FBI created in October 1991.

Chapter 5: The Cirillo Affair

1. *L'Unità*, 4 August 1988.

2. Quoted in G. Di Fiore, *Potere camorrista: Quattro secoli di mala-napoli*, pp220–22. (Guida, Naples 1993) Nonno was later convicted of libel.

3. The film, a fictional account of Cutolo's criminal career, was entitled *Il Camorrista* and starred Ben Gazzara in the title role. Cirillo, renamed Mesillo in the film, probably took offence to the following dialogue set in a prison, in which a leading politician appealed to Cutolo, using his real-life nickname of 'the Professor': 'Councillor Mesillo does not have a strong character; he has been in politics for thirty years in Campania and knows many things. If he should give in to the terrorists' blackmail, confidence in the institutions would be severely compromised. So Professor, my party is asking you to take action to save the Councillor's life.' Despite no legal action being taken against it, the film disappeared from cinema and home video screens for several years; it was shown on television for the first time in March 1994. See the fascinating account in *Narcomafie*, October 1993.

4. D. Moss, *The Politics of Left-Wing Violence in Italy*, p66. (Macmillan, London 1989)

5. Quoted in 'Sentenza-Ordinanza contro Cutolo Raffaele e altri', Tribunale di Napoli, 28 July 1988. The quotation from the Red Brigades' communiqué in fact comes from a shorter,

edited version of 250 pages, rather than the 1,500 pages of the original sentence. See V. Vasile (ed.), *L'affare Cirillo: L'atto di accusa del giudice Carlo Alemi,* p8. (Editori Riuniti, Rome 1989)

6. 'Sentenza n.11219 contro Fabbrocino Mario e 94 altri,' Tribunale Civile e Penale di Napoli, 29 August 1983, p23.

7. *L'Unità,* 2 August 1988, quoting an October 1984 Parliamentary Committee report on information and security written by Senator Libero Gualtieri. See also I. Sales, 'Ciro Cirillo,' p47, in N. Tranfaglia (ed.), *Cirillo, Ligato & Lima: Tre storie di mafia e politica* (Laterza, Bari-Rome 1994).

8. Quoted in an Anti-Mafia Commission report on the Camorra approved on 21 December 1993, published in book form by *L'Unità* and entitled *Rapporto sulla camorra,* (Rome 1994), p125. Hereafter referred to as *Rapporto sulla camorra.*

9. Quoted in Vasile, *L'affare Cirillo,* p47.

10. 'Sentenza-Ordinanza n.1140/81 contro Sabato Saviani e 261 altri,' Tribunale Penale di Napoli, 21 January 1983, p49.

11. M. Figurato, *Patto inconfessabile: Politica, crimine e affari dopo il caso Cirillo a Napoli,* p48. (Pironti, Naples 1993)

12. Ibid, p41.

13. See *Il Manifesto,* 22 September 1994.

14. *La Voce della Campania,* December 1998.

15. Vasile, *L'affare Cirillo,* pp183–192.

16. Ibid, p98.

17. Ibid, p99.

18. See Sales, 'Ciro Cirillo,' pp69–73, for a detailed reconstruction of the likely amount and contributors to the ransom payment.

19. See *Rapporto sulla camorra,* p140, and U. Santino and G. La Furia, *L'impresa mafiosa: Dall'Italia agli Stati Uniti,* p330. (Franco Angeli, Milan 1990)

20. Vasile, *L'affare Cirillo,* p218.

21. *La Repubblica,* 23 May 1989.

22. Vasile, *L'affare Cirillo,* p165. Giovanni Senzani was one of those who interrogated Cirillo in the Red Brigades' 'people's prison'.

23. *Oggi,* 12 August 1981.

24. Vasile, *L'affare Cirillo,* p7.

25. *Rapporto sulla camorra,* p147.

26. Vasile, *L'affare Cirillo,* pp239–40.

27. Ibid, p244.

28. F. Tarsitano and S. Pastore, *Il Caso Cirillo. Parola d'ordine: inqui-nare*, pp88–9. (Tribunale di Napoli, Naples 1990)
29. Vasile, *L'affare Cirillo*, p139. Emphasis in the original.
30. *La Voce della Campania*, April 1988.
31. Ibid.
32. Vasile, *L'affare Cirillo*, pp158–9.
33. *La Repubblica*, 2 July 1993.
34. Pasquale Galasso's revelations are probably more important for understanding the Camorra than Tommaso Buscetta's have been in terms of understanding the Mafia. When Buscetta decided to cooperate with the authorities he had been living abroad for several years, away from the nerve centres of power. Galasso had been in the eye of the storm until his arrest, and had arguably played a more important role within the Camorra than Buscetta had within the Mafia.

    The fact that he confessed to over twenty murders, and indicated to the police where many of his victims were buried, makes it highly unlikely that Galasso might have any motive to invent his involvement in other crimes, such as those connected to the Cirillo affair. His credibility is still accepted by investigating magistrates today, as several major trials in Naples still feature Galasso as a witness.

    We shall discuss Carmine Alfieri's gang, of which Galasso was a leading member, in later chapters.
35. Commissione Parlamentare di inchiesta sul fenomeno della mafia e sulle associazioni criminali similari, *Audizione di Pasquale Galasso 13 luglio 1993*, p2313. (Camera dei Deputati, Rome 1993)
36. Ibid, pp2314–15.
37. Quoted in Vasile, *L'affare Cirillo*, p26.
38. Quoted in F. Barbagallo, *Il potere della camorra*, p19. (Einaudi, Turin 1999)
39. The Oxford Dictionary defines symbiosis as 'an association of two different living organisms attached to each other or one within the other, usually to their mutual advantage'. It is a concept frequently used by Camorra supergrass Pasquale Galasso.
40. Tarsitano and Pastore, *Il caso Cirillo*, p50.
41. Originally quoted in 'Richiesta di autorizzazione a procedere nei confronti di Antonio Gava, Raffaele Mastrantuono, Vincenzo Meo, Paolo Cirino Pomicino e Alfredo Vito', Direzione Distrettuale Antimafia, Naples, 6 April 1993. The same

document has been produced in book form by M. Coscia (ed.), *Il patto scellerato – potere e politica di un regime mafioso,* p197. (Crescenzi Allendorf, Rome 1993). Hereafter referred to as 'Il patto scellerato'.

42. Coscia, *Il patto scellerato*, p242. Salvatore Alfieri, Carmine's brother, was murdered five months after Cirillo's release, in December 1981.

43. *Audizione di Pasquale Galasso 13 luglio 1993*, p2264. The Dorotea faction was formed in the 1950s, and was, roughly speaking, a centrist faction within the DC.

44. *Rapporto sulla camorra,* p145.

45. Coscia, *Il patto scellerato*, p248.

46. Alfieri was being questioned in February 1994. Cited in F. Barbagallo, *Napoli fine Novecento: Politici camorristi imprenditori*, p56. (Einaudi, Turin 1997) For an explanation of the Dorotea faction, see note 43.

Chapter 6: How the Camorra works

1. *Panorama*, 14 January 1994.

2. Interview with Judge Giuseppe Borrelli, 8 June 2001.

3. N. Tranfaglia, *La mafia come metodo nell'Italia contemporanea*, p99. (Laterza, Rome-Bari 1991)

4. The use of the masculine pronoun here and elsewhere is deliberate. However in recent years female activity within Camorra gangs, involving women such as Rosetta Cutolo and Maria Licciardi, has occurred at a far higher level than that of Sicilian women within the Mafia. See C. Longrigg, *Mafia Women* (Vintage, London 1997), and R. Siebert, *Women and the Mafia* (Verso, London 1996).

5. Commissione Parlamentare di inchiesta sul fenomeno della mafia e sulle associazioni criminali similari, *Audizione di Pasquale Galasso 13 luglio 1993*, p2233. (Camera dei Deputati, Rome 1993)

6. Ibid, p2236.

7. Rosario Stornaiuolo, secretary of the FILCAMS union, in *La Voce della Campania*, October 1999.

8. Quoted in F. Imposimato, 'Da camorra a mafia,' p34, in V. Faenza (ed.), *Cosa Nostra Napoletana. Rapporto 1992 sulla camorra.* (Publiprint, Trento 1993)

9. *Il Mattino*, 17 November 2000.
10. *La Repubblica,* 25 February 1992.
11. *Il Mattino*, 14 September 1999.
12. F. Feo, *Uomini e affari della camorra*, p145. (Edizioni Sintesi, Naples 1989)
13. Ibid, p146.
14. *Fortune*, (Italian edition), July/August 1991.
15. Interview with Francesco Cirillo, 2 February 1994. Cirillo is head of the Naples office of the Direzione Investigativa Anti-Mafia, the Anti-Mafia Investigative Commission, a kind of Italian FBI created in October 1991.
16. It is difficult to dismiss this hypothesis. In the 1986–87 season the Naples team had performed brilliantly, and they continued to do so the following year – five games before the end of the season they were four points clear of their closest rivals Milan. Then they suddenly collapsed, Maradona even refused to play in one match, and the team fell apart scoring just one point in five games, thus allowing Milan to win the League.

    Furthermore, there is considerable circumstantial evidence to link Maradona to the Camorra: he was photographed socialising with some of the Giuliano brothers on more than one occasion, he had relationships with women closely linked to Camorra clans, and developed a cocaine habit which eventually led to his rapid departure from Naples as a result of a ban on playing and the obligation to face a trial. See *Il Manifesto*, 12 March 1994.
17. *The Independent,* 29 December 1993.
18. *Il Mattino*, 17 November 2000.
19. *Liberazione* and *Il Mattino*, 2 February 1997.
20. Quoted in M. Coscia (ed.), *Il patto scellerato: Potere e politica di un regime mafioso*, pp218–9. (Crescenzi Allendorf, Rome 1993)
21. Quoted in ibid, p236.
22. Ibid, p237.
23. *The European,* 7 September 1990. See also G. Di Fiore, *Il palazzo dei misteri*, p90. (Il Mattino, Naples 1991)
24. *La Repubblica,* 6 October 1991. An even more sordid reality subsequently emerged concerning the same contract. According to the managers of the companies which won the new contracts, before signing, council politicians had demanded the right to choose the new workers. Three months

later three councillors – the Socialists Di Donato and Mast-rantuono and the Christian Democrat Vito – began demanding kickbacks totalling $1 million. See *Il Manifesto*, 16 March 1993.

25. *Il Manifesto*, 25 September 1992.
26. *Il Manifesto*, 13 July 1996.
27. Antonio Peduto, general secretary of the CGIL public sector union in Naples, in *La Voce della Campania*, October 1999.
28. Anti-Mafia Commission report on the Camorra approved on 21 December 1993, published as a volume by *L'Unità* in February 1994 and entitled *Rapporto sulla camorra*; p158. Here-after referred to as *Rapporto sulla camorra*.
29. Judge Aldo De Chiara, in *La Voce della Campania*, June 2001.
30. *Observer*, 13 February 1994.
31. *Il Mattino*, 21 April 1999.
32. Quoted in J. Haycraft, *The Italian Labyrinth: Italy in the 1980s*, pp199–200. (Secker & Warburg, London 1985) The Agnelli referred to is Gianni Agnelli, President of the Turin-based car multinational.
33. *La Repubblica*, 17 November 1991.
34. *La Repubblica*, 22 December 1991. The Lockheed scandal broke in 1976, when it emerged that the American aircraft company had been paying bribes to politicians in several major countries in order to gain contracts; one Minister, Mario Tanassi, was briefly sent to jail the following year. The first petrol scandal occurred in 1974, when it was discovered that major petrol companies were secretly financing parties in return for favourable legislation; whilst the second petrol scandal, in 1980, saw the involvement of politicians, finance police and petrol companies in tax frauds worth $1.6 billion. Zaza's outburst carries even more weight when one considers that it was made three months before the all-encompassing *Tangentopoli* scandal began to emerge in Milan.
35. *La Repubblica*, 3 March 1992.
36. G. Ruotolo, *La quarta mafia: Storie di mafia in Puglia,* pp147–8. (Pironti, Naples 1994) See also, *Rapporto sulla camorra,* p24.
37. Commissione Parlamentare di inchiesta sul fenomeno della mafia e sulle associazioni criminali similari, *Relazione sulla criminalità organizzata in Campania,* 24 October 2000, p63. (Camera dei Deputati, Rome 2000)

38. *Il Manifesto,* 19 December 1991.
39. Commissione Parlamentare di inchiesta sul fenomeno della mafia e sulle associazioni criminali similari, *Audizione di Salvatore Migliorino 12 novembre 1993,* p3136. (Camera dei Deputati, Rome 1993)
40. *Il Mattino,* 11 September 1999.
41. *Il Manifesto,* 20 December 1991.
42. *Il Manifesto,* 7 November 2000 and 18 January 2001.
43. *Relazione sulla criminalità organizzata in Campania,* 24 October 2000, p64.
44. *Narcomafie,* February 1994.
45. A. Lamberti, 'Le trasformazioni strutturali della camorra', p103, in F. Barbagallo and I. Sales (eds), *Rapporto 1990 sulla camorra.* (L'Unità, Rome, 1990)
46. A. Lamberti, 'La camorra: struttura, dimensioni e caratteristiche dei fenomeni di criminalità organizzata in Campania negli anni '90', p21, in *Osservatorio sulla Camorra,* no.2, June 1992.
47. A. Cipriani, *Mafia: Il riciclaggio del denaro sporco,* p23 (Napoleone, Rome 1989), and Feo, *Uomini e affari,* pp157–8.
48. *Il Manifesto,* 29 and 30 September 1992.
49. *La Voce della Campania,* April 1999.
50. Lamberti, 'La camorra,' p34.
51. *Relazione sulla criminalità organizzata in Campania,* 24 October 2000, p61.
52. Ibid.
53. Statistics published by the Anti-Mafia Commission, compiled from Ministry of the Interior figures. See www.camera.it/_bicamerali/antimafia/sport.../dossierdati.htm.
54. Gianfranco Donadio, an investigating magistrate at the Salerno Law Courts who specialises in money laundering investigations, writing in *La Voce della Campania,* May 1993.
55. *Rapporto sulla camorra,* p81.
56. Interview with Judge Giuseppe Borrelli. Pompeii and its surrounding area are the main centre for flower exporting in Italy.
57. See Coscia, *Il patto scellerato,* pp267–272.
58. *La Repubblica,* 9 November 1991.
59. *La Voce della Campania,* July 1998.
60. Interview with Judge Giuseppe Borrelli.
61. As regards Italian organised crime in the US, the fact that

Sicilian migration to North America in the early part of the last century was far higher than Campanian migration, gave many Sicilian-based *Mafiosi* a bolt-hole to run to during the fascist period. This large expat community then became a launching pad during the Allied invasion of Sicily of 1943. The smaller number of Neapolitans residing in the US has always meant that the Sicilians have dominated Italian organised crime in the US.

62. Interview with Robert Elliott, detective at the Organised Crime Unit, National Criminal Intelligence Service, 4 February 1993.

63. 'Ordinanza di custodia cautelare n.2667/96/A contro Antonio Baldascino e 85 altri,' Tribunale di Napoli, 22 October 1996, p333.

64. See *La Repubblica,* 13 January 1991.

65. *Il Manifesto,* 2 July 1992.

66. 'Ordinanza di custodia cautelare n.2667/96/A,' p330.

67. Interview with Judge Raffaele Cantone, 11 June 2001. Although he appears to have been in contact with known criminals both in Italy and in Venezuela, La Torre has never been arrested or questioned in Britain. See *The Guardian,* 14 March 1992.

68. *The Guardian,* 14 March 1992.

69. *The Independent,* 3 February 1993.

70. A report written by Leonid Fituni, Director of the Centre for Global and Strategic Studies at the Moscow Academy of Science, reproduced in *Narcomafie*, November 1993.

71. *Il Mattino*, 6 February 1994.

72. These wars have also led to the rapid growth of the *Sacra Corona Unita*, or Holy United Crown, in Apulia. In the period 1992–2000 arrest warrants were issued for 966 members of this organisation, compared to 1,579 for the Mafia and 1,739 for the Camorra. Available at: www.mininterno.it/dip_ps/dia/

73. *Il Mattino*, 18 June 2001.

74. *Il Manifesto*, 8 August 2000.

75. *Il Mattino*, 19 April 2000.

76. *Il Manifesto*, 8 August 2000.

77. *Il Manifesto*, 9 December 1999.

78. *Avvenimenti*, 26 September 1999.

79. *Il Mattino*, 11 September 1999.

80. *Avvenimenti*, 26 September 1999 and *Il Manifesto*, 9 December 1999.
81. Interview with Francesco Cirillo.

Chapter 7: Criminal politics

1. The 1901 report of Giuseppe Saredo's Commission of Inquiry into Naples, quoted in an Anti-Mafia Commission report on the Camorra approved on 21 December 1993, published as a volume by *L'Unità* in February 1994 and entitled *Rapporto sulla camorra*; p96. Hereafter referred to as *Rapporto sulla camorra*.
2. G. Di Fiore, *Potere camorrista: Quattro secoli di malanapoli,* p191. (Guida, Naples 1993)
3. *Rinascita*, 20 January 1984.
4. Amato Lamberti, interviewed in *La Repubblica,* 31 May 1991.
5. Interview with Antonio Menna, Communist Refoundation councillor in Marano, 9 May 2000.
6. I. Sales, 'Gli Enti Locali tra illegalità ed inefficienza,' p11, in *Enti Locali in Campania: radiografia di un malessere.* (Editrice Sintesi, Naples 1985)
7. Ibid, p12.
8. Ibid, p14.
9. See *La Repubblica*, 13 April 1990, and *Il Manifesto*, 18 April 1990.
10. Judge Paolo Mancuso, interviewed in *La Repubblica*, 14 April 1990.
11. Ibid.
12. G. Di Fiore, *Il palazzo dei misteri*, p140. (*Il Mattino*, Naples 1991)
13. Ibid, p56.
14. *La Repubblica,* 5 December 1991. Masciari later faced charges relating to a $5 million bank account he was unable to find an explanation for; magistrates suspect it derived from bribes paid for a fast-tram line planned but never built, and for works connected with the 1990 World Cup; see *Il Manifesto,* 27 February 1993. After two years on the run, in March 1993 he finally turned himself in to face a series of charges, including membership of the Camorra.
15. *The Guardian*, 14 September 1990.
16. *La Repubblica,* 4 June 1992.
17. *Rapporto sulla camorra*, pp91–2.

18. *Il Manifesto*, 30 March 1993.
19. Statement made to the Anti-Mafia Commission, quoted in *Rapporto sulla camorra*, p95. Tagliamonte was mayor from April to July 1993.
20. *Rapporto sulla camorra*, p199, note.
21. Ibid, p93.
22. F. Barbagallo, *Il potere della camorra*, p108. (Einaudi, Turin, 1999) The successes and limitations of his party, the DS, will be discussed in greater detail in the next chapter and the conclusion.
23. 'Richiesta per l'applicazione di misura cautelare contro Del Sorbo Leandro e 9 altri,' Procura della Repubblica presso il Tribunale di Napoli, 26 July 1996, p6.
24. 'Comune di Afragola, Relazione della commissione di accesso,' Prefettura di Napoli, 13 March 1999, p20.
25. Ibid, p18.
26. Ibid, p81. Despite evidence such as this, and many equally serious accusations made by the investigating commission, the authorities inexplicably decided not to disband the council.
27. 'Ordinanza di custodia cautelare in carcere n. 638/93 contro Carmine Alfieri e 22 altri,' Tribunale di Napoli, 3 November 1993, p131 (hereafter referred to as 'Ordinanza contro Carmine Alfieri').

    Interestingly enough, the town is named after an Egyptian Saint who, apart from advocating a semi-hermitic lifestyle, is often represented in popular tradition as fighting against demons, particularly domestic ones.
28. Ibid, p132.
29. Ibid, p223.
30. Ibid, p226. Administrative decisions such as these contributed to the $8 million debt which the council had accumulated when it was finally disbanded in 1993.
31. Ibid, p137.
32. Ibid, p140.
33. Ibid, p138.
34. Ibid, p144.
35. Ibid, p192.
36. Ibid, pp268–9.
37. *Rapporto sulla camorra*, p168.
38. 'Ordinanza contro Carmine Alfieri,' p196.

39. Ibid, p185.
40. 'Sentenza-Ordinanza n. 148/88 contro Catello De Riso, Ciro D'Auria, Bernardo Santonicola, Gaetano Mercurio e Diodato D'Auria,' Tribunale di Napoli, 20 April 1989, p8.
41. 'Ordinanza contro Carmine Alfieri,' p191. Abagnale was also the father-in-law of Aniello Rosanova; see F. Barbagallo, *Napoli fine Novecento*, p99. (Einaudi, Turin 1997)
42. Ibid, p193.
43. *Roma*, 7 August 1993.
44. Reproduced in the *Gazzetta Ufficiale della Repubblica Italiana*, 6 September 1993.
45. *Il Manifesto*, 19 November 1995. Tomato growing and canning is the main activity in this area, and accounts for over 15% of all national output.
46. 'Richiesta di custodia cautelare nei confronti di Ferdinando Cesarano e 69 altri,' Procura della Repubblica di Napoli, 31 January 2001, p4197.
47. Ibid, p4191.
48. See R. D. Putnam, *Making Democracy Work: Civic Traditions in Modern Italy,* p211, note. (Princeton University Press, Princeton 1993)
49. S. Minolfi and F. Soverina, *L'incerta frontiera: Saggio sui consiglieri comunali a Napoli 1946–92,* p52. (E.S.I., Naples 1993)
50. *Making Democracy Work,* p27.
51. See ibid, p73, pp201–4.
52. ISTAT, *Le Regioni in cifre*, p24. (ISTAT, Rome 1993)
53. Patriarca also faced charges of illegally favouring the application for a cleaning contract by a company owned by his nephew, worth $320,000 annually between 1983–90. See *Il Mattino*, 8 April 1993.
54. The most detailed account of ASL 35 is by G. Martano, 'L'Usl malata,' pp115–122, in V. Faenza (ed.), *Cosa Nostra Napoletana. Rapporto 1992 sulla camorra.* (Publiprint, Trento 1993)
55. *Avvenimenti,* 3 February 1993. In the same period primary schools in Castellammare also found themselves without school dinners, due to Camorra intimidation aimed at winning the contract for supplying the food. See *Il Giornale di Napoli,* 18 November 1994.
56. *Il Manifesto*, 24 and 30 April 1994.
57. Quoted in *Il Manifesto*, 4 June 1999.
58. *Il Manifesto*, 18 April 1990. Evidence has also emerged of a

photograph taken in 1980, which shows Gava together with Alfieri and Galasso at the opening of a local school. See *Il Manifesto*, 22 September 1994.

59. See M. Figurato, *Patto inconfessabile: Politica, crimine e affari dopo il caso Cirillo a Napoli*, p28 (Pironti, Naples 1993), and M. Coscia (ed.), *Il patto scellerato – Potere e politica di un regime mafioso*, p207. (Crescenzi Allendorf, Rome 1993)

60. *L'Espresso*, 25 September 1983. Patriarca is currently appealing against his conviction of Camorra membership at the Appeal Court of Naples, see Commissione Parlamentare di inchiesta sul fenomeno della mafia e sulle associazioni criminali similari, *Relazione sulla criminalità organizzata in Campania*, 24 October 2000, p94. (Camera dei Deputati, Rome 2000)

61. *Il Mattino*, 8 January 1994.

62. Figurato, *Patto inconfessabile*, pp14–15. Like Patriarca, Mastran-tuono is currently appealing against his conviction of Camorra membership.

63. *Napoli fine Novecento*, p169.

64. S. Messina, *Nomenklatura*, p54. (Mondadori, Milan 1992)

65. See *Relazione sulla criminalità organizzata in Campania*, p36.

66. *La Repubblica*, 23 April 1994. Emphasis in the original.

67. *L'Espresso*, 30 September 1994.

68. *Corriere della Sera*, 19 June 1995, and *Il Manifesto*, 27 July 1995.

69. Quoted in *Il Manifesto*, 9 March 1996.

70. Quoted in *La Voce della Campania*, March 1998.

71. Quoted in *Il Manifesto*, 4 June 1999.

72. Interview with Francesco Cirillo, 2 February 1994. Cirillo is head of the Naples office of the *Direzione Investigativa Anti-mafia*, the Anti-Mafia Investigative Commission, a kind of Italian FBI created in October 1991.

73. Interview with Antonio Menna.

74. Commissione Parlamentare di inchiesta sul fenomeno della mafia e sulle associazioni criminali similari, *Audizione di Pasquale Galasso 17 settembre 1993*, pp2748–49. (Camera dei Deputati, Rome 1993)

75. Interview with Massimo De Siena, Marano branch secretary of Communist Refoundation, 8 May 2000.

76. Quoted in Messina, *Nomenklatura*, p53.

77. See G. D'Agostino, 'Voto e camorra,' pp86–91, in F. Barbagallo (ed.), *Camorra e criminalità in Campania* (Liguori, Naples 1988), for a discussion of electoral trends influenced by the Camorra.

See also F. Imposimato, 'Potere politico e criminalità', pp63–70, in F. Barbagallo and I. Sales (eds), *Rapporto 1990 sulla camorra* (L'Unità, Rome 1990) for a slightly more impressionistic view.

78. Commissione Parlamentare di inchiesta sul fenomeno della mafia e sulle associazioni criminali similari, *Audizione di Pasquale Galasso 13 luglio 1993*, pp2277–78. (Camera dei Deputati, Rome 1993)

79. Coscia, *Il patto scellerato*, p275.

80. *La Repubblica,* 23 April 1993.

81. *Il Manifesto*, 20 May 2001.

82. Isaia Sales, writing in *La Voce della Campania,* May 1992.

Chapter 8: Who will stop the Camorra?

1. National Appeal Court statistics, quoted in *Panorama*, 27 February 1997.

2. *La Repubblica,* 4 April 1990.

3. Ibid.

4. Senato della Repubblica-Camera dei Deputati, X Legislatura, Commissione Anti-Mafia, Doc. XXIII, no.9, pp38–9. (Tipografia del Senato, Rome 1989)

5. Prisons Department statistics, cited in *Narcomafie*, March 1994. The situation became so dramatic that in August 1994 the 'Victims of Injustice Association' organised a three-day work and hunger strike, and could subsequently claim that 70% of inmates had supported the action; see *Il Mattino*, 17 August 1994.

6. *La Voce della Campania*, January 2001.

7. *La Voce della Campania*, June 2000.

8. [Various authors], *Sbilanciamoci: Rapporto sulla Finanziaria 2001*, pp74–5. (Lunaria, Rome 2000) All of this helps to explain why there were 59 suicides, 920 attempted suicides, 100 deaths after hospitalisation and 83 suspicious deaths in Italy's jails during 1999–2000. See *The Observer*, 3 September 2000.

9. *Il Manifesto,* 27 April 1994.

10. Amato Lamberti, interviewed in *Il Mattino*, 18 November 2000.

11. A. Jamieson, *The Antimafia*, p85. (Macmillan, Basingstoke 2000)

12. *Il Manifesto* and *Il Mattino*, 2 December 1998.

13. *Il Manifesto*, 22 June 2000.

14. *Il Manifesto*, 22 March 2001.

15. *Corriere del Mezzogiorno*, 2 June 2001.

16. Commissione Parlamentare di inchiesta sul fenomeno della mafia e sulle associazioni criminali similari, *Relazione sulla criminalità organizzata in Campania*, 24 October 2000, p95. (Camera dei Deputati, Rome 2000)

17. G. Locatelli, *Mazzette e Manette: Dizionario di politici e imprenditori beccati a Napoli e a Milano*, p108. (Pironti, Naples 1993)

18. *Il Manifesto*, 21 May 1993.

19. *Il Manifesto* and *Il Mattino*, 22 May 1993.

20. *Il Mattino*, 29 May 1993.

21. Commissione Parlamentare di inchiesta sul fenomeno della mafia e sulle associazioni criminali similari, *Audizione di Pasquale Galasso 17 settembre 1993*, p2735. (Camera dei Deputati, Rome 1993)

22. See M. Coscia (ed.), *Il patto scellerato: Potere e politica di un regime mafioso*, p208. (Crescenzi Allendorf, Rome 1993)

23. Ibid, pp209–10.

24. *Audizione di Pasquale Galasso 17 settembre 1993*, p2737.

25. *The Independent*, 12 March 1994. This has also been confirmed by ex DC senator and lawyer Dino Bargi, who admitted to being the contact between Galasso and Cono Lancuba. He also stated that 'the three of us spent many evenings together' in a house at Positano, i.e. a *camorrista*, a lawyer and a judge. See *Il Manifesto*, 13 March 1994.

26. Commissione Parlamentare di inchiesta sul fenomeno della mafia e sulle associazioni criminali similari, *Audizione di Pasquale Galasso 13 luglio 1993*, p2314. (Camera dei Deputati, Rome 1993)

27. G. Di Fiore, *Il palazzo dei misteri*, p14. (*Il Mattino*, Naples 1991)

28. *Il Manifesto*, 9 March 1994.

29. Commissione Parlamentare di inchiesta sul fenomeno della mafia e sulle associazioni criminali similari, *Audizione di Salvatore Migliorino 12 novembre 1993*, p3118. (Camera dei Deputati, Rome 1993)

30. *Audizione di Pasquale Galasso 17 settembre 1993*, p2738.

31. *Relazione sulla criminalità organizzata in Campania*, p96.

32. The High Council of Magistrates plenary session of 9 April

1988. Quoted in *Rapporto sulla camorra*, p98. (L'Unità, Rome 1994) Regina Coeli and Poggioreale are the two main jails of Rome and Naples respectively, while the backstreets of Via Toledo are a particularly poor area of Naples.

33. *Panorama*, 14 January 1994.

34. *L'Espresso*, 14 September 2000.

35. *The Guardian*, 14 September 1990.

36. The 'historic compromise' was first formulated in late 1973 by PCI leader Enrico Berlinguer in response to the military coup in Chile. He argued that Salvador Allende's left-wing government had gone too far and had antagonised the right-wing opposition. For Berlinguer, therefore, '51% [of the electorate] wasn't enough' for the left to govern, an alliance must be built with the centre or right parties at all costs, i.e. a 'historic compromise' must be made. The closest this policy came to actual practice was the PCI's promise not to 'no confidence' Giulio Andreotti's Christian Democrat government of 1976–79. In exchange the Christian Democrats frequently hinted that communists might join their government, but the agreement was dropped once the DC regained strength.

   In many ways the 'historic compromise' was a more modern version of the 'Popular Front' policies followed by western communist parties during the 1930s. See P. Ginsborg, *A History of Contemporary Italy,* pp354–8. (Penguin, Harmondsworth 1990)

37. A. Galdo, 'Il lottatore stanco,' p9, in *Nord e Sud*, no.17, Jan–March 1982.

38. Ibid, p13.

39. See F. Barbagallo, *Napoli fine Novecento*, pp106–7 (Einaudi, Turin 1997), and M. Figurato, *Patto inconfessabile: Politica, crimine e affari dopo il caso Cirillo a Napoli,* p92. (Pironti, Naples 1993)

40. *Il Mattino*, 8 April 1993.

41. *Il Giornale di Napoli* and *Il Manifesto*, 24 April 1993.

42. *Il Manifesto* and *La Repubblica*, 20 April 1993.

43. 1999 figures. Quoted in DS Federazione di Napoli, *Insieme per continuare a cambiare: Assemblea congressuale provinciale*, p14. (DS Federazione di Napoli, Naples 2001)

44. Quoted in *Il Mattino*, 21 April 1999. Naples' position as regards general quality of life actually decreased under Bassolino,

314 SEE NAPLES AND DIE

according to this survey: from 88th in 1991, to 94th in 1996 and 100th in 1997.

45. *Il Giornale di Napoli,* 26 January 1993.

46. *Audizione di Pasquale Galasso 13 luglio 1993*, p2283. The use of inverted commas here is intended to highlight the incongruity of professionals dedicating themselves to the cause of communism.

47. See: *Il Manifesto* and *Il Mattino*, 2 December 1998; and *Il Mattino*, 3 February 1999.

48. *La Voce della Campania*, October 2000.

49. Press statement, Procura della Repubblica di Napoli, 23 April 2001; and *Il Manifesto*, 24 April 2001.

50. *Il Mattino*, 6 May 2001.

51. 'Richiesta di custodia cautelare nei confronti di Ferdinando Cesarano e 69 altri,' Procura della Repubblica di Napoli, 31 January 2001, p711.

52. Ibid, p713.

53. Ibid, p741.

54. Traditions of mass resistance extend back through the last century, and notably include the four-day insurrection of October 1943 which forced the Germans to withdraw from the city.

    Naples has also experienced the longest and probably largest movement of the unemployed of any major western city. The *movimento dei disoccupati organizzati* was formed in Castellammare in 1972; although it has undergone many changes since then – the most disturbing being Camorra infiltration – demonstrations of thousands of unemployed are still regular events. See P. Basso, *Disoccupati e Stato: Il movimento dei disoccupati organizzati a Napoli (1975–81)* (Franco Angeli, Milan 1981), L. Ferrara, *E` qui la festa* (Ediesse, Rome 1997) and F. Ramondino (ed.), *Napoli: I disoccupati organizzati.* (Feltrinelli, Milan 1977)

    Until recently Naples has had a significant industrial working class, mainly centred on the massive Bagnoli steelworks. See F. Mazzucca, *Il mare e la fornace* (Ediesse, Rome 1983), and the Istituto campano per la storia della Resistenza, *Italsider: Una fabbrica, una città* (Naples 1983). Indeed it is no coincidence that the rise of the modern Camorra has generally coincided with the decline of an industrial working class: not only has the level of unemployment and underemployment risen as a result of factory closures, the relative absence of organised labour has been a critical weakness in Naples from the early 1980s onwards.

55. *Il Mattino*, 25 November 1982.
56. *L'Unità*, 28 November 1982.
57. *L'Unità*, 10 December 1982; *Il Mattino* and *Paese Sera*, 11 December 1982.
58. *Paese Sera,* 18 December 1982.
59. *The Guardian* and *Il Mattino*, 27 January 1983.
60. *Il Manifesto, Il Mattino, Paese Sera* and *La Repubblica*, 12 February 1983.
61. See *Il Manifesto*, 20 March and 17 May 1994; and U. Santino, *Storia del movimento antimafia*, pp308–9. (Editori Riuniti, Rome 2000)
62. *La Repubblica*, 22 and 23 October 1996.
63. *Il Manifesto*, 12 December 1995.
64. *Il Mattino*, 28 September 1997.
65. *La Repubblica*, 11 October 1998.
66. *Il Mattino*, 31 January 1999.
67. *La Repubblica*, 1 May 1997.

Conclusion: Ha dda passà 'a nuttata

1. This phrase, in Neapolitan dialect, is one of the best-known sayings associated with the city's most famous actor and playwright, Eduardo De Filippo. Roughly translated, it means 'the bad times must come to an end'.
2. F. Feo, *Uomini e affari della camorra,* p25. (Edizioni Sintesi, Naples 1989)
3. F. Imposimato, 'Da camorra a mafia', p32, in V. Faenza (ed.), *Cosa Nostra Napoletana: Rapporto 1992 sulla camorra.* (Publiprint, Trento 1993)
4. See M. Coscia (ed.), *Il patto scellerato: Potere e politica di un regime mafioso*, p210. (Crescenzi Allendorf, Rome 1993)
5. Feo, *Uomini e affari*, p34.
6. Commissione Parlamentare di inchiesta sul fenomeno della mafia e sulle associazioni criminali similari, *Audizione di Pasquale Galasso 13 luglio 1993,* p2233. (Camera dei Deputati, Rome 1993)
7. See Coscia, *Il patto scellerato,* p211.

8. J. Walston, 'See Naples and Die: Organized Crime in Campania,' p143, in R. J. Kelly (ed.), *Organized Crime: A Global Perspective.* (Rowman & Littlefield, New Jersey 1986)

9. Ibid, p153.

10. Interview with Francesco Cirillo, 2 February 1994. Cirillo is head of the Naples office of the *Direzione Investigativa Anti-mafia*, the Anti-Mafia Investigative Commission, a kind of Italian FBI created in October 1991.

11. Interview with Judge Giuseppe Borrelli, 8 June 2001.

12. *Audizione di Pasquale Galasso 13 luglio 1993*, p2327.

13. Anti-Mafia Commission report on the Camorra approved on 21 December 1993, published in book form by *L'Unità* in February 1994 and entitled *Rapporto sulla camorra*, p185.

14. Throughout the 1980s there were a succession of super-grasses, beginning with Pasquale Barra who, realising that Cutolo was prepared to let him be killed, decided to reveal details of NCO murders in order to gain greater protection. He was then followed by Giovanni Pandico, one of the NCO's 'brains' whose accusations led to many of the arrests in the 1983 'maxi-blitz'; many of his accusations, however, were later proved to be unfounded. The third major NCO super-grass was Mario Incarnato, who confessed to a series of murders in late 1983. In the mid-1980s Giovanni Auriemma exposed the NCO's links with the secret services, whilst Pasquale D'Amico revealed Cutolo's links with Calabrian organisations.

15. *Il Manifesto*, 1 May 1994 and *Il Mattino*, 7 June 2001.

16. The eldest of several brothers, Nunzio Giuliano is best described as a 'disassociate' *camorrista* rather than a super-grass. Over the last twenty years the Giuliano gang has always been amongst the top five Camorra gangs in the city of Naples, and is probably the longest-surviving clan in exist-ence today. Their stronghold, Forcella, is an area of central Naples between the station and the cathedral.

 Those who disassociate themselves from a Camorra gang let it be known both to the judiciary and to their ex gang that their criminal activities are now over. Although this stance may lead to considerable judicial interest for several years, and the risk of retribution from gang members, once this crit-ical period is over there is the possibility of full rehabilitation into society. Somebody who chooses to 'grass' on former gang members either has to build a new identity or live with the permanent threat of retribution.

Nunzio Giuliano's disassociation was prompted by the death of his eldest son Vittorio in October 1987 after a heroin overdose. Interviews conducted on 21 and 25 January 1993.

17. Interview with Giuseppe Borrelli.

18. See Commissione Parlamentare di inchiesta sul fenomeno della mafia e sulle associazioni criminali similari, *Relazione sulla criminalità organizzata in Campania*, 24 October 2000, pp16–22. (Camera dei Deputati, Rome 2000)

19. *Corriere del Mezzogiorno*, 15 June 2001.

20. Alberto Ziparo of Catania University, writing in *Il Manifesto*, 8 July 1993.

21. Earthquake expert Professor Rocco Caporale, quoted in *The Guardian*, 16 October 1993.

22. *Relazione sulla criminalità organizzata in Campania*, p75.

23. *La Repubblica*, 19 September 1997.

24. *Il Messaggero*, 2 February 1999.

25. Diego Gambetta, writing in *L'Indice*, December 1993.

26. N. Tranfaglia, *Mafia, politica e affari 1943–2000*, p22. (Laterza, Rome 2001)

27. G. Falcone with M. Padovani, *Men of Honour: The Truth about the Mafia*, p141. (Warner Books, London 1993)

28. 'La relazione di minoranza nella Commissione Parlamentare Antimafia,' published in book form as *Mafia e politica in Italia (1984–1990)*, p79. (Edizioni Associate, Rome 1990)

29. G. Martano, 'Comuni senza governo,' p63, in Faenza (ed.), *Cosa Nostra Napoletana*. It is interesting to see how earlier laws have been modified: until 1977 the commitment for trial of a mayor or the head of a council committee was enough to lead to their suspension from office, yet as a result one council out of eight in Italy had its mayor suspended; the law was therefore changed to allow councillors to stay in office until convicted.

30. *Relazione sulla criminalità organizzata in Campania*, p63.

31. Interview with Nunzio Giuliano.

32. *Il Mattino*, 9 May 2000.

33. Vito Mattera, quoted in G. Di Fiore, *Il palazzo dei misteri*, pp119–20. (Il Mattino, Naples 1991)

It is interesting to compare the realistic views of Italian policemen and politicians concerning strategies to beat

organised crime to those of their counterparts in Britain and
the US. In Italy the discussion revolves around political
honesty and material conditions; moral crusades about 'back
to basics' and 'family values' are almost entirely absent from
the debate. The strong traditional family structure in
southern Italy, together with its high level of crime, is clear
evidence that it is not the lack of a 'traditional family life'
which causes crime.

34. *Il Manifesto*, 1 April 2001.
35. *Panorama*, 10 July 1997.
36. According to Agostino Cordova, Naples' Federal Prosecutor,
interviewed in *Il Manifesto,* 21 November 1994.
37. *La Repubblica*, 16 June 1997.
38. *Il Manifesto*, 19 September 2000.
39. Report compiled by the state-run research institute SVIMEZ.
Quoted in *Il Manifesto*, 13 July 2001.
40. Interview with Nunzio Giuliano.
41. F. Ramella and C. Triglia, 'Associazionismo e mobilitazione
contro la criminalità organizzata nel Mezzogiorno,' p36, in L.
Violante (ed.), *Mafia e società italiana: Rapporto '97.* (Laterza,
Rome 1997)
42. I. Sales, 'Introduzione,' p7, in Faenza (ed.), *Cosa Nostra
Napoletana*.
43. Interview with Nunzio Giuliano.
44. Imposimato, 'Da camorra a mafia,' p39, in Faenza (ed.), *Cosa
Nostra Napoletana*. Imposimato is a magistrate specialising in
fighting organised crime, and has also been a consultant for
the UN task force against the drugs trade.
45. The general climate of illegality tolerated and even encouraged by the ruling class is closely related to the existence of
criminal gangs. Many people live in an environment characterised not only by powerful criminal gangs, but also by a
general disregard towards many day-to-day laws and regulations that is shared by both institutions and people in
general. The existence of these two elements side by side
naturally creates a political climate of fear, cynicism and
passivity.
46. The question of the illegal or 'submerged economy' does not
concern the South alone. See P. Mattera, *Off the books: The Rise
of the Underground Economy,* pp84–97 (Pluto Press, London
1985) for a broad discussion regarding the whole of Italy.

47. Interview with Giovani Sannino, Naples provincial secretary of the CGIL-FILLEA union, 20 June 2001.

48. Interview with Ciro Crescentini, 20 June 2001.

49. *Audizione di Pasquale Galasso 13 luglio 1993,* p2309.

50. Coscia, *Il patto scellerato,* p257.

51. *Audizione di Pasquale Galasso 13 luglio 1993,* p2278.

52. Interview with Nunzio Giuliano.

Index